Praise for
Let It Bang

"We need more books like this: personal, emotional meditations on gun ownership . . . showing us all the ways in which guns take on meaning for people, and what happens when those meanings collide."   —*Pacific Standard*

"RJ Young's *Let It Bang* is a penetrating and personal look at America's gun culture that hits the mark, finding what brings us together as much as what tears us apart."
                      —Glenn Stout, author of *Young Woman and the Sea* and
                               series editor of *The Best American Sports Writing*

"It's easy to stand outside the fray and criticize the gun-hung whites and radical rednecks defending the Second Amendment. It takes real courage to grab a pistol, head to the range, and try to understand where they're coming from. This is RJ Young's success with *Let It Bang.*"
                      —Ben Montgomery, author of *Grandma Gatewood's Walk*

"In the often muddled debate over gun possession and gun violence, *Let It Bang* resonates with common sense."
—Charles E. Cobb Jr., author of *This Nonviolent Stuff'll Get You
                    Killed: How Guns Made the Civil Rights Movement Possible*

"Honest and heartbreaking, Young's raw account of being a [B]lack gun owner in America will mesmerize readers."
                                                                —*Publishers Weekly*

Requiem
for the
Massacre

ALSO BY RJ YOUNG

Let It Bang: A Young Black Man's
Reluctant Odyssey into Guns

Requiem
for the
Massacre

A Black History on the
Conflict, Hope, and Fallout of
the 1921 Tulsa Race Massacre

RJ Young

Counterpoint
BERKELEY, CALIFORNIA

This is a work of nonfiction. However, some names and identifying details of individuals have been changed to protect their privacy, correspondence has been shortened for clarity, and dialogue has been reconstructed from memory.

First Counterpoint edition: 2022

Library of Congress Cataloging-in-Publication Data
Names: Young, R. J. (Writer) author.
Title: Requiem for the Massacre : a Black history on the conflict, hope, and fallout of the 1921 Tulsa Race Massacre / RJ Young.
Other titles: Black history on the conflict, hope, and fallout of the 1921 Tulsa Race Massacre
Description: First Counterpoint edition. | Berkeley, California : Counterpoint, 2022. | Includes bibliographical references. | Identifiers: LCCN 2022016663 | ISBN 9781640095021 (hardcover) | ISBN 9781640095038 (ebook)
Subjects: LCSH: Young, R. J. (Writer) | African Americans—Oklahoma—Tulsa—Biography. | African Americans—Oklahoma—Tulsa—Social conditions. | Tulsa (Okla.)—Race relations—History. | Tulsa (Okla.)—Biography. | Tulsa (Okla.)—Social conditions. | Tulsa Race Massacre, Tulsa, Okla., 1921.
Classification: LCC F704.T92 Y68 2022 | DDC 305.8009766/86—dc23/eng/20220414
LC record available at https://lccn.loc.gov/2022016663

Jacket design by Lexi Earle
Book design by Laura Berry

COUNTERPOINT
2560 Ninth Street, Suite 318
Berkeley, CA 94710
www.counterpointpress.com

Printed in the United States of America

10 9 8 7 6 5 4 3 2 1

For my brother Ron, who never left

I would like roses to come out of the ground somewhere any time a person's voice cracks under the weight of what it has been asked to carry. I would like to do this while the living are still the living, and I don't want to hear from any motherfucker who isn't with the program.

—HANIF ABDURRAQIB

I ain't scared of you motherfuckers.

—BERNIE MAC

Requiem
for the
Massacre

1921–2020

N 1921, OTTAWAY W. GURLEY WAS THE RICHEST AND MOST powerful Black man in Tulsa. He had been among those on the starting line at the edge of Kansas and Oklahoma Territory for the Land Run of 1893. He was a Black man among thousands who traveled west and made stakes with their names written on them to stick into the ground and claim their parcel. He was twenty-five years old then, the son of two former slaves, born on Christmas Day 1868 in Huntsville, Alabama, though he grew up in Pine Bluff, Arkansas, where he finished enough school to become a teacher and then an employee of the United States Post Office Department. He was ambitious and enterprising. Learning that the U.S. government had recently purchased 6,361,000 acres of land from the Cherokee Nation, Gurley sensed an opportunity to make his family upwardly mobile and seized it. Gurley believed what Massachusetts senator Henry L. Dawes believed. Dawes saw the Cherokee Nation as a capitalist's nightmare and a socialist's utopia. Only one of those ideas has been allowed to flourish in the United States, and he was, like Gurley, determined not to let the future state of Oklahoma be an outlier. Upon returning from a visit to the Cherokee land in Indian Territory that would later become the state of Oklahoma, Dawes delivered his thoughts before a group at Lake Mohonk in New York: "The head chief told us that there was not a family in that whole nation that did not have a home of its own. There was not a pauper in that nation, and the nation did not owe a dollar. It built its own capitol . . . and it built its schools and hospitals. Yet the defect of the system was apparent. They have got as far as they can go because they own their land in common. It is Henry George's system, and under that there is no enterprise to make your home any better than that of your neighbors. There is no selfishness which is at the bottom of civilization." This was a philosophy Gurley believed in, too, this enterprise of taking what was once communal and sectioning it into a district powered by capitalism. For him, Dawes was prescient, not pernicious. Six years after the formation of the Dawes Act of 1887, which led to the creation of the Land Runs of 1889 and 1893, Gurley, former postal worker, an employee of one of this nation's oldest institutions, wanted a parcel of this manifest destiny.

On September 16, 1893, fifty miles south of the Kansas state line, Gurley drove his stake into the ground just outside what would become one of the first towns of Oklahoma. Five days later, the town of Perry was incorporated. Gurley ran for county treasurer, though he was defeated. He became the town's school principal. As Perry expanded with cattle ranches and wheat farms, bars and restaurants opened to accommodate the growing citizenry. Gurley opened a profitable general store, yet he wanted more for his family, wanted to continue moving up, hunting the American Dream.

In 1905, just outside an Oklahoma town called Tulsa, oil was discovered.

The oil boom created jobs and opportunities for businessmen, including Black businessmen. Black visionaries like Edward P. McCabe, Robert Reed Church, and W. E. B. Du Bois implored Black folks to move from the South, where the promised Reconstruction was failing, to Oklahoma. Gurley recognized a unique opportunity in Tulsa: an all-Black district on the outskirts of a town, creating oil-baron millionaires overnight. Black folks flocked to Tulsa, which citizens nicknamed "Magic City." In swift order, Black folks worked together to transform forty-acre lots into a city within a city, nearly forty blocks of Black-owned and Black-operated businesses, from movie theaters to clothing stores, and including offices for local doctors, lawyers, and clergymen.

In 1905, Gurley sold his general store and land in Perry and moved his family. He bought forty acres just outside Tulsa, north of the train tracks that ran through the city limits. It was Gurley who opened the first grocery store in the area. In that same area, he met John the Baptist Stradford, who went by J.B. The two became friends and informal partners while building a Black community on a foundation of pro-business as philosophy. But Gurley and Stradford were no fools. They knew racial animus would find them—politically, socially, violently—outside of their enclave. Each sought to insulate himself, his businesses, and the growing district in an area that city architects called Greenwood.

Greenwood was annexed to Tulsa in 1909 and stretched north from the Frisco railroad tracks to Independence Avenue, east to the Midland Valley railroad tracks, and west to Cheyenne Avenue. The Greenwood District grew faster than the city of Tulsa, outpacing the growth of Tulsa at large by 2 percent. In 1907, the year Oklahoma achieved statehood, 1,422 Black folks lived there. By 1910, three years later, 2,754 Black folks lived in Greenwood; by 1919, more than ten thousand.

The district was home to two high schools, Dunbar and Booker T. Washington; two newspapers, the *Tulsa Star* and the *Oklahoma Sun*; and three lodges, two theaters, a hospital, a library, and thirteen churches. Outside the district, Tulsa lacked both job and housing opportunities for Black folks. If they were fortunate to find work at all, it was as domestics and live-in servants for rich, white households. Greenwood's rapid development filled this absence, providing a pathway to wealth and stability. Journalist and publisher Andrew Jackson Smitherman wanted to see a pathway to racial equality too. Smitherman, who went by A.J., called his most famous newspaper the *Tulsa Star*. He was born December 27, 1883, in Childersburg, Alabama, the second-born of eleven children. His parents were James and Elizabeth Phillips Smitherman, and they moved the family to Indian Territory when A.J. was still a boy. Smitherman's father owned a general store and coal mining outfit in Lehigh, Oklahoma. His mother was a schoolteacher. They were of mixed race, and they were not poor when the family moved to what would become Muskogee, Oklahoma. If not for his mother, Smitherman probably would have kept working in the mines. She sought an education for him at a time when many universities did not admit Black folks. He attended the University of Kansas, Northwestern University, and the law school at LaSalle University in Philadelphia, and began his newspaper and law career in 1909.

After first working in Muskogee, he accepted seed money from one of the richest men in Tulsa, J. B. Stradford, to publish the *Tulsa Star*. His political ideology was one of Black self-reliance. He wanted Black folks not just to take care of each other but to harness their power to affect change in a country that had recognized us only as second-class citizens. In 1917, he interceded on behalf of Black folks in Dewey, Oklahoma, when a mob of angry white folks burned nearly two dozen Black homes to the ground. Smitherman petitioned the governor on behalf of Black Dewey residents and saw thirty-six white folks—including the mayor—arrested for the crime. At a moment when most Black folks called themselves Republican after Abraham Lincoln issued his proclamation, Smitherman announced himself as a Democrat. When President Woodrow Wilson traveled to Tulsa, Smitherman was selected as a member of the delegation to greet him.

Even as he was a Democrat and a Roman Catholic, he wanted his paper to be known as politically independent. As the *Star*'s circulation grew, so too did the respect engendered by Smitherman's name. At one point in his career, he was elected president of the Western Negro Press Association for more than a decade straight.

As editor of the paper, he suffered no fools, punched up at elected officials, parried segregationist rhetoric, relentlessly campaigned against lynch law, and encouraged Black folks to see not just what they'd accomplished but that there was still more to do. Change in attitude was needed, as he would later find out.

*

In Greenwood, a Black man could be a preacher, a doctor, a businessman, a lawyer, or a teacher—but only in Greenwood. As Danney Goble notes in *Tulsa! Biography of the American City*, a 1916 Tulsa ordinance "forbade persons of either race from living in or maintaining a public facility in any city block in which three-quarters or more of the population was of the other race." While the U.S. Supreme Court later overturned such laws, Tulsa kept that ordinance among its statutes, codifying a segregated way of life.

Meanwhile, Gurley and Stradford subdivided their land north of the railroad, creating lots for housing and retail outlets and carving out streets. On the new Greenwood Avenue, Gurley built brick boardinghouses near his grocery store, as well as the African American Methodist Episcopal Church. He built apartment buildings and detached homes and the Gurley Hotel. By 1914, his net worth was estimated by the *Muskogee Cimeter*, a nearby Black-owned newspaper, at $150,000 ($4.5 million in 2021). As he grew rich, so did Greenwood, which benefited from the closed-circuit nature of separate but equal: Black folks patronized each other, in part, because they were socially unacceptable in Greater Tulsa.

Gurley promoted this behavior, claiming to be a follower of Booker T. Washington and his philosophy of his conciliatory compromise with white folks. Many Black Tulsans also followed Washington's philosophy. They left Greenwood to work as domestics, but returned home, wages in hand, to patronize businesses ran by their own.

Still, Greenwood was not rich, even at its height in 1921, in comparison to St. Louis and Atlanta. But Greenwood was special because Black folks could live a respectable life, even without being wealthy. With the oil barons' high demand for employees, a Black maid, a Black chauffeur, a Black bootblack, a Black porter could earn enough of a living to live well. Living well meant seeing a Black doctor and being respected by him. Those same professionals sent their kids to schools like Fisk, Tuskegee, Spelman, or Oberlin. Most residents of Greenwood walked through the front door of a bar, saloon, or nightclub. They paid rent to a Black man, likely Gurley.

In 1921, Gurley "was landlord to almost half of Greenwood's residents and shopkeepers, collecting $5,000 a month in rents ($77,000)," according to Shomari Wills's *Black Fortunes: The Story of the First Six African Americans who Survived Slavery and Became Millionaires*. "With more than a hundred properties in Greenwood, he was worth between $500,000 and $1 million ($7.5 and $15 million). His net worth could only be guessed at in Greenwood, as Gurley kept his own money across the tracks in white banks in downtown Tulsa. His hotel, valued at least $99,000 ($1.5 million), was one of the busiest in the district."

In spring 1921, Gurley was symbolic of what Greenwood could be, stood for, represented: a place where a Black man could rise and Black folks could live good lives. Nearly all of it went up in fire and decades of institutionalized silence.

*

Most people, Black and white, were off work on Memorial Day, May 30, 1921. But Dick Rowland, a former Booker T. Washington High School student, was at work. For him, it was just a Monday. He left Greenwood, his Black enclave, to work downtown where he shined shoes on white men's feet to a high buff. But even he had to use the bathroom. Tulsa was segregated, and there was no restroom nearby where he worked that Black Tulsans were allowed to use. This is the most reasonable rationale for why he entered the Drexel

Building, located at 319 South Main Street, a block away from a white storefront. The restroom was on the Drexel's top floor.

To get there, Rowland had to use the elevator in the back of the building, which was operated by a seventeen-year-old white girl named Sarah Page. Did she know him? Almost certainly yes; she would have recognized all the shoe-shiners who needed to use the restroom. She ferried Rowland to the fourth floor and back down again. Then someone, who remains unnamed to this day, heard this white girl scream, and saw this Black boy running away. And someone—perhaps the same unnamed someone—called police.

A white shop clerk at Renberg's, a high-end clothing store on the ground level of the Drexel, swore he knew what happened, though he said he did not witness what he later said must have happened. Based on this heresy, two Tulsa police officers showed up to Dick's mama's house on the morning of May 31. They told Damie Rowland they needed to arrest her son, which they did.

Later, no one would much care that Page refused to press charges or that Dick was exonerated, which begs the question: Was white mob violence in Greenwood about a Black boy and a white girl at all? What happened inside the elevator isn't known. When the elevator opened, Page screamed. It was assumed by a white man who heard the scream—and white folks who heard this white man claim he heard her scream—and saw Rowland run away that he had attacked her, attempted to rape her, and then had run down Archer Street back to Greenwood.

Whether Rowland and Page were romantically entangled is unclear. But sexual assault was alleged, and a police report was filed. A Black man sexually assaulting a white woman was news enough to merit an article in the one of the city's two white-owned newspapers, the *Tulsa Tribune*.

The *Tribune*'s May 31 story about Rowland's alleged assault of Page was five paragraphs long, headlined "Nab Negro Attacking Girl in Elevator." The initial police report didn't mention Page by name. Rowland was arrested the same morning the *Tribune* published its account. The following day, Rowland was taken into custody. He was jailed at the police station at 109 East Second Street, where he admitted to stepping on Page's foot.

The *Tulsa World*, the other white-owned newspaper in the city, ran a story about Rowland's arrest in its June 1 edition: "There was movement afoot, it was reported, among white people to go to the county courthouse Tuesday night and lynch the bootblack."

Tulsa police commissioner James Adkison answered an anonymous phone call the day Rowland was arrested. "We're going to lynch that negro tonight," the caller told him. Adkison said the threat was credible enough that he asked Tulsa police chief John Gustafson to move Rowland to the Tulsa County Jail, because the city jail was much easier to break into than the county one. That also meant Rowland legally changed hands from the city police to the Tulsa County Sheriff's Office. Rowland was turned over to Tulsa sheriff Bill McCullough, who called on his deputies to fortify the jail on the fifth floor of the county courthouse.

As news of Rowland's arrest spread, Black and white Tulsans organized and gathered outside the courthouse where Rowland was now being held. They formed two segregated groups. Black men, some with guns, stood outside to defend Rowland, while white men sought to disarm their Black counterparts. Many of these men, both white and Black, were veterans of World War I. Upon finding out Rowland was in jail and there was a rumor of white folks looking to lynch him just before 7:00 p.m. on June 1, a Black veteran taking in a show at the Dreamland Theatre, a space that seated up to 750, leapt up. "We're not going to let this happen," he said. "We're going to go downtown and stop this lynching. Close this place down."

C. F. Gabe, a Black man, said he was first apprised that white folks were going to lynch Rowland while he was on his way to see friends around 6:30 p.m. on May 31.[1] He'd lived in Greenwood for fifteen years. When he heard about Rowland, he said he "went home and pulled off his gun," heading to the courthouse later that evening. He saw Deputy Barney Cleaver, O. W. Gurley, and seven to eight hundred people outside the building. A white person whom Gabe couldn't identify told him to "get these niggers away from here," noting tension was building. Not long after, he saw a carload of white men drive up to the courthouse. "Let's go to the armory," he heard one of them say.

When another white person pointed a gun at him, Gabe decided to go back to Greenwood. Coming to the intersection of Boston and Archer, he found a frenzied group of what he estimated was about five thousand Black folks. Here, he turned around yet again and made for the courthouse, then decided to leave the courthouse once more, perhaps feeling boxed in. He walked four blocks and heard gunfire. He turned around one last time to head to the courthouse again but was stopped by Police Commissioner Adkison, who told him to leave the area or risk getting hurt. He encountered Deputy Sheriff John Smitherman shortly thereafter. Gabe said Smitherman asked for assistance to "help stop the thing." Gabe thought perhaps J. B. Stradford could help. He walked to Stradford's hotel to ask him to use his influence to end the conflict, but Stradford refused to help him. Gabe left Stradford and walked to Cincinnati and Archer by himself. There, he saw two white men shot while attempting to set fire to a house. A third white man accomplished what the first two had attempted. Upon seeing the house ablaze, Gabe made his way back to his home at 422 East Easton Street and went to sleep. Greenwood, however, began to burn.

At 7:00 p.m., Sheriff McCullough was joined by the only Black deputy in Greenwood, Barney Cleaver, and implored both Blacks and whites to go back home. Cleaver was fifty-four in 1921 and was the first Black member of both the Tulsa Police Department and the Tulsa County Sheriff's Office. He tried to assure his Black neighbors that no harm would come to Rowland and went inside the jail to be sure. In August 1920, eighteen-year-old Roy Belton had been ripped from jail and lynched by white Tulsans after pleading not guilty to the murder of Homer Nida. Police Chief Gustafson and his officers had arrived in time to stop the lynching but he had ordered his men not to intervene, telling the *World*, "any demonstration from an officer would have started gun play and dozens of innocent people would have been killed and injured."

The Black men of Tulsa resolved not to leave Rowland's life in the hands of police. Their number outside the courthouse only grew between 7:00 and 9:00 p.m. In her book *Race Riot 1921: Events of the Tulsa Disaster*, Mary Elizabeth Jones Parrish, a secretarial teacher, recounted what she saw outside the courthouse as she let out her class around 9:00 p.m. on May 31: "I am told this little bunch of brave and loyal [B]lack men who were willing to give up their lives, if necessary, for the sake of a fellow man, marched up to the jail where there were already 500 white men gathered, and that this number was soon swelled to a thousand."

The Oklahoma National Guard was under the command of Adjutant General Charles Barrett. Three National Guard units—a rifle company, a supply company, and a sanitary unit—were stationed in Tulsa in 1921.[2] Colonel L. J. F. Rooney was the senior National Guard officer in Tulsa. National Guard Major Charles Daley was first made aware of the crowd at the courthouse at 8:30 p.m. Barrett told Rooney to make his troops available to local police if need be. In theory, Major Daley had several hundred veterans and servicemen at his disposal across Tulsa and the neighboring towns of Bristow, Broken Arrow, and Cleveland. Crucially, Guardsmen wore a khaki uniform.

As news spread about the crowd outside the courthouse, William Redfearn, a white man who owned two buildings in Greenwood, closed his Dixie Theater, a space that seated more than a thousand, at 9:30 p.m.[3] He took it upon himself to find out what was going on at the courthouse, said he saw nearly sixty people turning violent, and turned around to go back to his theater, where he claimed he was going to try to prevent more from coming to the courthouse. National Guard Captain Van Voorhis was at the armory when local police called and asked for assistance. He called Colonel Rooney at 9:30 p.m.

After an attempt by three white men to take Rowland from the sheriff's custody, the sheriff decided to barricade the jail. He locked Rowland, his men, and himself inside his office. As a small number of white men pushed their way to the courthouse interior, a white man named E. S. MacQueen tried to disarm a Black man identified as Johnny Cole. MacQueen grabbed Cole's gun. Cole refused to let go, and the gun fired. The June 1 edition of the *World* reported that 150 white men and 300 Black men were at the courthouse at 10:15 p.m. on May 31 when fighting and shooting began in earnest, and the number of white men joining in was still growing as Black men at the courthouse had begun to fight back.[4] Tulsa police officer J. L. Wilson told the *World* that a group of Black men threatened to lynch him at Second Street and Cincinnati, but he was let go when a Black man talked them down.

*

National Guard Major Byron Kirkpatrick saw armed men in cars speeding past his house on Sixth Street, then heard gunfire at Fifth and Elgin and called Rooney. Rooney and Voorhis met at Kirkpatrick's home, where Rooney called Barrett in Oklahoma City at 10:13 p.m. and told him about the violence taking place. Barrett told them to guard the armory and assist local authorities, but that no one could mobilize without the governor's approval. After the phone call, Rooney told Voorhis to take sixteen men to the police station. Barrett called and got through to Oklahoma governor James B. A. Robertson shortly thereafter. He telephoned Chief Gustafson and asked if he needed assistance from the Guard. Gustafson told Governor Robertson no help was needed.

Between fifteen hundred and two thousand white folks had convened outside the courthouse by 10:30 p.m. "Governor Robertson, however, felt that more action was needed, and since the Tulsa authorities were apparently content with matters as they stood, he took the initiative," according to Scott Ellsworth's *Death in a Promised Land: The Tulsa Race Riot of 1921*. "Shortly after midnight, he ordered Major Kirkpatrick in Tulsa to draw up a telegram—addressed to the governor—requesting that the National Guard be sent into the city. He then ordered Kirkpatrick to get Gustafson, McCullough, and any district judge he could find to sign it, since at that time Oklahoma law required that a request for the National Guard to be sent into any area needed the signatures of the local police chief, the county sheriff, and a local judge." Kirkpatrick completed his task hours later. While he tracked down signatures, Black families fought or fled.

Kenny Booker was eight years old, one of five children living at 320 N. Hartford Avenue. "We had a lovely home, filled with beautiful furniture, including a grand piano," he told the Greenwood Cultural Center.[5] "All our clothes and personal belongings—just everything—were burned up during the riot. Early on the morning of June 1, 1921, my parents were awakened by the sounds of shooting and the smell of fire, and the noise of fleeing [B]lacks running past our house. My dad awakened us children and sent us to the attic with our mother. We could hear what was going on below. We heard the white men ordering dad to come with them; he was being taken to detention. We could hear dad pleading with the mobsters. He was begging them 'please don't set my house on fire.'

But, of course, that is exactly what they did just before they left with dad. Though dad went outside the house with the mobsters, he slipped away from them when they got preoccupied splashing gasoline or kerosene on the outside of the house to speed up the burning. He rushed to the attic and rescued us. We slipped into the crowd of fleeing [B]lack refugees. Thank God we did not burn up in that attic!"

Otis Clark was nineteen, like Rowland, and was trying to find a way out of the carnage with a friend. "I got caught right in the middle of that riot!" he told the Cultural Center. "Some white mobsters were holed up in the upper floor of the Ray Rhee Flour Mill on East Archer and they were just gunning down [B]lack people, just picking them off like they were swatting flies. Well, I had a friend who worked for Jackson's Funeral Home and he was trying to get to that new ambulance so he could drive it to safety. I went with him. He had the keys in his hand, ready for the takeoff. But one of the mobsters in the Rhee building zoomed in on him and shot him in the hand. The keys flew to the ground and blood shot out of his hand and some of it sprayed on me. We both immediately abandoned plans to save that ambulance! We ran for our lives. We never saw my stepfather again, nor our little pet bulldog, Bob. I just know they perished in that riot. My stepfather was a strong family man. I know he did not desert us. I just wish I knew where he was buried."

The governor's order to mobilize the Guard in Oklahoma City to Tulsa came at 3:00 a.m. on June 1. But the National Guard in Tulsa had already arrived at the police station at 11:00 p.m. on May 31. The Guard received reports that white men had broken into McGee's Hardware Store and stolen guns and ammo. The store owner later said he thought Tulsa Police Captain George H. Blaine was the leader of the group of men who robbed his store.

Beulah Lane Keenan Smith had just celebrated her thirteenth birthday when white men destroyed her family's home. "Mobsters had kicked a hole in the side of the store and had set it on fire. That was the saddest day of my life. That riot cheated us out of childhood innocence."

Delois Vaden Ramsey was a toddler during the massacre. She was born in March 1919. "My father, Hosea Oscar Vaden, owned one of the most popular pool halls in Tulsa at the time of the Tulsa riot," she told the Cultural Center. "Vaden's Pool Hall was located on Greenwood Avenue next to Art's Chili Parlor. Across the street was another pool hall, Spann's Pool Hall. Younger people went to Spann's, and older people came to dad's pool hall. Famous people were always coming to play pool at Vaden's Pool Hall. Boxer Joe Louis always came by my dad's pool hall to buy newspapers. Dad sold 'Black Dispatch' newspapers and white Tulsa newspapers. My parents also owned a home on Elgin Street, which burned to the ground in the riot. I was too young to personally remember details of the riot, but I heard my parents talk about the riot—how bad it was, how it destroyed so much property that [B]lacks had worked so hard to acquire."

*

Past midnight and before 2:00 a.m., a group of white Tulsans smashed the front windows of a pair of businesses and set the insides afire on Archer Street in the southwestern corner of Greenwood. Firefighters at Fire Station No. 2 answered the call to extinguish the flames. They were stopped before putting their hoses into action by the same group of white men who set the fire. They wanted to see the building burn.

Farther north in Deep Greenwood, white Tulsans snuck across the Santa Fe and Frisco railroad tracks. They shot out the Williams

Building and the office of the *Oklahoma Sun,* one of two Black-owned newspapers that would be forced to shutter due to the damage and denial of insurance claims. The other, the *Tulsa Star,* was decimated along with A. J. Smitherman's livelihood. "Nine p.m. the trouble started," he later wrote. "Two a.m. the thing was done."

Mary Elizabeth Jones Parrish was wide awake, clutching her child in her apartment, as the fighting began to leak into Greenwood past midnight. "About 1:30 o'clock the firing had somewhat subsided, and it was hoped that the crisis was over," she wrote. "Someone on the street cried out, 'Look, they are burning Cincinnati!' On looking, we beheld columns of smoke and fire, and by this we knew the enemy was surging quickly upon Greenwood." She watched as Black men stood and defended their community, defended her, from white men shooting and setting fire to the place they called home. "Our boys stood 'like a stone wall,'" she wrote, "offsetting each and every attempt to burn Greenwood and the immediate vicinity." White men coming in behind those pierced through to the Frisco railroad tracks, punctured at least one passenger train, and set fires at the southwestern boundary of Greenwood. At 3:15 a.m., Major Daley said he saw to it fires were extinguished at the Boston and Frisco railroad tracks. But right afterward, he said in his report five weeks after the massacre, he saw white men climb onto platforms at the Frisco depot on the tracks' south side. "I immediately went to the depot and found a large crowd gathered on the platform of the Frisco station also on the Frisco tracks where several of the men were firing over into the black belt." He said he organized twenty volunteer guardsmen with rifles to stop white attackers "further firing into the negro district."

Gunfire was exchanged across the street from Booker T. Washington High School and at a brickyard off Lansing Avenue and at Pine Street and Peoria Avenue. Another firefight took place at Mount Zion Baptist Church. As Black folks defended their place of worship, the all-white National Guard arrived on scene and pointed their machine guns at the church. The church's stained-glass windows were shattered, and the church was filled with holes. Suddenly, the church erupted in sound and flames, ensuring the desolation of a house of worship with the help of the military on American soil. No Black Tulsan attended church that Sunday. White Tulsans had burned them down.

Mabel Little, twenty-five, who owned an eatery called the Little Café on East Cameron, later wrote, "airplanes dropped incendiary bombs to enhance the burning of Mt. Zion Baptist Church and business buildings." W. I. Brown was a porter on a train taking the Katy Railroad and arriving in Tulsa on June 1. "Two airplanes were doing the most work," he said. "They would every few seconds drop something and every time they did there was a loud explosion, and the sky would be filled with flying debris."

B. C. Franklin, an attorney who had just moved to Tulsa, recounted seeing men urging one another to set fires in parts of white Tulsa in the throes of the massacre. James Leighton Avery, a teenager then, said decades later, "there was a mob of [B]lack and white men in confrontation, lots of yelling, screams and women, and the firing of many guns. Cars sped by haphazardly, and no policing of the streets could be seen."

By 4:00 a.m. on June 1, Dick Rowland was the safest Black man in Tulsa. When the mob that initially set out to take Rowland turned its attention to Greenwood, Rowland was all but forgotten by nearly every white man except those charged with protecting him. From the fifth floor of his barricaded jail and office, Sheriff McCullough believed the situation was well under control when a reporter from the *World* made his way up to the jail in the middle of the night. "We believe we have the situation well in hand without further help from the national guard or state militia," he said. "While I do not feel the situation warrants help from the outside, yet it is always best to play safety first."

After finding out Rowland was secure in the courthouse, Deputy

Barney Cleaver walked toward home in North Greenwood to get his family and take them to a farmhouse he owned outside the city limits. He saw armed Black and white groups, hostile and prowling. He was joined by two other Black men on his way. The trio were stopped by carloads of white men asking who they were and where they were coming from. Once back in Greenwood, Cleaver happened upon "fifteen or twenty boys with guns" asking if Rowland had been lynched. Cleaver told them no, Rowland had not been lynched. He asked them to go home. They waved him off. "White man lover," one of them called him.

All night, Black folks stood ready to fight. Some stood in their own front yards with guns, preparing for the attack they knew was coming to their homes. At a building Cleaver owned, some Black folks had climbed to the second floor overlooking the intersection at Easton and Greenwood. Cleaver said he joined them and waited until nearly 5:00 a.m. Then they heard a shrill whistle.

The high pitch of the whistle woke C. F. Gabe from his sleep. A carpenter at Dreamland Theatre, Green Smith, said he heard a siren blare as he was installing a cooling system and went to the window to peer around after hearing the whistle. James T. A. West told Parrish he heard the whistle too, while staying with Booker T. Washington High School principal Ellis Walker Woods at his home on Detroit Avenue. "About five o'clock a very peculiar whistle blew," he said. "This seemed to be a signal for a concerted attack by the whites, for immediately a terrible gunfire began. Aeroplanes also began to fly over very low; what they were doing I cannot say, for I was in my room." Dr. R. T. Bridgewater heard the whistle while he, his wife, Mattie, and their niece left their house. He'd received a phone call just minutes earlier imploring him to attend to two wounded men. As he opened the front door, a bullet hit his leg. He fled back inside his home. His wife stuck her head out the front door and fled back inside as bullets hit the door. They escaped out the back. "Shortly after we left a whistle blew," Bridgewater said. Some Black folks did not hear the whistle. Some white folks have said the noise came from a steel plant near Greenwood. Others have said the noise came from the "fire steam whistle" at the Public Service Oklahoma plant installed in November 1920. The *World* reported the PSO whistle could be heard within a twenty-mile radius and was used when "announcing changes of shift, 'election returns,' and other 'news' of public interest." Not everyone in Greenwood heard or mentioned hearing the whistle, but the people who did thought what West and Bridgewater did: "The shots rang from a machine gun located on the Standpipe Hill near my residence and aeroplanes began to fly over us, in some instances very low to the ground," Bridgewater said. "A cry was heard from the women saying, 'Look out for the aeroplanes, they are shooting upon us.'"

"There was a great shadow in the sky," Parrish wrote, "and upon second look, we discerned that this cloud was caused by fast-approaching aeroplanes. It then dawned upon us that the enemy had organized in the night and was invading our district, the same as the Germans invaded France and Belgium."

The terror continued from the ground into the early morning. Parrish, watching from her apartment in the Woods Building at Greenwood and Archer, "saw carloads of men with rifles unloading up near the granary, which is located on the railroad tracks near First Street. Then the truth dawned upon us that our men were fighting in vain to hold their dear Greenwood."

"About 5:30 someone called up our home and said for the men not to fight," West told Parrish, "that the Home Guard were visiting the homes and searching them but that they would harm no one. A few minutes after that, some men appeared with guns drawn and ordered all men out of the house." West was made to raise his hands, searched, and then put into line with other Black men on the street. In all, he said, thirty to forty men were rounded up and marched through the street to the Convention Hall while "some ruffians would shoot at our heels and swore at those who had difficulty keeping up."

Green Smith watched a "gang" "knocking on the doors and setting the buildings afire." Who were the men in these gangs? "Policemen, I guess," he said. He was harassed by "ten or twelve." They wore "what they call special police and deputy sheriff's badges . . . Some had ribbons and some of them had regular stars."

Gurley's hotel was raided by men "wearing khaki suits." They were clear in their warning to him: "You better get out of that hotel because we're going to burn all of this Goddamn stuff." Upon leaving, Gurley was met with a hail of gunfire sprayed down Greenwood Avenue. He took shelter at Dunbar School on North Hartford Avenue but was forced to leave that place too after it was set ablaze.

Ernestine Gibbs was eighteen in 1921. A family friend fled to her house after the fighting broke out. "He was so scared he could not sit still, nor lie down. He just paced up and down the floor talking about the 'mess' going on downtown and on Greenwood. When daylight came, [B]lack people were moving down the train tracks like ants. We joined the fleeing people. During this fleeing frenzy, we made it to Golden Gate Park near 36th Street North. We had to run from there because someone warned us that whites were shooting down [B]lacks who were fleeing along railroad tracks. Some of them were shot by whites firing from airplanes." Survivors said they saw turpentine bombs dropped from airplanes onto Greenwood, likely used to control the flames so that the fire did not escape the district and threaten Greater Tulsa. A train pulling into Union Station was shot up as Tulsa's fire department put out only those fires that threatened white businesses downtown.

Near 8:00 a.m. on June 1, Dr. A. C. Jackson, a person the Mayo Clinic founders called "the most able Negro surgeon in America," according to the Greenwood Cultural Center, was one of those who surrendered at gunpoint. With his hands in the air, a group of white men shot him as he was headed to an internment camp. "I heard him holler and looked up and saw him coming about twenty-feet away from me or thirty, with his hands up, and he said . . . Here I am, I want to go with you, or words to that effect," Jackson's white neighbor and former police commissioner John Oliphant said in his testimony. "I said to the fellows, 'That's Dr. Jackson, don't hurt him.'" Oliphant, who lived just around the corner, thought he could get the police to stop these seven or eight "fellows" from killing Dr. Jackson. Oliphant never identified Jackson's murderers, and they were never caught.

Oliphant said he was trying to stop arsonists from torching his home rather than just trying to save Dr. Jackson's life. "I wanted to get some policemen to help me. I thought I could stop that whole business, but I guess I was mistaken." Near mid-morning, Oliphant thought the violence had finished. "The fight was all over and had been for an hour and a half. There was no shooting at that particular time because there were no negroes to shoot at." The two men who shot Dr. Jackson were dressed as civilians, but Oliphant said several more wore "khaki uniforms." Looters arrived at the property quickly and in force. Oliphant said they were "a hundred or two" in number—men, women, and children. "Some were singing, some were playing pianos that were taken out of the buildings, some were running victrolas, some dancing a jig and just having a rollicking easy good time in a business which they thought . . . was upright." Oliphant went on: "They absolutely sacked all the houses and took everything out . . . Pianos, victrolas, clothing, chairs, musical instruments, clothing of all kinds [;] men, women and children would go in the house and fill up pillow cases, sheets and clothing and carry them out and carry them away."

*

Guy Ashby was a young white clerk at Cooper's Grocery on Fourteenth Street. When he showed up to work on June 1, his boss told him to go back home. "The boss told me there would be no work today as he was declaring it 'Nigger Day' and he was going hunting niggers," Ashby said. "He took a rifle and told me to lock up the store."

A gang of white Tulsans "went to the home of an old couple and the old man, eighty years old, was paralyzed and sat in a chair and they told him to march and he told them he was crippled, but he'd go if someone would take him, and they told his wife (old, too) to go, but she didn't want to leave him, and he told her to go on anyway," a person told *The Chicago Defender* for a story appearing less than two weeks after the massacre. "As she left one of the damn dogs shot the old man."

White Tulsans burned down Frissell Memorial Hospital and the Colored Library Branch at 429 E. Archer. White Tulsans took books from the library and burned them in the street.

There are many substantial but anonymous eyewitness accounts. These accounts are nearly impossible to verify using empirical means, but I have little doubt that most, if not all, are true: white Tulsa women looted Black homes with shopping bags in hand, shoving silverware, clothing, and jewelry into those bags while remarking how much better Black Tulsans lived than they did; white Tulsans swept through recently abandoned homes, loaded Black Tulsans' furniture into trucks, and threw Black family Bibles into flames; white Tulsans snapped photos in front of Black-owned ruins; gangs of white Tulsa men cornered Black couples and Black families, killed Black fathers and husbands, separated Black wives and mothers from their children and raped them behind a brick wall just close enough so that those children could hear their mothers' violent screams.

*

Governor Robertson declared martial law in Tulsa at 11:29 a.m. on June 1, leaving the National Guard's Charles Barrett in charge. One of Barrett's most consequential acts as officer in charge was banning funerals. His next was interning Black Tulsans at the Convention Hall, baseball park, and fairgrounds. Nearly all Black Tulsans who were held captive needed a white person to vouch for them to gain release. Some wouldn't gain release for a week. Some Black Tulsans managed to escape involuntary imprisonment by hiding in the woods on the outskirts of town or disappearing into the woods altogether.

*

By noon on June 1, the fighting had ended. All but just a few Greenwood residents had been taken into custody and interned. The National Guard, with more forces from Oklahoma City, patrolled the edge of the district. Greenwood was in ashes, piles of bricks where six hundred businesses, twelve hundred buildings, and thirty-six blocks, home to ten thousand people, used to be. "Greenwood avenue, principal business district in the negro district, is a mass of broken bricks and debris," the *World* reported the following day. "Only gas and water pipes, bath fixtures, bedsteads or other metal fixtures remain to mark the places where homes once stood. The negro residences remaining intact can almost be counted on one's hand. There is not an undamaged business building owned by negroes in the entire district."

"I watched this awful destruction from where I sat on the hillside," said an unidentified person in Parrish's book, later believed to be Mrs. C. L. Netherland. "As I sat and watched my modern 10-room-and-basement home burn to ashes, an old white man came by. Addressing me as 'Auntie,' he said, 'It's awful, ain't it?' and offered me a dollar to buy my dinner with."

With the district bathed in black smoke and fires still smol-
dering, Barrett's seven companies of Guardsmen, having already
rounded up thousands of Black Tulsans and interned them at the
county fairgrounds, awaited further instruction. At 8:30 a.m. on
June 2, the situation was "well under control," Barrett declared
to the *World*. "We do not anticipate any further rioting, although
nothing has been overlooked as a precaution against its recurrence.
With Tulsa under martial law, which is now in force, we expect to
see rapid readjustment of conditions." Nearly the entire population
of Black Tulsans who had not been killed or escaped had been de-
tained at the fairgrounds.

Less than a month after the massacre, an all-white grand jury had
been assembled and submitted its findings. "We find that the recent
race riot was the direct result of an effort on the part of a certain
group of colored men who appeared at the courthouse on the night
of May 31, 1921." It further stated, "there was no mob spirit among
the whites, no talk of lynching and no arms." Neither the *World*
nor the *Tribune* acknowledged the massacre or its anniversary for
thirty years. "At *Tribune*," Ellsworth wrote in his 1992 book-length
account, *Death in a Promised Land*, "someone removed a front-
page article and part of the editorial page from the May 31, 1921,
edition in the bound volumes of the newspaper before they were
microfilmed by the Works Progress Administration in the 1930s."
    The *Oklahoma Eagle*, a Black newspaper that picked up the
spiritual mantle left after the demolition of the *Star* and *Sun*,
made its first reference to the massacre in 1946: "In 1921 racial
bitterness, which had been brooding for several years, culminated
in one of the most disastrous race riots in the nation's history."
Also in 1946, Loren Gill published a detailed account of the massacre for his master's thesis. Gill's work, called "The Tulsa Race
Riot," is notable because, as Dr. Rachael Hill pointed out in her

work "The 1921 Tulsa Massacre," Gill's thesis is "an unusual in-
quiry into an event that was largely censored.⁶ While Gill gave
an account of the white mob-led violence against Greenwood in
a way that certainly represented a more balanced view than the
blatantly prejudiced and sensational 1921 newspaper articles, he
affirmed the Tulsa Grand Jury Report's assessment that armed African Americans were a principal cause."

*

In 1948, Nancy Feldman, a sociology instructor at the University
of Tulsa, met Robert Fairchild, a Black Tulsan in his fifties, while
working on behalf of the League of Women Voters in Tulsa. She
was attempting to find a doctor for Tulsa's county health department when she met Fairchild, a recreation officer who studied at
the University of Nebraska and held a master's in public health.
Born in Arkansas and raised in Tulsa, he was the first person to
tell Feldman about what was then called the Tulsa Race Riot. It
happened when he was seventeen, and he'd survived it. Being from
Chicago, Feldman was so fascinated by this history she'd never
heard before that she brought a conversation about the riot to a
class she taught at TU. She was surprised to learn her students
had never heard of the event. When she asked their parents and
other older adults she knew, some said they had no idea the riot
happened, and others denied that the riot had occurred. So she
brought Fairchild in to talk to her class, and he told her students
about the carnage wrought beginning that Memorial Day in 1921.
He told them about walking on the railroad tracks alongside his
brother to escape being killed. In an oral history Feldman gave
for *Voices of Oklahoma* with John Erling in 2012, she said a TU
dean of students called her into his office and told her to not let
Fairchild speak to her class again.⁷

John Erling asked, "Why did the dean not want Mr. Fairchild
[to speak]?"

"He didn't want to create any troubles," Feldman said.

In fewer than thirty years, the massacre had been erased from the memory of white Tulsans, as white folks were the only people Feldman taught at TU, a university that had not integrated and would later become my alma mater.

N EARLY ONE HUNDRED YEARS LATER, I STOOD ON ONE of the plaques embedded in the sidewalk on Greenwood Avenue. Some brick buildings survive next to an urban renewal that threatens to engulf what the flames did not claim in the district. *The Oklahoma Eagle* office was just behind me. The Black Wall Street Gallery was just ahead of me, though it, like most good things in Tulsa, has left us too, now that the gallery is in New York City. As I walked the sidewalk, stepping from plaque to plaque, I saw one that honors Bayer Grocery at 304 N. Frankfort Avenue, and another for Dr. P. I. Travis at 122 N. Greenwood Avenue. There are dozens of them—several for doctors—alongside the Dreamland Theatre, once at 127 N. Greenwood, and Duncan and Clinton Grocers at 123 N. Greenwood. There is a plaque for A. J. Smitherman's offices at 115 N. Greenwood, and one for Commodore's (Knotts) Cotton Club at 232a N. Greenwood. There are plaques for tailors and clothing stores, restaurants, a barbershop, a printing shop, a shoe store, a cigar store, a bakery, real estate offices, hotels, and a hospital. Greenwood was so much bigger, so much brighter, than this block that's slowly being squeezed, pushed, and priced out.

On May 29, 1921, this space was a vibrant and exploding city within the city of Tulsa. It was a prosperous community for Black folks looking to escape the racist values—the American values—that had plagued them for so long. For about twenty years, this place offered them hope, community, and respite.

A mob of white Tulsans burned Greenwood to the ground, which led to the deaths of thirty-nine people, according to the 1921 Tulsa Race Riot Commission. Twenty-six of them were Black; thirteen of them were white. All thirty-nine are listed as male. "It should be added, however," said the final report of the Oklahoma Commission to Study the Tulsa Race Riot of 1921, "that at least one credible source from the period—Maurice Willows, who directed the relief operations of the American Red Cross in Tulsa following the riot—indicated in his official report that the total number of riot fatalities may have run as high as three hundred."

The bodies of Black Tulsans were piled onto flatbed trucks. Some were buried without a monument to mark them. Still more were buried in unmarked mass graves. According to some accounts, bodies were dumped into the Arkansas River. The Oaklawn Cemetery in south downtown was said to hold mass graves, as was Newblock Park in west downtown. When families went to claim life insurance policies, most were denied. An article in the June 5, 1921, edition of the *Columbus Dispatch* noted that former Tulsa mayor L. J. Martin chaired a committee, established by the Tulsa Chamber of Commerce, to investigate Black Tulsans' claim to reparations, since the insurance companies denied their claims. "Most of this damage was done by white criminals who should have been shot and killed. As the final outcome, we must rebuild these houses, see that the negroes get their insurance, and get their claims against the city and county." The committee followed with a suggestion of $500,000 to pay Black Tulsans for property lost. Tulsa mayor T. D. Evans held fast to his claims that Black Tulsans had caused the massacre, and the committee was forced to announce the city would not financially recompense its Black citizens. Martin and the committee members tendered their resignations on July 15. They were replaced by a new committee created by the City Commission.

O. W. Gurley lost more than $250,000 in the massacre (over $3.8 million in 2021 dollars). Months afterward he moved to Los Angeles, bought a four-bedroom home, and opened another hotel. He eventually sold his land in Greenwood to other Black folks who stayed.

Mayor Evans and the City Commission pressured Black residents to sell their land so that the city of Tulsa could redistrict Greenwood for industrial use. In a meeting with members of the City Commission, Evans wrote, "Let the Negro settlement be placed farther to the north and east." *The Nation* called this "Tulsa's shame." Gurley, Cleaver, Green, and Gabe were a few who testified in a lawsuit brought by William Redfearn, the owner of the Dixie Theater, against the American Central Insurance Company. The Oklahoma Supreme Court ruled for the insurance company on January 12, 1926, which extinguished Greenwood property owners' best chance for restitution.

To make even more money from the carnage, photos of the damage were turned into postcards with captions like "Little Africa on Fire" and "Running the Negro out of Tulsa."

*

The exact number of people killed during the massacre remains unknown, with the best educated guesses numbering in the hundreds, and damages approaching millions of dollars. Complicating the idea of the massacre is still the thought that it was a premeditated, conspired real estate scheme and not just a hate crime. The difference between "attempted genocide" and "chaotic violence" is the difference between "riot" and "massacre." A riot implies that Black Tulsans destroyed our own community. A massacre implies a brutal and deliberate slaughter of one group of people perpetrated by another group.

It took only twenty-four hours for white Tulsans to decimate thirty-six city blocks and burn down more than twelve hundred homes of beautiful Blackness. The American Red Cross estimated white Tulsans took hundreds of Black lives they decided did not matter. Some scholars estimate the number of Black lives lost is higher—so much higher, in fact, that an earnest search for mass graves filled with Black bodies began ninety-nine years later. Damage to property and generational wealth is estimated in the tens of millions of dollars by twenty-first-century standards. Statutes of limitations have mostly put a stop to justice for the Black lives and Black property lost in American court systems, though a few are still trying to force the state to financially atone for its barbarism. Institutional racism and housing discrimination have made certain that Black Tulsans mostly live in the section of the city known as North Tulsa, and only in North Tulsa. North Tulsa provides fewer job and enrichment opportunities and a worse standard of living than its white counterpart, South Tulsa. Human Rights Watch recognized the damage done in a massive report in May 2020:

> Under international human rights law, governments have an obligation to provide effective remedies for violations of human rights. The fact that a government abdicated its responsibility nearly 100 years ago and continued to do so in subsequent years does not absolve it of that responsibility today—especially when failure to address the harm and related action and inaction result in further harm, as it has in Tulsa . . . Human Rights Watch supports the conclusion of the Oklahoma Commission to Study the Tulsa Race Riot of 1921 (recently renamed the Tulsa Race Massacre Commission)—a commission created by the Oklahoma state legislature in 1997 to study the massacre and make recommendations—that reparations should be made.

*

I was ten years old in 1997. My parents were reaching for the American Dream they had been promised. We were living in Hattiesburg,

Mississippi, when a moving company truck emerged at the dead end of our block, in front of the first house I have memory of, at 800 Mable Street. My younger sister, Denise, who we all call Nise, and I never knew life without having our own rooms. We were so indulged in our individuality that we took to the idea of a bunkbed because we thought that might be fun. I slept on the top bunk and Nise slept on the bottom for just a couple of weeks before she decided she'd made a mistake. I moved to the bottom. The movers had no trouble taking down the bed, packing its firetruck-red railing and two twin mattresses into what I believed was the largest trailer in the world, for it held my entire life and that of my family. When the movers hoisted our velvet red couch and then our matching sofa, I scurried outside to stand in the street. I couldn't believe one would fit, let alone both. When I saw not only did they fit, but there was ample room to spare, I thought the world was surely too big, never that my view of it was too small.

I was born at Tinker Air Force Base in Oklahoma City—an Okie by birth. My mother, Felecia, was a captain in the United States Air Force, and my father was a buck sergeant when they met. Mama gave birth to me just before leaving the military, and my father finished his service just as Nise was brought into this world twenty-three months later. Having enlisted as soon as he graduated high school in Graceville, Florida, my father's plan a decade later was to go to college at Southern Miss and open a computer repair business while he pursued his degree. He wanted to move closer to his home, a small town outside of Graceville called Campbellton, but my mother had implored my father to move us all to Hattiesburg, to her hometown, so that her mother, my Grandmomme, could help raise us. I couldn't have known then that both of my parents would get what they wanted.

*

I have little recollection of the drive from Oklahoma City to Hattiesburg, only that my mother found the whole ordeal harrowing. They'd packed themselves, loaded their home into a U-Haul, put my sister and me in the back of their car, and departed. Mama drove the car with my sister and me strapped into car seats in the back. My father followed in the U-Haul. I don't remember arriving at the house. I don't remember what the house looked like without furnishings. I only remember my red bike with training wheels in the driveway of the carport. I was happy. The first school I was ever enrolled in was Jefferson Davis Head Start. My first teacher, Mrs. Moore, greeted me and my four-year-old classmates—all of whom were Black—with the most perfect welcome I've ever heard for a preschool class. After the last parent had left on the first day of school, she shut the door, lifted her nose, quickly looked down it in one motion, and said, "I'm your mama now." I was shook.

When I told my mother this story later, she smiled at me. "You'll be all right," she said. Mama had chosen Mrs. Moore for me and later my sister because Mrs. Moore was a strict disciplinarian. Mama was always at Head Start, or downtown at the local Head Start headquarters. She split her time between pursuing a terminal master's degree in marriage and family therapy at Southern Miss— where she'd also earned her undergraduate degree in special education nearly twenty years prior while also participating in the USM Reserve Officers' Training Corps—and raising my sister and me. Her plan was to help my father get situated as a part-time student. He worked at FedEx as a courier while trying to get his computer business off the ground. But my father didn't like school. He liked making money and having a sense of purpose, and his job at FedEx allowed him both. Soon, he rose from courier to operations manager. He learned there was a career for him at FedEx, and he didn't have to have a college diploma to pursue it. As he excelled at his job, Mama proved outstanding in her graduate work. Just two years after she began the program, she graduated and took a job at Pine

Grove Behavioral Health & Addiction Services, one of the premier drug and family rehab clinics in the country. In my family, we were each finding our way in Hattiesburg. As my parents found success, Nise and I were allowed to pursue any activity within driving distance. We took karate classes. I was in Cub Scouts, Nise in Girl Scouts. I played baseball in the Dixie Youth Baseball League, won a fall city title on my U10 soccer team. Two years after we moved to Hattiesburg, my mother had not just made herself integral to Head Start but made sure I attended private school at Presbyterian Christian School—one of the best schools in the area, in the whitest part of a city in the legally integrated, socially segregated South. Two years later my sister followed. There was one other Black child I saw in the school, and he was not in my class. The only friends I made there were white. I wouldn't realize what a cruelty this was until I was an adult. The white boys didn't always want to play with me, but one of the white girls always did. The first one who didn't ask to rub my head was Hartley. She said she asked her mom about my hair, and she'd been told it'd be impolite to ask to touch it. And she never did. I liked her best.

The older I grew, the more I came to understand Grandmomme was the reason my family thrived. Grandmomme babysat Nise and me. She bought our Easter clothes each year out of the JCPenney catalog. She took us to run errands all over town and introduced us to every person she spoke with along the way. We were "Jean's grandbabies," a moniker that felt royal in speech. This was as true when Grandmomme drove us downtown to the bank in her beige Plymouth Acclaim as it was at Zion Chapel AME Church, my first church. Here I learned the tradition of Black church, of Denmark Vesey and what Black folks can do, must do. Services began at 10:00 a.m. on Sundays and were interminable. I spent whole Sunday mornings on my feet staring at the backs of men and women in the pews in front of me. I couldn't see the choir, let alone the person leading it, and I was constantly looking up at the mouths of adults next to me, to try to decipher the words I was supposed to sing. When a person—never the pastor—began the offering, I felt only a few minutes of relief as I was able to sit down and get off my feet, which hurt so much. Grandmomme would remind me I was much too young to be complaining about my feet hurting. I'd stare at the gold offering plate as it was passed over my head, thinking there must be all the money in the world in that plate, never knowing how close to the truth I was. What little people had in the world went into that plate along with their hope for their future. The tithe you owed, the offering you prayed.

Through years of her own work, and the work of many others in Hattiesburg over the previous forty years, Grandmomme carved out space for us by sacrificing more than I would come to realize until adulthood. But I tasted the depth of respect people possessed for her. While at PCS, my third-grade teacher, Mrs. Malone, helped me into Grandmomme's car one day after school. When Mrs. Malone met eyes with Grandmomme's, she looked startled.

"Can I help you?" Grandmomme said.

"No, Ms. Connor."

I had no idea Mrs. Malone knew Grandmomme, and from the look on Grandmomme's face, she didn't know Mrs. Malone either. My elementary teacher took in my grandmother for a moment longer, smiled, then shut the door. Later, when Black History Month was discussed in class, my classmates and I were assigned to write reports about Black historical figures. The white kids got to pick folks like Martin Luther King Jr., Garrett A. Morgan, George Washington Carver, and Sojourner Truth. I did not. Mrs. Malone told me to write a report about Grandmomme. I was angry about that. I wanted to write about Frederick Douglass, "a real historical figure," I said, and I told Grandmomme as much when I told her Mrs. Malone said I had to write about her.

Grandmomme chuckled. "Well, I ain't no Frederick Douglass," she said. "But some folks think I did a few things worthwhile—like be your Grandmomme." She smiled at me. She always smiled at me. She told me her stories, and I filled my loose-leaf binder for my third-grade report, and later my journals, with them. By sixth grade, Grandmomme was the first subject I wanted to talk about every February and each month thereafter. By the time I was twelve years old, she'd told me so much for my sixth-grade history class paper that it's archived among the Peggy Jean Connor Papers at the University of Southern Mississippi McCain Library and Archives. From Grandmomme, I learned that the civil rights movement was my birthright. Black activism, as tradition, was my birthright. The tradition ran through my veins. I learned a dream promised was being achieved, and my parents, my sister, and I were the proof, realized. We didn't start out attending white schools, but that's where we ended up. We enunciated when we spoke, like white folks. We played baseball and soccer, like white folks. My parents haven't divorced, and their children were not raised in poverty. We were the future that Booker T. Washington's bootstraps promised and the talented tenth that W. E. B. Du Bois anointed. This is what my parents demonstrated with their every breath, their every action.

I wouldn't understand what my Grandmomme gave, sacrificed, so that I could live as I do until it was clear to me that she lost not just her livelihood, her business, and many so-called friends but her daughter for the half measures that civil rights legislation turned out to be.

My Grandmomme was Peggy Jean Connor. She was raised in Hattiesburg, Mississippi, where the right to vote was expressly denied to Black men and women like her, from the drafting of the 1890 state constitution until the 1965 Voting Rights Act. In 1890, 57 percent of Mississippians were Black. The state maintained 134 delegates, of which 130 were Democrats and 133 were white. Mississippi, where racist Democrats took over the state legislature and formed policy around white supremacist ideology. "The Negro is not a white man with a black skin," they said. "He is a different race. He is a

REQUIEM FOR THE MASSACRE 37

barbarian, and barbarians cannot rule civilized people." This same constitution made laws enacting a two-dollar poll tax that must be paid two years in advance of any election a citizen wanted to partic- ipate in; two years of residency in the state with at least one year of residency in the voting precinct; a literacy test that involved reading a portion of the state constitution and a willingness to demonstrate comprehension of that portion to any registrar who required such. Poll taxes remained law in some states until 1965. In 1898, the U.S. Supreme Court took up the charge that these restrictions are ille- gal and found they "do not on their face discriminate between the races, and it has not been shown that their actual administration was evil, only that evil was possible under them." This form of voter suppression continued well into the 1960s, when my Grandmomme was a civil rights activist in Hattiesburg as a single mom of two; had built, owned, and operated Jean's Beauty Shop; and was building toward becoming the woman who sued the governor and state of Mississippi for voting rights reapportionment because registration was made nearly impossible for most Black voters in the state by the registration procedure.

"The applicant must complete the form perfectly without any as- sistance. Questions 1-17 request such information as the applicant's name, age, occupation, residence, citizenship, and criminal record. Question 18 requires him to copy a section of the Mississippi Con- stitution selected by the registrar. Question 19 requires him to write an interpretation of the section he has copied. Question 20 calls for a description of duties of citizenship under a constitutional form of government." In at least one county in Mississippi, Black citizens who wanted to register to vote were never shown the registration form. Grandmomme was arrested and jailed twice for picketing outside the Forrest County Courthouse. She was once asked if she was upset about being thrown in jail.

"Oh no," she said. "I thought I was getting freedom."

Once, when she received a notice for jury duty, she showed up among the prospective jurors and was asked a question. "Have you ever sued anyone?"

"I filed suit against the state of Mississippi," she said.

She was a delegate in the Mississippi Freedom Democratic Party at the 1963 Democratic national convention alongside Fannie Lou Hamer as she questioned America. When a group of racists threatened violence toward her and a busload of Black folks, Lawrence Guyot said she gave the bus driver courage that comes from a kitchen knife inches from his face. She was married once. I found her marriage license at the courthouse she picketed, in the colored section.

Twenty-six days shy of her thirty-third birthday, Grandmomme strutted to cheers at the Masonic Temple in Jackson, Mississippi, as she was joined by members of the MFDP in 1965. She and seven others signed their names to a suit filed against the Mississippi state legislature to begin a journey legally called *Peggy J. Connor v. Johnson*. Johnson in this matter was Mississippi Governor Paul B. Johnson, and this case began a fourteen-year journey with eight trips to the U.S. Supreme Court that would result in reapportioning voting districts in the state. The case created a policy that meant Black votes would be meaningful by not only counting the number of voters in a district, but which voters were in those districts. The case changed how voting rights laws were made at the federal level. In *Mississippi Politics: The Struggle for Power 1976–2008*, Grandmomme's contribution to this country—to me, her grandson—is summed up: "The imposition of small, single-member legislative districts and the presence of a significant number of [B]lacks in the legislature would transform the way power was exercised at the state capitol."

For this, Grandmomme is remembered in these pages and others. There is a research grant in her name at my mother's alma mater, the University of Southern Mississippi, and she received numerous awards, including the Carter G. Woodson Award for Courage in Civil Rights. What is not remembered is that she lost her business because she was labeled an agitator by white supremacists in

Hattiesburg, who told her friends not to patronize her business lest they lose their own livelihoods. She was forced to raise my mother, Felecia Young, who lost Grandmomme to the Movement and to unemployment for years. When Grandmomme died in 2018, all she owned was the dilapidated home my great-grandfather built, and we could not afford to keep that in the family.

The ignorant life I lived through my teens, the magical thinking that Black folks had won something *like* self-determination, was ripped away as soon as the last piece of furniture was loaded into the trailer that was eventually driven away from Hattiesburg.

The drive took just over three hours. I would think about it for the next twenty years. I only needed to watch how carefully these men and women from the moving company wrapped my karate trophies is brown paper and gently set them inside boxes. When those monotonous actions began to take their toll on my nine-year-old attention span, I was allowed my imagination in the front yard. The last of my toys came with me. The last of my protected childhood came with me too. We arrived in Panama City, Florida, and the movers began to unpack our things at our new house. I called Grandmomme. I told her about seeing pine trees, just like in Mississippi, about the sand everywhere, even so far inland. "Inland, it's a word," I said. "Mama said that's where we live. Inland." I told her it wasn't so bad because I was going to get to play baseball. I loved baseball. We were thirty minutes from the beach, even though we were "inland," and I couldn't wait for her to see it.

We'd moved here to follow my father's job. He'd earned a promotion from operation manager to senior manager to a station in Panama City. My parents did not have to sell my sister and me on Panama City. As soon as they mentioned "beach," we were in. I loved the water, loved to swim. In Panama City, I'd learn to surf and skateboard. I'd learn so much more, too. The beach was just over the Hathaway Bridge, when in Hattiesburg it was an hour and a half away. The house my parents found had an in-ground pool in the backyard. We arrived at the house on my birthday, and I was allowed to forgo any unpacking to ride the new mountain bike my parents bought me. I didn't notice how few Black folks there were in the neighborhood. I did not know the Black part of town from the white one, and I didn't care to know. I just knew I wanted to play baseball, and I still thought I could do that professionally. Mama always believed I could. "If someone has done it, you can do it too," she'd say.

I'd take my catcher's mitt and ball with me to school until my fourth-grade teacher, Mrs. Mixon, told me I had to leave it at home. I played little league at R. L. Turner, a city league that had recently become renowned for earning a trip to the Little League World Series in Williamsport, Pennsylvania. When we were allowed to play outside at school, I tried to be wherever there was a ball. Once, during the fall that year, I found a group of white kids—they were nearly all white kids—playing catch with a tennis ball. Just tossing it around in a circle. I tried to insert myself, but they refused to throw me the ball. I was so angry that I intercepted the tennis ball like Deion "Prime Time" Sanders and ran toward the tree line at the edge of the field. The white boys—always they were white boys—caught me, wrestled the ball away from me. Only one of them spoke.

"You're lucky we don't Rosewood your butt," he said.

I told the teacher on duty what happened. She deduced that it was I who caused the "fracas." I was admonished but no one got into real trouble. By the time I got home that afternoon, I'd forgotten about the incident. I was thinking about being Ken Griffey Jr. when the bus dropped me off on the corner. I couldn't wait to get to practice. I loved baseball.

Mama taught me to love the game. She'd played competitive fast-pitch softball and was keen on fundamentals. She taught me if I fielded a ground ball on the first hop that no one would ever be able to outrun my throw to first base. Catch fly balls with two hands. Watch the ball hit the bat. She, not my father, was the person who played catch with me in the front yard of our house. During one of these catch sessions, I asked about Rosewood as I threw the ball back to her. She didn't know either, but her tone was leery. She didn't like how the story sounded as I told it to her; like she knew there was something sinister in the use of "Rosewood" as an action verb. When I came home from school one day the next week, she told me were going to watch a movie. I asked which movie, and she told my sister and me to hush. Just watch it. As the credits began to roll, I learned the movie was called *Rosewood*.

*

Rosewood was an all-Black town four hours south of Panama City, hugging the western edge of Florida's Gulf Coast. A little over three hundred people lived there in 1923 when a white woman named Fannie Taylor said "a nigger" broke into her house in Sumner, just a few miles southwest of Rosewood, and beat her, stopping short of saying he raped her. She was sure about her assailant. She said he was Black. But he was not Black. None of the white folks who heard her story wanted to investigate her claim, though. They simply wanted to find that Black man and lynch him. Taylor's false claim led to six days of violence in Rosewood that culminated in twelve Black homes burned to the ground, eight deaths—six Black, two white—and the lynching of a Black Rosewood resident, Sam Carter.[8] The movie *Rosewood* dramatized this story for the first time on screen.

This atrocity had been forgotten for nearly a half century until 1982, when *St. Petersburg Times* (now *Tampa Bay Times*) reporter Gary Moore stumbled onto the story that had been suppressed into silence. Black folks were scared white folks would burn their homes and kill them again if they spoke about the 1923 massacre. Twelve years after Moore wrote the story, in 1994, Florida's legislature passed a law to distribute $2.1 million reparations to survivors,[9] and director John Singleton set out to make the movie Mama now put in front of me. As I watched Don Cheadle and Ving Rhames act the part of Black men trying to protect Black families, their homes, from white violence, I encountered a new feeling: fear. I was not safe. We were not safe. That white boy at school had threatened to do this to me, and it quickly dawned on me that there was little I could do to stop him. I was outnumbered.

After finishing fourth grade at Northside Elementary, I began to see the world and see how it saw me. In fifth grade, I was one of just two Black children in my class. The other was Ashley. Ashley's mother worked at FedEx, where my father worked. I spent a lot of time at the FedEx station, building forts out of cardboard boxes with Nise. I saw lots of Ashley and her mom, too, and we became close at school, looking out for each other, eating lunch together. But we didn't bond over being Black. Not at first. We bonded over our mutual hate for our fifth-grade teacher, Mrs. Gilbert. Mrs. Gilbert was harder on us than the rest of the class. We couldn't prove it. But we knew it. When the entirety of the class was loud, talking when she'd asked everyone to be quiet, Ashley or I would be labeled instigator, agitator, the reason the class was unruly. She came down hard on us when we misread a word aloud in class. She asked us to wait to get in line until everyone else was in line to go to lunch or recess. We hated being at the back of the line, but we ranked ourselves accordingly. Getting a pass to go the bathroom was always the worst, so much so that I always made sure to pee before entering Mrs. Gilbert's class because I didn't want to be caught having to hold it while she admonished me or flat told me no, I couldn't go.

One day Ashley couldn't hold it. She looked ready to burst next to me. She pleaded with Mrs. Gilbert to let her go to the bathroom.

Mrs. Gilbert said no. Ashley cried out, yelled, she couldn't hold it. Mrs. Gilbert looked taken aback. "You will learn to treat me with respect, and you will hold it until lunch." Ashley couldn't hold it, and her face contorted with anger until she looked stricken, afraid. Then all at once I saw tears well in her eyes and softly roll down her brown cheeks. I followed the tears down her cheeks and saw her shuffle her feet. The floor around them had pooled with yellow water. Instinctively, I got up to go get paper towels. Ashley tried to stop me. "RJ!" I stopped and turned, but so did the class and Mrs. Gilbert. With every eye in the room on her, Ashley burst into tears and all-out wailing. Mrs. Gilbert told her go to the bathroom. Three days later, I was the only Black child in Mrs. Gilbert's class.

I didn't cope well. I had lost my friend, the only person I felt connected to. I didn't want to go to school. I didn't want to be around any of my classmates. I didn't want to read aloud for Mrs. Gilbert. Mama made me talk about my feelings after weeks of what she called "being blue." Not long after talking to Mama about my feelings, she arranged for me to transfer to another school. I finished fifth grade at Highland Park Elementary.

My teacher at Highland Park, Ms. Burt, was a white lady in her sixties who my parents and I knew from church. We attended Faith Christian Family Church across the Hathaway Bridge in Panama City Beach. My father had heard about FCFC at work while getting oriented at FedEx. Ashley and her mom went to church there. Ashley stopped talking to me after she left Mrs. Gilbert's class.

We attended our first service, and we were welcomed. We were invited to participate, to be a part of the church and to work in the church—always "the church." We were offered membership to the church, and my parents eagerly accepted. They did not question how white the church was, or our white pastor. They were happy to have a church home. Mama worked as a greeter and later in the church bookstore. My father worked as an usher. I started in the nursery. FCFC became a second home for my family and me. Our pastor, Markus Bishop, was an Auburn football fan, and the first charismatic evangelical Christian pastor in my life. Until I saw this white man with blond hair parted down the middle and curling up at his shoulders, I didn't appreciate that this was the first church my parents ever picked for us, and our pastor was white.

I didn't question that. I didn't know enough to ask good questions then, either. I knew that I liked being at the church, and I liked working with people who were happy to see me and wanted to see me do well. Mrs. Burt was such a person. This older white lady became friends with my mother in a short number of months, and they believed it was God's will for me to be in her fifth-grade class. So did I. God's will was viewed as a panacea in my parents' house, and the more you did in his name, the better the cure worked.

As a preteen, I went to the teenage service called "Oneighty," then helped with the children's service in addition to working in the nursery. I relished helping my mother complete her tasks at the bookstore, and I never wondered where the money from tithes and offerings ended up.

I never asked why Mama would tune the radio to Rush Limbaugh's show as we drove to Publix for groceries, to R. L. Turner for baseball practice, or why, when I complained about talk radio, she'd put a sermon tape into the cassette player in the car. When I learned Pastor Bishop's home was a $4 million mansion in a tony gated community in Panama City Beach, I asked Mama how our preacher could afford such a nice house. "God showers down his riches on those who love him," she said. She assured me that if I loved God and worked hard, good things would happen to me. She believed my father, our home, our upward mobility among white folks, was proof of that. And so I loved God with all my heart because I wanted to be rich too.

At our home, the Trinity Broadcasting Network was on our living room TV as often as ESPN. Through this cable network, I got to know televangelists like they were relatives. Joyce Meyer became one of my mother's favorites, while my father gave his attention to Creflo Dollar and Bishop Carlton Pearson. Televangelists Kenneth Copeland, Kenneth Hagin, Benny Hinn, Leroy Thompson, Dr. Fred Price, and Bishop T. D. Jakes were men I regularly saw on TBN, and my parents encouraged my viewership. Being right with Jesus was one of the proudest moments I ever gave my parents.

We listened to Vickie Winans, Alvin Slaughter, and Fred Hammond on CD and cassette in my house. My father took great pride in blasting Slaughter from the car speakers when we were driving an hour-plus from Panama City to his boyhood home, Campbellton, yelling out "Get slaughtered!" when we'd protest. Campbellton did not appear on most maps in the summer of 1998. There were about as many people who lived there then as lived in Rosewood in 1923. But in this tiny town, my father became the eleventh of twelve children. His promotion was the primary reason for moving to Panama City, but the prospect of being just an hour from his hometown was enough to convince him and my mother that this was a move worth making. He was happy and proud when we pulled into the front yard of my grandfather's house, a shotgun shack with no central heat or air-conditioning, in the very hot month of June in Northeast Florida.

This was the first opportunity I ever had to meet my cousins on my father's side, and I had no idea there were so many. Most of my father's siblings had at least two children, and they were all older than Nise and me. There was nothing I could tell them they didn't know, and I was shaken by what they already knew that I didn't.

Three of my cousins were the daughters of another cousin of my aunt Earnestine: Latisha, Lakisha, and Ashley. Latisha and Lakisha are twins, and Ashley is their baby sister. They ran together as a group, like a country-ass TLC. When I first met them, I told them that Ashley looked nothing like her sisters, and she reared back and punched me. I dropped to the ground, grabbing my chin as she stood over me. "Watch how you talk to me, li'l nigga." I had heard that word before. My house was one in which we'd watch *Coming to America* or *Harlem Nights*, and then repent for it in prayer later in the week. But this was the first time I had heard that slur hurled *at* me like the epithet it is, and it came from someone who was family. My cousins laughed after I stayed on the ground for too long, and my father cackled on the porch as the rest of my relatives looked on. When I stood up, my mama was first to me and came over to console and protect me. The twins remarked how I needed my mama to save me, and I don't think they understood how right they were. I vaguely remember meeting my grandfather for the first time and his taking me out on his tractor during that weekend. I certainly remember how hot it was in Campbellton, sweating through the night on an air mattress and my parents waking my sister and me up to get into the car at five in the morning. And I vividly remember my father cackling on the drive home about Ashley punching my face.

*

In 1999, I matriculated to Jinks Middle School, and I was enthusiastic about it. I couldn't wait to go from one class to another; to have not one teacher but six—one for each subject. Mama was thrilled to see me excited about school and happier still to know that my principal, Mr. McAllister, was not just Black but a graduate of an HBCU, Florida A&M University, where he'd played football. I'd discovered Black superheroes then too. The movie *Blade* came out in August 1998, and my parents made the rare exception to take Nise and me to see the film at a movie theater. Entranced, I watched a Black man with a samurai sword, a half vampire who walked around during the day wearing a high-top fade. I watched him leap from one rooftop to another, defeat a basement full of vampires, vanquish a bloodthirsty god with a sword while wearing sunglasses indoors. He was who I'd decided I wanted to be when I grew up. I wrote that down near the end of my second-semester, fourth-hour English class and volunteered to read my work aloud. School was almost out that May, and I felt good about my first year in middle school. My classmates clapped dutifully and my teacher let me have my fantasy. I rode the bus home with one of my classmates in fourth hour, a tall-for-our-age white boy named J.R. He told me he liked my story "about the nigger vampire." I pushed him. He pushed me back. The bus driver stopped the bus almost immediately to break us up. He threatened us, and that was enough to stop us coming to blows. But when we got off the bus J.R. tried to fight me again. This time, the instinct I had wasn't to push him, but to run. I ran home as he chased me for two blocks. When I got to the door and let myself in, Mama was home and asked me what I was so worked up about. I pointed to the front door. "J.R. is trying to kill me." Mama went outside and told J.R. to go away, and that if he came back, she was going to call the police. When she settled me and asked me what happened, I told her. She hugged me close and told me everything would be OK. I don't know how my father found out about this incident. I've only ever assumed that my mother told him. I only know he threw open the door to my room that night. He looked around the room, crazed. His eyes settled on me sitting on my bed, grew larger as he closed the distance between us. He pushed in my chest so that I fell backward, and then pointed a finger at me. He was shaking.

"It's bad enough that you wear a white man's name on your back," he said. "I won't have you run from them. Not and live under my roof. Do you understand?"

I nodded. He waited for a moment. Then I understood. He needed me to say the word. "I understand."

He turned around and left, slamming the door behind him.

I thought about Blade that night, what he might do if someone called him nigger. I'd asked for a black trench coat, like the one he wore in the movie, for Christmas, and my parents bought it for me. I got black loafers with a silver buckle on top, black corduroy jeans, and a black button-down shirt and vest to complete the look. The day after J.R. chased me home I pulled that outfit out of my closet and decided to put it on like Blade would. I got off the bus, walked to my locker, and settled into my first-hour class, math. Not long after the bell rang, I was summoned to the principal's office. Mr. McAllister asked me to sit tight in his office while he called my mother. I started to worry. Was I in trouble? I knew you got called to the principal's office only if you were in trouble. What had I done? I don't remember how much time went by before my mother walked into Mr. McAllister's office. Later, I learned he asked my mother to hold on for just a minute, and then he called my math teacher. When my math teacher walked in, she explained to my principal and my mom that she thought I was going to hurt someone at school that day.

"What evidence do you have to support this claim?" Mr. McAllister asked like he was a judge at trial.

"He dressed today like the kids who shot up Columbine," my math teacher said.

This was in May 1999. In April 1999, two students at Columbine High School in Columbine, Colorado, murdered twelve students and a teacher. The gunmen killed themselves less than an hour after they began killing fellow students. Both killers wore black trench coats to the school that day.

Mr. McAllister sent school officials to search my locker for guns or anything else that might lead someone to believe that I was going to commit such a heinous and horrible act. When they found none, he asked me why I chose to wear my outfit, Mama stopped me from talking and spoke up for me. "Blade, James." Then she looked at my sixth-grade math teacher. "The boy's favorite superhero is a comic book character called Blade, and he dressed like him today."

Just then I missed my Grandmomme. I couldn't help thinking she'd know what to say, what to do. I'd seen her just twice since moving away. Mr. McAllister apologized to my mother first and then to me. He told my mother she could take me home with an excused absence if she wished. Mama asked me if I wanted to go home. I did. The next day I was assigned to a new math teacher, a new math class. I felt shunned, disoriented, angry. That day I called Grandmomme on our cordless phone, and I cried to her. What was wrong with me? Why was this happening to me? "Sugar, there is nothing wrong with you. I love you, and I know you are sunshine."

*

Following that year at Jinks, my parents took my sister and me out of public school. They decided I needed a more Christian education. After all, I was thriving at FCFC, like they were. I was becoming more involved in the church and beginning to believe I'd been called to serve as a minister. Mama relished the idea of homeschooling us, and my father was in no position to object. He was getting everything he wanted, and I had had enough of Bay District public schools. I spent four hours studying in the morning, with a half hour a day devoted to Bible study, and got to play baseball, join a children's theater troupe, and continue being a Boy Scout in the evenings once a week.

After one troop meeting, my mother took me home and told me to get undressed out of my uniform, into my sleeping clothes, and come to her and my father's bedroom. I did as I was told. My sister was already there. My parents grabbed our hands and began to pray. I closed my eyes, bowed my head, and listened. "Lord, we know you will take care of us," Mama said. "We know you'll provide a way. That is why we are coming to you, where two or more are gathered, and asking for your favor in picking the right numbers." My parents were praying to hit the Florida Lottery and using my sister and me to increase their chances of being granted favor from God. That was the first time I ever believed my parents might not be right about something. The ritual struck me as wrong, but I could not articulate why, not to myself, not in my journal, and especially not to my parents. After all, weren't we supposed to ask God for what we wanted, what we needed? Was it not his job to provide for us? Doesn't God help those who help themselves, who are among his blessed and highly favored? At twelve, I was lost in what was right, who was right, and I did not have the tools to test these questions. So I put them out of my mind and did my best to settle into my new homeschool routine.

I was just getting used to this Christian homeschool education full of extracurricular activities when parents told my sister and me that the Lord had blessed my father with another opportunity for advancement at FedEx, an upward mobility. He accepted another senior manager position, with more responsibility and more money, in Tulsa, Oklahoma.

My eyes lit up. I knew Tulsa by reputation, through TBN. They called it "Tulsarusalem," equating this city in the middle of the country to Jerusalem. There were churches all over with superstar televangelist pastors everywhere. There was Oral Roberts and his Oral Roberts University. There was Billy Joe Daugherty and his Victory Christian Center. There was Willie George and his Church on the Move. There was Bishop Carlton Pearson and his Higher Dimensions. Bishop Pearson and Dr. Fred Price were the only Black men with a national television audience among the evangelical community. I knew that Bishop Pearson graduated from ORU, and I was thinking about going to college there too, with an eye toward the ministry as a career. After hearing him campaign for George W. Bush to be president, my parents had no doubt in their minds about who they'd vote for. Mama would tell us as much during homeschool lessons with us during seventh and eighth grade. "All the God-fearing men in your life believe in George Bush," she said. "We will too."

The move to Tulsa wasn't as glamorous as the move to Panama City. After just three years in Florida, I was unprepared to pack up and leave again. The immediate elation of moving to Tulsa was overcome by the knowledge of what I'd leave behind: the church, my troop, my baseball team, and our in-ground pool. A moving company packed us up again, and I expected us to move into a house not unlike the large three-bedroom home we enjoyed in Florida. When my parents pulled up to the duplex that I learned was our new home, I was visibly disappointed. Mama said they'd picked this half-a-house as our home because the duplex was close by my father's new station. Sure, that was great for him, I thought. But what did it mean for us? In the short term, for me, that meant finding a church. Finding a Boy Scout troop. Finding a baseball team. Continuing with school.

Mama found everything but a baseball team for me, but I stumbled into a love of bowling. At first, it was Mama's idea of a field trip. Then it was a field trip we just kept taking. Mama would take Nise and me to the bowling alley, Riverside Lanes, and let us roll for two hours. Nise grew tired of bowling, but I didn't. Sometimes Mama would take me by myself as soon as it opened if I'd worked through two lesson plans in one day. I started to spend so much time there that she'd drop me off to run errands with my sister and pick me up on the way home. I was there as often as I was allowed and would get upset when the place closed for holidays. I was there on a Tuesday morning when planes crashed into the World Trade Center. There was a TV monitor on every pair of lanes, and every one of them was tuned to live coverage of what I later learned was a terrorist act. What kind of God would let this happen? I left the lanes and went to the front desk where a Black lady called Ms. Jackie worked. She was in tears. She told me the attack was the worst thing she'd seen since the Oklahoma City bombing. I asked if there could ever be something like that in Tulsa. She told me there already had been. She told me it was called the Tulsa Race Riot. I was fourteen. I'd start high school the next year.

*

I had heard about the Tulsa Race Riot just once before. My father kept having bad luck finding a Black barber to cut our hair. We visited two barbershops before he took me to Tee's on Greenwood Avenue. The area looked old-timey to me. Like someone had tried to re-create a moment past, and made sure that moment was always present to future-proof the area for generations that followed. There were signs claiming this place was once called Black Wall Street. I never thought to ask why, and I wouldn't until I was fifteen.

After two years of homeschooling, I'd had enough of my mama's lesson plans and just my little sister for a classmate. So had Nise. Mama didn't fight us. She was tired of us too, I think. She hadn't worked for nearly five years, and she wanted to move out of the duplex. So Nise went to Byrd Junior High, I went to Booker T. Washington High School, and Mama decided to look for work. Booker T. is a magnet school, and because I didn't live inside its districted area in North Tulsa, I needed to apply and be accepted. The draw was the rigorous and prestigious International Baccalaureate program the school offered. If I completed the program, I could essentially leave high school with two years of college credit. I was excited to get in, excited to go back to school with other kids, excited to have a chance to enter the IB program. Finishing the IB program in the next four years was my goal when I walked into Robyn Thomas's ninth-grade English class.

*

Ms. Thomas was the youngest teacher I ever had in my life. She was warm, embracing, and she delighted in her little brother, Levi, just a year older than me, walking into her class just before ours began to say hi. These were all things I learned through my year with her as well as why she wore a hijab on her head and a jilbab on her body. She told us we could ask her questions if we were at all curious about her, and she was gloriously patient with me. She encouraged free writing as an activity in class, and she recognized I enjoyed writing about sports. She was the first person who told me that I could not only make a career in writing, but could do so as a sportswriter. Ms. Thomas also was the sponsor for the school book club, and she introduced me to writers like Patricia Cornwell, Janet Fitch, Bernhard Schlink, and J. M. Coetzee. She told me about James Baldwin, Ralph Ellison, Zora Neale Hurston, and Toni Morrison, authors unlike any I'd read before. I read them quickly.

Ms. Thomas didn't so much hand me books and novels to read as she encouraged me to follow my curiosity, and it was piqued when she told me about a book called *Death of a Promised Land: The Tulsa Race Riot of 1921*, by Scott Ellsworth. It was a thin volume, fewer than two hundred pages, but I read it and reread it. During the second semester of my freshman year, in 2003, Tim Madigan published his book about the massacre called *The Burning: Massacre, Destruction, and the Tulsa Race Riot of 1921*, and I read that too. By its end, I was sure that Black folks were not safe in Tulsa. Awash in this history, I called Grandmomme in tears. I told her about the massacre. I talked and talked and talked, and when I was through, there was silence. The silence was so long that I asked Grandmomme if she was still there. I heard her sniffle back tears. "Oh, sugar, it's going to be all right." That was the first time in my life that I didn't believe her.

I RAN INTO DR. REBECCA SIMCOE'S RUMP AND FELL OVER. When I looked up, this white woman with blonde hair softly draping over her shoulder, a black blouse, and black skirt rubbing just above her matte open-heel shoes turned around like she had committed some egregious mistake but with a smile that could power the Eastern Grid. Her power radiated through Booker T. Washington High School.

"Oh, honey, are you OK?" she said.

I said I was. I think so. I thought so. I was just running late. I'd missed the bus, my mom had just dropped me off outside, the security guard made me show my school ID, the lady in the office needed to write me a pass to class. I was flustered and brimming with excuses. I was still new enough then not to know exactly where I was going in what everyone I met in my first few days at Booker T. kept calling the "old building." She helped me up, nodded with every word of my explanation, and personally escorted me to my first class while explaining how anyone could get perfectly lost in this byzantine blueprint. After opening the classroom door for me, Ms. Thomas smiled.

"Thanks, Doc," she said. Then to me: "Isn't Dr. Simcoe lovely?"

And she was. Shortly after I learned about Ellsworth's book about the massacre from Ms. Thomas, she pointed me to Doc

Simcoe, who had fought for the opportunity to teach it in class. Soon, I was popping in and out of her class so often that some of her students thought I was in class with them—not a chance. Doc Simcoe taught all the difficult English classes as well as Humanities I, II, and III. In conversation, she could weave in and out of Beckett and Baldwin, lead me around the corner to the massacre, over the bridge to Greek tragedies, back through the massacre, and send me off on my own to battle the *Epic of Gilgamesh*, Seamus Heaney's translation of *Beowulf*, and Homer's *Iliad* only to see me walk in the next day, hear me say I had no idea what was going on, and then gently show me that yes, I did—*see?* Ms. Thomas whetted my appetite for books I never knew were there as weaponry fit for a Black boy to wield. Doc Simcoe took me into the armory, outfitted me, and demonstrated how to parry with fiction like it was a shield, lunge with nonfiction like it was a short sword, and pierce with language like it was a spear.

"You can write it," she said.

She introduced me to those who wrote it, too. After J. M. Coetzee won the Nobel Prize in Literature for *Elizabeth Costello* and had already achieved much with *Waiting for the Barbarians*, he was invited to read and give a public lecture at the University of Tulsa. Doc Simcoe gave extra credit for attendance. When she saw me, after he was done, she didn't speak. She charged over to me in the audience, took me by the hand, and dragged me to the front of the room to a group of people surrounding Coetzee. There, we waited. We waited for what felt like long enough that I wanted to be anywhere else when he turned to us. She spoke.

"This is RJ Young," she told him. "I thought he should meet you." Years later, I know this was the kindest gift I ever received in high school.

Coetzee shook my hand and smiled. "It's very nice to meet you, RJ. Are you a writer?"

Was I?

*

Doc Simcoe showed me that McFarlin Library and its many treasures were open to me if only I showed my TPS ID. She talked about TU like it wasn't the lily-liberal elite university it sold itself as, but the city college that belonged to me, to the children of this place it once shot at, murdered, and burned out because they looked like me. This, TU, was our birthright as much as the city of Tulsa was, and she wanted me to claim it.

At McFarlin, the "One Hero" parable prevailed upon me, made itself known to me. When the Japanese invaded, many Koreans reached for weaponry. One hero, though, reached toward the tool of the wordsmith. A shooter could fire a gun and put down an enemy. But a writer, a publisher, could fire a mimeograph once, kill a soul, regenerate an ally, ignite a revolution. From Doc Simcoe, I learned that writing lines was not punishment but sorcery. To tell a story, to argue within an essay, to wrestle in revision, was to engage, to charge and animate language with vibes eternal. And to read, and read widely, was to strengthen my vibe, turn up the quality of those vibrations until what was written could not be read without transferring wavelengths into another body. Earthy as she was, Doc Simcoe believed in the long memory of the land—this land. The ruins of Greenwood, the prosperity that once cloaked North Tulsa, the animus that erupted in bullets and flame, the amity of the few who chose to stay, who chose to move here, to rebuild North Tulsa, she believed it was all here if only I would look.

"Where do I start?" I asked.

"Here!" she said. "You can start right here at Booker T."

The Booker T. Student Creed starts with a fool's hope and ends with a pledge of allegiance that feels as nationalistic as the one we were all made to stand and say in front of the American flag:

I believe in honest work, in generous
Comradeship, in the courage of high
Convictions. I believe in the inspiration
That come from contact with all that is
Truest and best, in books, in people, in life.
I believe in loyalty to our high school,
The fostering mother of these ideals, and I
pledge her my allegiance in all her under takings,
In all that will make her a stronger
And nobler school.

I was among the last group of students to attend in what alumni and faculty at Booker T. call "old building." The tone teachers and students uttered "old building" with was loaded with reverence, drenched in a particular tradition, with a rhythm that felt like a reverence to original man. The "old building" that was once propelled by teachers and students and called Booker T. Washington High School was erected in 1958, but "old building" was not original. It was derivative, diluted. Its address was 1631 E. Woodrow Place, and I was an adult before I knew how rich that address was with history that was becoming my own. The original Booker T. predated the massacre.

The first building where students and teachers congregated for class at Booker T. was just four rooms at 507 E. Easton Street in Greenwood. Among fourteen Black students and two Black teachers was a Black principal, E. W. Woods. Such was Black Tulsans' thirst for educating their children that the space became too small for such Black abundance. Seven years after the first class was taught, Booker T. took over a brand-new edifice three stories tall. The "old building" was one of a handful that survived the massacre, and in that space, Black minds flourished, thrived, for nearly forty years on a street called Zion. The school song was written by race massacre survivor and Booker T. vocal instructor C. B. Neely. She held it down at the Hive—the community made of alumni, students, and faculty at Booker T.—from 1918 to 1960, and she wrote these words:

> *Dear Booker T. Washington High School*
> *The pride of the great south west*
> *You're a symbol of light for many a youth*
> *By pointing the way to life's best.*
> *You stand as a beacon in Tulsa,*
> *By teaching the ideals of truth*
> *You inspire us with all that is worthy*
> *And gird us for life's greatest test.*

Black excellence ran a steady stream from North Tulsa without a single white student at Booker T. for sixty years. Nineteen years after *Brown v. Board of Education* overturned separate but equal and nine years after the Civil Rights Act was made law, Booker T. endured selection as one of six pioneer schools for Tulsa Public Schools' forced bus integration program. This is also how Booker T. became Tulsa's first "magnet high school," a term to shroud an intention toward integrating that made desegregation in schools easier to swallow for white folks. The point was never to make the school better for Black students, merely a by-product. In fact, the term "magnet" was not applied to Booker T. until 1975, two years after it began operating as such.

Tasked by federal mandate to integrate Booker T., TPS superintendent Bruce Howell used his office to empower administrators to recruit the best faculty in the metro area, like Director of Senior High Schools for TPS Roy Lewis, after learning from the mistake of closing Black schools and forcing Black children to bus to white schools elsewhere in the city.

The first school TPS tried to integrate was Burroughs Elementary School, called Burroughs Little School, with TPS administrators trying to convince white folks to send their kids to school with Black kids on the north side. A white lady, Nancy McDonald, led the integration effort among whites using a simple method: she recruited friends, who recruited friends. They'd try to do the same at Booker T.

"We wanted faculty members who were perceived to be the best in that school and who we felt, the two of us felt, would attract White students to Booker T. Washington High School," Lewis said in James Adrian Ferrell's doctoral dissertation, "A Magnet School and Desegregation: A Case Study of Booker T. Washington High School, 1975–1980."[10]

The day the school opened as an integrating public school was no small event in 1971. Television stations from as far as London, England, sent journalists to observe on the ground while white kids walked into a previously segregated Black elementary. But as the school opened for voluntary integration, TPS decided to close nearby Carver Junior High because federal district judge Fred Daugherty said it must be integrated by the 1972 fall semester, and TPS administrators believed that couldn't be done. After closing Carver and forcing those Black students to attend junior high schools across the city, community leader Julius Pegues, a Booker T. alumnus and the first Black basketball player at the University of Pittsburgh, led a protest against forcing North Tulsa kids to attend TPS schools outside the North Tulsa community. The protest led to the formation and brief existence of the Carver Freedom School in 1972.

The freedom school operated for a full semester out of Saint Monica's Catholic Church until Pegues, then–Tulsa mayor Bob LaFortune, Williams Company president Joe Williams, Nancy McDonald, and others found a deal. That compromise culminated in the reopening of Carver Junior High in the spring of 1973 along with a commitment that two hundred and fifty students would enroll and a pledge from TPS and the city to renovate Carver and provide faculty and busing. But TPS said it would not create the bus routes that white students would need to take to reach Carver. So McDonald and others created a grid system, with students attending Carver meeting at local pickup stations. The legacy of that plan was still in action when I attended Booker T., and I benefited from it, along with kids attending Carver into the twenty-first century. A better plan was needed to ensure white students attended Booker T. in 1973, though. But what was clear was that Tulsa's Black community would not stand for its educational beacon to be closed, especially after the attempt to close its junior high school. "[W]e as a community told them, 'You are not going to close our high school,'" Pegues said. "When schools close, communities die. Schools are key components of viable communities."

TPS held informal meetings it called "coffees" to find out what courses and extracurricular activities would need to be taught at Booker T. for white students to bus to North Tulsa. They found that teaching foreign languages was tremendous recruiting tool. "Russian was a big deal and Japanese was a big deal," then Booker T. principal H. J. Green said, "so we ended up with a foreign language department that offered French, Spanish, Japanese, Russian, Chinese, Latin, and German."

To further entice white students and their families to attend school with Black ones, Roy Lewis pushed the Advanced Placement courses Booker T. taught and, crucially, told other high schools they could not emulate Booker T.: "I probably made some enemies by telling the principals, 'No, you can't do anything that is going to detract from the accomplishments from Booker T. Washington High School or anything to cause parents not to want to or not to elect to let their students go there.'"

More surveys of what white folks wanted in return for sending their kids to school with Black ones revealed a desire for courses in aeronautics, geology, archaeology, women's studies, multicultural studies, and "an incredible fine arts program." TPS cratered and catered.

By 1975, Booker T. included eighteen AP courses and had begun its International Baccalaureate program. TPS enrolled 550 white students at Booker T. in its first year and 550 Black ones, for a total enrollment of 1,100. However, the application process left out about 250 Black students who were once districted for Booker T. From 1974 on, every student had to apply to earn admission to the school. Booker T.'s zoned area shrank to nothing, with students, in some cases living across the street from the school, being reassigned to East Central, Will Rogers, Nathan Hale, and Memorial senior high schools. "Every student in the Tulsa Public School system has the right to go to their neighborhood school except the students that live in the Booker T. Washington High School attendance area," Pegues said. "[T]hey have to qualify to go to their neighborhood school . . . You had students living right across the street from the school who couldn't go to their school. Like I said, I didn't like it then when they started it and I don't like it now because they are treated differently . . . This is discrimination."

This was still true at Booker T. when I graduated high school in 2006, while it was not true at the magnet school that opened inside Edison Preparatory High School in 2002. Unlike Booker T., students who lived near Edison didn't have to apply to the magnet school to attend the high school. "Edison has a magnet school, very much different from Booker T., OK?" Pegues said. "[E]very child who lives in the Edison High School district has the right to go to Edison High School. They can either qualify to be in the magnet program or they don't have to, but they can go to their high school without any qualifications." And he knew this was hypocrisy.

*

In 1973, 50 percent of the Booker T. student body identified as white and was unaccustomed to the rich tradition the previously all-Black school enjoyed. H. J. Green went to great lengths to keep Booker T.'s traditions intact. "We had two missions going on at the same time," Green said. "One is to maintain the traditions of BTW and its importance in that community. The second was to demonstrate that Black and White can work together and go to school together and be productive together. A lot of people today think well, gosh, what is so big about that, but in the 1970s that was a major issue, especially in the South."

Those courses and programs first installed during forced de-segregation were the reason I wanted to attend Booker T. and why I rode a bus for my first year of high school to get there. I don't recall the process to apply, only the result. Mama was told by a TPS administrator that I was the only one of seventy homeschooled applicants to earn admission in 2002. I was buoyed by that fact until I learned that every other homeschooled applicant was white. I walked into my first class with the crushing understanding that I might not be at Booker T. because I was good enough, but because I was Black enough.

My over-eagerness, though, roared out of me. I was aggressive in pursuing relationships, friendships, with people I thought might share my love of bowling, my desire to play snare in the march-ing band, the visceral reaction I had to hearing Dr. Dre's *2001*. Channel-surfing when Mama wasn't paying attention, I stumbled across MTV and have never once forgotten about Dre. Had they? I doubted it as the yellow bus wound through the parts of the city the white folks don't know, don't go.

The bus route started out right where they were most comfort-able, just down the street from Seventy-First and Memorial where Woodland Hills Mall was kept sterile, modern, solidly lily-white to price out most who were not. As the bus snaked off, the trees hid less of the houses, revealed more of the dirt and the height of the fences. The gates around Southern Hills, a country club I will never be able to afford to patronize, kept out the children who populated McClure Elementary, just two blocks west, where nearly half of the five hundred students looked like me. Nearly all the kids who got on the bus were Black. I met one Black boy's eye. "The fuck you lookin' at, nigga?" I did not answer. I stared at the brown fake leather bus seat in front of me for the rest of the ride to Booker T. on that first day. It'd be four days before I felt like I could bring myself to talk to any of the Black kids who boarded at McClure, Grissom Elementary, and Nimitz Middle School. It'd be four days before I saw how the houses deteriorated in appearance and became smaller in size the farther north the bus route traversed. I was ashamed of my own people; didn't know my own people; wasn't known by my own people.

On the ride home from school that fourth day, the kids who chose to ask me about myself, engage with me, were white. As the bus took the same route in the opposite direction after school, they were the kids still on with me when the wheels on the bus rolled round out of North Tulsa into South Tulsa. The fewer people around, the more likely strangers are to talk to each other, no matter their backgrounds, is what Grandmomme told me on the phone during the first weekend following my return to public school. She was happy to know I was making friends, never mind if they were white or not. I counted the Black bodies on the bus and in every room I ever entered, and the way white kids treated me laid bare truth I was too afraid to write down, to bring to my parents.

"I don't think they see me," I told Grandmomme on the cordless phone.

"See you how?" she asked.

"See *me*. I'm Black. I'm dangerous too."

"Who said you have to be dangerous to be Black?"

"That's how I know when white folks see me. It's when they think I'm dangerous."

"And how do you think your Black classmates see you?"

"I don't."

"You don't think your Black classmates want to see who you are?"

"I don't think they see me at all."

*

At school, I wasn't immediately enrolled in AP courses or the IB program. The entirety of my freshman year was spent learning exactly how much I didn't know about people, my people. My sophomore year, I'd decided, would be different. I would be different. I turned sixteen just a month before school began; taking part in the back-to-school ritual, my parents bought Nise and me new school clothes. We were each allotted $200, and we were encouraged to use whatever money we earned working part-time to supplement our wardrobe. My sister spent her allotment at Abercrombie and Fitch, American Eagle, JCPenney, and Sears. I pleaded with Mama to let me drive myself to shop exclusively at the Springdale Shopping Center in North Tulsa—just a few miles east of Booker T. I did not have a car, and parents did not offer to buy me one. Mama's gold Chrysler Town & Country minivan was the only option.

"There isn't but one clothing store over there, right?"

I nodded.

"Fine," she said. "Don't wreck my van, and don't whine to me when your off-brand clothes start unraveling in my washing machine."

Bet.

I hopped into the driver's seat of this minivan I wished wasn't one and onto Route 169 to the B. A. Expressway, to Route 75 North, believing I was about to be fresher than Andre 3000 and Big Boi on *Stankonia*. By the time I exited on Peoria and turned right onto Pine, I was feeling myself as 105.3 K-Jamz buzzed as Big Tymers thumped my mama's factory speakers with "Still Fly." Tops & Bottoms was the store where the people I hoped would become my friends shopped. Where I could find the otherwise undiscoverable in Tulsa, a town where "hip hop" was two words and came with the loud clap of a gallop. At Tops & Bottoms, I wasn't left to put together an outfit out of Levis, plaid button-downs, and Ralph

Lauren polos. At Tops & Bottoms, I bought FUBU and Vokal. I decked myself out with Big Bird–yellow cargo shorts, yellow Converse knockoffs; purple Converse knockoffs; white Converse knockoffs. I bought three G-Unit tank tops, brown Dickies, and a black T-shirt with a picture of Tupac, his hands forming a pyramid of prayer with Old English script spelling out ONLY GOD CAN JUDGE ME. The only set of jeans I bought were a size too big so I could wear basketball shorts underneath them, and the jacket I bought had a picture of Aaliyah on the back of it with Old English script spelling out R.I.P. I thought I was Jet Li in *Romeo Must Die* when I bought that jacket. Before walking up to the register, arms full because there were no shopping carts, I stopped off in front of the do-rags, headbands, gold neck chains I knew would turn my skin green, and fake diamond earrings I knew would inflame my earlobes. I bought them anyway. The look was all. The cashier tallied me up. I'd spent $304.54 on clothes. Forking over the money, I knew I was going to pick up another shift at Reasor's, the grocery store I rode my bike to on weekends to sack groceries.

The first day of school sophomore year Mama dropped me off in front of the "new building," where I felt everyone got to start fresh. The new building was new to everyone. No one really knew where any room was, even though we'd gone through orientation a week prior. I thought the disadvantages I suffered as a freshman— knowing no one, not being Black enough, being a *freshman*—were gone. I was ready when I walked into my AP and IB classes. As I took my seat in AP U.S. History, I noticed most of the room was made of white kids. As I took my seat in AP/IB English, I noticed most of the room was made of white kids there too. The same was true in AP Spanish.

The AP/IB program was one in which you needed to opt in, and I was devastated by how few of the kids who chose to looked like me. There was no pressure from faculty or administration to enroll. Indeed, many students had picked Booker T. for that reason. At the time, the Hive was still home to the only magnet school in the district. The kind of education you could receive there was on par with the well-to-do private schools in the city like Bishop Kelley, where tuition was over $12,000 a year; Cascia Hall, over $16,000 a year; and Holland Hall, over $22,000 a year. Passing AP/IB tests to be rid of prerequisite qualifications for almost any four-year degree program in the world could be worth six figures in student loans, plus interest. This was the selling point for many of my white classmates at Booker T., some of whom routinely earned acceptance letters and financial aid from Ivy League institutions. These were facts that teachers and guidance counselors threw out as parents leaned forward at informationals about the school. That was how the pressure cooker at Booker T. trapped its steam, and how I became one of those kids who would slowly evaporate inside the program. I wasn't prepared. I wasn't ready. Most Black kids are not, even now. A white teacher charged with shepherding a predominantly Black school needed to investigate that. His name is Chris Mahnken.

In 2015, Mahnken was a white principal at the KIPP Tulsa charter school when he found himself asking questions about the criteria the state of Oklahoma used to evaluate whether or not his students succeeded in the classroom. He was looking for a way to accurately show how his students performed relative to their Oklahoma peers so he could better sell the charter school to parents who were skeptical. When he looked at the data as reported by the state's department of education, compared to the raw data gathered, he grew angry.

"I uncovered it in plain sight," Mahnken said. "Because I was, you know, as a founding school leader, and of course, wanting to make sure that we look good publicly, in the eyes of a state report card. So, I needed to have a deep understanding of where the data came from. And, of course, because [KIPP Tulsa] serves predominantly Black low-income students." As many as 90 percent of his students were Black and live in North Tulsa. "Ultimately, what I found was just, in my viewpoint, blatant systemic racism at play."

Oklahoma's Department of Education uses what it calls the "Oklahoma Academic Achievement" to measure individual performances of its students. In high school, the department evaluates how prepared those students are for post–high school life in math, reading, and English as assessed either by the ACT or the SAT. Students' raw scores are converted into what are called Oklahoma Performance Index scores. Using OPI conversion,[11] the Department of Education allows students' achievement to be compared regardless of which test they take.

OPI conversion uses what the department of education calls "priority groups" when giving points for achievement, and sets different "scaled scores" for those priority groups.[12] The scaled scores are ways the schools can still receive the majority of "1 point" for a student based on their achievement. Students who do not hit "proficient" or a scaled score earn zero points. Students who hit the scaled score, but not "proficient," earn 0.95 points. Students who hit the proficient score earn 1.0 points. Students who hit the advanced score earn 1.25 points. The state did not overinflate the scores of non-white students who earned an advanced score.

This means a large portion of a school's grade on Oklahoma School Report Cards, the metric the state uses to comply with the federal Every Student Succeeds Act, comes from raw student achievement, but schools will receive 0.95 points even if a student scores significantly below "proficient" *solely because of their race*. The result is that schools have highly inflated academic achievement scores, even if a large majority of their population is not scoring anywhere even close to "proficient."

In the 2018–19 academic year, Booker T.'s Black students comprised 30.2 percent of its population. Just 25 percent of those Black students scored "proficient" or "advanced." Economically disadvantaged students comprised 46.8 percent[13] of Booker T.'s population; just 36 percent of those students scored "proficient" or "advanced." However, Oklahoma's OPI conversion of ACT and SAT scores of

Booker T.'s population equaled an academic achievement composite score of 89.3 percent. This, despite 75 percent of Black students at Booker T. not scoring "proficient."

In the Oklahoma Department of Education's report cards, minority students who reach the OPI "scaled score" are assigned 0.95 and reported as "basic" in the student performance metric. Those not reaching the "scaled score" are assigned zero and reported as "below basic." Fifty-three percent of Booker T.'s Black students did not meet criteria for proficiency in English, math, or science. Just 25 percent did. Seventy-eight percent of Booker T.'s white students scored "proficient" or "advanced," while just 22 percent scored "basic" or "below basic."

"Booker T. Washington, on paper, looks great," Mahnken said. "However, part of the reason why they look great is that if a Black kid gets a 17 [on the ACT], he is counted the same as a white kid who scores a 21. And the school gets 0.95 points for the Black kid."

Oklahoma public school districts have no incentive to push their non-white students to succeed. "So what this means," Mahnken said, "is that it has essentially disincentivized schools, school administrators, and the system as a whole in the way funding is distributed and on and on. It disincentivizes schools from wanting to push that Black child to a 21 versus the white students. Of course, they want to push the white student there so that they capture that one point rather than a zero. But the Black kid? They get 95 percent of that point just by him hitting a 17. So why would they go through all of the tremendous additional work to be able to get that kid to proficient. Well, they go, 'Okay, well, 0.95 out of 1 is pretty damn good.'"

We asked for self-determination, and we got integration. We asked for liberation and received Reconstruction. We asked to not be slaves and, tucked inside the Thirteenth Amendment, received prison. We asked to be left alone, and the white Tulsans shot and killed us. Those of us who survived don't even have the intellectual beacon in Booker T. that we were promised, and so we cling to its tradition.

*

The "T" in Booker T. Washington High School ought not stand for "Taliaferro" but for "tradition," its academic reputation being the heart from which all tradition flowed. Historian Dr. John Hope Franklin was a Hornet, as was GAP Band cofounder Charlie Wilson. In 1967, Wilson and his brother, Ronnie, gave their band the name from an abbreviation of Greenwood, Archer, and Pine on the north side—because "The Greenwood, Archer, and Pine Band" didn't fit on a flyer. The Wilsons did this to harken to how they grew up, where they grew up, and just how Tulsa treated them, as explained in Charlie's autobiography, *I Am Charlie Wilson*: "It was a clever homage to the Tulsa race riot of 1921, the catastrophic, racially motivated insurrection in which whites attacked [B]lacks in their most prominent community, the Greenwood district, known back then as Black Wall Street." This is yet another legacy of the massacre, and perhaps its most artful. When the massacre was not discussed, all but omitted, the GAP Band made it their name. "The nickname felt good," Wilson said. "It stuck." And they wore it proudly, even as the meaning was obscure to the people who claimed to love them.

*

Booker T. claimed seventeen academic bowl state championships from 1991 to 2013 and two national titles in '92 and '08. Ten Speech and Debate state titles were won by Booker T. students from 1978 to 2015.

The tradition courses through the Hive, blood through a body willing this spirit to survive. The school's talent show, "Hi-Jinks," has been an annual affair for ninety years, and it is the longest-running show of its kind in the district. Tyson McNulty won the show singing "Gin and Juice" while playing acoustic guitar during my sophomore year. He went to MIT.

The football and men's basketball teams were other arteries pulsating tradition. The jerseys of past greats who played college and pro football bedeck the fieldhouse, later renamed for one of the school's best basketball coaches and my U.S. government teacher, Nathan Harris. In the lobby are uniforms worn by college and NFL greats Kevin Lockett and R. W. McQuarters, and college and NBA great Wayman Tisdale. My freshman year was the senior year of Robert Meachem and the sophomore season of Felix Jones. Both played football in the SEC—Meachem at Tennessee and Jones at Arkansas—and in the NFL. But while that program has won just nine state championships since 1968, the boys' basketball program has won sixteen since 1973. In wrestling, Kenny Monday stood alone. After graduating Booker T., he won two NCAA titles, made three Olympic teams, and won the 1988 welterweight gold medal.

The T-Connection Marching Band and its drumline, the Funky D's, was the draw for me, though—a band modeled after an HBCU. Band camps took place at schools like Prairie View A&M, Langston University, and the University of Arkansas–Pine Bluff. Watching the drumline perform at an MLK parade two years prior was enough for me to use the money I made working at Reasor's for my first set of Vic Firth marching sticks. I watched how the boys in orange and black made those drumheads rattle. I felt the sticks crack and reverberate in my sternum. I began teaching myself to play a year before I matriculated to the Hive. When I got there, I had no idea who I needed to talk to or with to play that freshman fall. The band director then, Elmer Davis, told me to come back in the spring. When three female students accused him of sexual harassment, though, he was fired the following spring. Harold Craig was hired to replace him. I waited a full year before trying out, this time as a sophomore, to try to make the line as a snare, to make like Nick Cannon in *Drumline* and show these folks how I do.

I was so nervous, so ill-prepared for the environment, that not only did I not make it, but I was also asked to play tenor—a bastardized bass drum that didn't keep time, didn't share pace, and was a completely different percussive instrument. I was angry enough to cry and did. Mama told me if I didn't want to play tenor, that I shouldn't.

"No use in making yourself even more upset than you are," she said.

As badly as I wanted to play snare and as hard as I worked to learn the school fight song by ear to try out, I wanted to be a part of that band in a way that ached. I wanted my Black classmates to see me. And so, when roll call came for summer trip to band camp in 2003, I packed a bag, bought a pair of marching tenor mallets, and showed up ready to attend camp at Prairie View A&M University.

The first thing I learned about band camp is the bus ride is too long. The drive from Tulsa to Prairie View, Texas, is seven hours-plus in my mama's minivan. In a legitimate tour bus, carrying eighty teenage kids, six chaperones, and one band director, the drive is about eight hours. Picking the right seatmate is important, and I was not about to hit the number in that lottery. I was left all by my lonesome until Zorah *told me to my face* I was sitting with her. And dumbass that I was, I asked her why me? Even protested that I might want to sit with a dude. She said no, you're with me, and I hadn't the faintest idea what that meant when I sat down with her.

Zorah was a flautist, which at that moment meant she was in the front of the formation while I was at the back of it—a whole galaxy between us. On the bus, though, the distance was closed from cosmos to centimeters. As we boarded and others did too, she waved hello and shouted out to other girls I'd never met, was scared to talk to, and was too scared to tell anyone I was too scared to talk to too. Maybe I was looking at her with awe as she displayed such gregariousness. Maybe

I looked at her as if she was one of the last survivors of Alderaan. When she settled on me, her topaz irises cut through me like Scott Summers's ruby quartz, her cheeks swelled, warmth rising from them like fresh-baked bread, and her full lips revealed sectioned pearls for teeth. "You're cute when you're nervous."

"How do you know I'm nervous?"

"You're a Black boy and a virgin. Of course you're nervous." She took a tube of lip gloss and a pink makeup mirror out of her flower-upholstered handbag, all sunflowers and lilies, and lined her top and bottom lips with the cotton tip. When she finished, she turned to me. "You like?"

I didn't know what to say. In fact, I couldn't say anything. So I nodded.

"Good," she said.

As the bus began to roll out of Tulsa and down the highway toward PV, I found myself flipping my snare sticks around, unwilling to touch my tenor sticks until I could absolutely no longer avoid them, and wondered just what might await me at this HBCU. I had so many questions about band camp, its rules and etiquette, the music we'd learn. When I thought to lob these questions at Zorah, she was already on her knees on her seat, turned toward the back of the bus and in deep discussion about how fine 50 Cent was in his G-Unit tank top in "In da Club." I looked down at my pecs just then. I didn't have any. Not a vein nor sinew could be found on that body, and such was my being. A Black boy who was athletic but not cut like an athlete. The first sixteen years of my life were spent in a body Grandmomme called "husky," like the section in the JCPenney catalog. How I longed to look like Wesley Snipes, my birthday twin. I cussed about these genes in the jeans over and over again. As I looked at Zorah leaning over the head of the seat, a personified Coke bottle, brown like milk chocolate with hair straightened back into a ponytail, I allowed myself to wonder why she'd chosen me.

And what was she pointing out I was virgin for? Wait. How did she know I was a virgin? I thought then about the first time I'd met her.

Outside of Coach Potocnik's room, between classes, she'd bumped into a bruh I later learned was an upperclassman. "Watch where you goin', bitch."

I saw her sprawled out on the floor, books on the other side of the hall, and went to pick them up.

She popped up, talkin' her shit. "Don't tell me how you talk to your mama."

He took a step to her, and I instinctively moved in front of him, a barrier to her. I summoned Ice Cube in *Friday*, talking back to Deebo, knowing I was about to eat flo'. "That's female."

He stood over me, looked over me to Zorah and then back to my eyes, still on his. He began to nod. "OK, OK. That's shawty then, huh? I see you, li'l nigga." He took two steps back and walked on. Zorah snatched her books from my hands and walked on too. On the bus, I thought that had to have been three weeks ago. When she finally turned around in her seat, exhausted and elated with talking, I tapped her on the arm. She recoiled like I was a spider crawling up her shoulder.

"What?" she asked.

"Why'd you pick me?"

"Pick you for what?" Saying it like an accusation.

She waited for a response, gestured like I should come out with it, and then gave up. I'd given up too. What was I thinking about? She took out her CD player and I took out mine, grateful for its gold finish and anti-skip technology. I never needed to hear Eminem's verse on "Patiently Waiting" more than I did then. Never mind that my parents didn't know I owned the record, that God might have some things to say about this secular music pumping into my ears, circulating through my veins, pushing what I thought was Black through my heart—irritated, angry, filled with something like gas and unable to see past a hazy light, wondering what exactly was real just then.

One of the dudes on tenor line tapped me on the shoulder. His name was Napoleon. I met him during tryouts for the Funky D's. He taught me the music, trying out for the first time too, but with an older brother on the snare line. I was quickly coming to learn that tenor was a stand-in instrument for those looking to play in the drum section, the rock in the hard place of percussion in the T-Connection band.

"That your girl?" He pointed at Zorah.

She ripped open half of her headphones, showing us exactly what she was listening intently to. "Why can't he be my man?" Ownership could go either way.

He put his hands up like he didn't mean her any offense. Then he smiled at me. "That's your girl."

He punched me in the shoulder. Zorah rolled her eyes. I was too afraid to smile and unable to stop my cheeks from burning. Only as the bus slowed to a stop and our bodies filled with a need to stretch and be freed of that rolling sardine can did Zorah deftly turn my cheek and kiss me on the lips without warning. She rubbed my cheek, heard ooohhs from chorus of girls behind us, and yelled back at them, "*Any*way." She exited the bus in front of me, and I didn't see her again for the rest of the week at band camp.

At Prairie View A&M, I glimpsed life on a Black college campus and wondered if this was the picture beyond the veil Du Bois had written so about, where the double consciousness met its community. We Black folks among Black folks at a place of higher learning. This was what Booker T. once was. This was what every school once was. Given inferior textbooks, inferior facilities, the tradition of a nation of people who thirsted after formal education after four centuries without had pushed us, Black folks, to bend the culture to our needs, among each other. To do less with more is a bloody birthright and one Greenwood, Booker T., and PV all proved. Just fifteen years after the Thirteenth Amendment abolished enslaving those called free and established enslaving those called criminals, Black folks had spent over $1 million on schools, raised through church and donations from laborers and craftsmen. The Texas Constitution of 1876 made way for "Agricultural and Mechanical College[s]" while mandating "separate schools shall be provided for the white and colored children, and impartial provisions shall be made for both." Article 7, section 14: "The Legislature shall also when deemed practicable, establish and provide for the maintenance of a College or Branch University for instruction of colored youths of the State, to be located by a vote of the people; provided, that no tax shall be levied, and no money appropriated out of the general revenue, either for this purpose or for the establishment and erection of the buildings of the University of Texas." Lest Black folks afford themselves the audacity to believe their school was equal to UT or, heaven forfend, a flagship university.

That piece of legislation led to erecting the Alta Vista Agricultural and Mechanical College of Texas for Colored Youth on land previously owned by white planters and maintained by enslaved Black bodies—the Alta Vista plantation—in 1876. A three-member committee for the newly founded Agricultural and Mechanical College at Bryan, later renamed Texas A&M University, was tasked with finding land for "the colored children." Jared Kirby, owner of Alta Vista, had died. His widow, Helen Marr Kirby, was no planter, but she fancied herself a teacher in the great cliché of white mistresses on plantations. She sought to flip the Alta Vista plantation into a school for girls. When that venture failed, she made the committee aware that she owned 1,388 acres still ideal for the growing and producing of cotton, timber, and rice. Add that the mostly Black population of Hempstead, a community of refugees from surrounding plantations, was close by. Not only did the committee buy her land, but Kirby became the University of Texas's first dean of women.

Three years on, the school in Waller County renamed itself Prairie View Normal and Industrial Training School, a veritable mecca for Black Texans who succeeded at the highest athletic and academic standards, just forty miles northwest of Houston. The first students enrolled on March 11, 1878. They were eight, paying $130 in tuition for nine months that covered room, board, education, and a uniform. In 1879, the school reorganized and renamed itself once more: Prairie View State Normal School, "normal" being the preferred moniker for a teacher's college, and equitable manner for every student was to be taught. The term was first created in France—*école normale*—in the seventeenth century, and most HBCUs were created first as normal schools. The school took its last and most important step forward in 1919, when it implemented a four-year program. Its final name change came in 1973, to Prairie View A&M, the place I wandered around three decades later between taxing sessions to learn T-Connection canon in the band hall and sweating beneath the south Texas sun learning foundational formations, shocked and embarrassed. By the third day, when I hadn't seen another white person except the four in the marching band, two on the drumline, I realized that not only was I not alone, but we outnumbered those white folks in every space my eyes could see. We were the majority.

We were encouraged to look around campus, to ask questions of it, and to meet with admissions counselors about what we might do to earn acceptance. They knew we were on campus. I and others had made appointments to meet them. I was bold enough to ask one of the counselors about the veil, about Du Bois, about how PV existed in the twenty-first century. She blinked. "Honey, you go to Booker T. You live there now. This is yours." The release I felt in my chest then aerated through my fingertips, out of my toes. The pitch was comfort, community in an understood code of experience unique to Black folks, at a school birthed out of a freedom we understood to be fleeting.

Dorm rooms were segregated, boys to one hall and girls to another. Groups were even more fractioned by specialty. I didn't find Zorah for two days. When I did, I felt codependently pulled toward her magnetism. She must have seen I was ashamed, not knowing what I should do or how I should do it. But I was grateful that she seemed to try when she took me by my hand and led me away. We sat with a bag of chips and a sandwich each on the grass.

"Whatchu think?" she said.

"About what?"

She waved her hands at buildings, the people, the adults someone had the nerve to call kids, college kids. "This."

"I like it."

"You gonna go to school here?"

"Maybe. You?"

"Nah," she said. "My mama went to UAPB. You know where that is?"

"Arkansas?"

"Where in Arkansas?"

"I'on know."

"Pine Bluff. Like, almost Mississippi. I don't think I want to be that close to Mississippi. Mississippi is nasty."

"What's wrong with Mississippi?" I felt a brief swell of indignation rise.

She saw it, named it. "I'm talking about your people or something?"

"My grandmother is from Mississippi."

"So?"

"So Black folks got it bad in Tulsa too, just like Arkansas, just like Mississippi, just like here."

"Nowhere is like Tulsa. White folks tried to kill every last Black person in Tulsa." She stared hard at me. "I thought you knew that." She kept staring at me, reappraising me. "I liked you." She stood up, walked away from me, and melted into a group of girlfriends.

★

When Mama picked me up, I told her about PV. That I thought I could see myself going to college there. She sat with that for a moment, at a red light leaving North Tulsa to take the on-ramp to 75 and home. Then she almost blurted, words biting like machine gunfire, "For what? No, you're going to a good school. You're not going there. Why go there when you can go anywhere else? You're an Eagle Scout. You're a good student. Rethink that."

PV was not a good school, not good enough for her. I could not go against my mama, not like that. So PV wasn't good enough for me, and I was too good for a Black education. A predominantly white school, a school closed to her and, half a century ago, closed to me. That was what Mama wanted for me. The culture I'd spent the past week in, learning a little more about who I was in America and the great value drawn from the struggle, meant little to nothing when I got back home. When I looked around, I failed to see me, and that began to terrify me.

And there was Mama reminding me what courage she mustered to enter ROTC, to come out a captain. There was my father, whose entire adult life was military precision from the moment he could jump onto the bus down the road from the only home he'd ever known. The road would lead him to Greenland before his duty ended. Duty. I felt the mass of that word at sixteen, just as I was drifting toward the part of Blackness that could not harbor any person who might wage war against another oppressed people. Muhammad Ali was only as good as the gloves on his hands in my parents' house. The moment he chose to act in defiance of the United States, he was no hero of theirs. Mama implored me to pick one of the three military academies, spend a half decade of life as an officer, and then choose law school. A foolproof plan for acceptance, honor, and rank in this country, and how I wanted to please her, never to fight with her. And I craved financial and social security.

This space, its whiteness, surrounded me, and to make a way in Tulsa was to make a way with white folks. The red, black, and green of Garvey had no standing here. There were cowboy boots, Bob Wills and his Texas Playboys, and stories about cowboys and country. The enclave carved out by a mere ten thousand Black Tulsans was smaller now than it was then, and each year we lost a little more of ourselves to assimilation I could feel but could not articulate. As I made my way from Baldwin to Fanon, I found fewer and fewer (Black) people to discuss the texts with and more and more (white) people who could essay about the merit of Cormac McCarthy, James Joyce, Faulkner, and Plath.

Had I kept machete-slashing a path from Tulsa, Oklahoma, to Conscious Black man, perhaps I could've fought for me and PV. Perhaps even made the journey to Harlem, to Oakland, to D.C. But I was not built to falter alone in the chaos, grasping at the knowledge in the works of Toni Morrison, Audre Lorde, and Amiri Baraka. Unable to summon the courage to use these spell books to spin magic won through survival from Middle Passage to this midcontinent, I felt the weight of the wayward, the dizziness of the disoriented, and clung to nothing. A brief search for self that set me aflame was now burning me up from the inside. I retreated to video games and solitude, hoping no one would find me as I limped toward the kind of college that Mama wanted me to attend but could not afford to send me to. But I first needed to graduate from Booker T., and six months after this conversation I knew that was impossible for me.

I prayed about it. My grades got worse, and I fell behind when learning the quadratic equation, telling protons from electrons. I read, though, and Mama still showed an ability to read me then. She found a psychologist for me, another doc in my life, but I didn't like talking about what made me sad, what made me angry. I didn't like talking about how felt, what I felt. I wanted to write it all down and let that serve, beginning by writing stories, telling essays, that became metafiction before I knew what that word meant. The rest

I only wanted to tell Grandmomme. This writing did not help me in school. Neither did working through Harry Potter just as Mama tossed my hardbacks in the trash after claiming Joyce Meyer told her J. K. Rowling's world of witches and wizards were tools of the devil. I argued with Mama about it, right there in her living room, raised my squeaky voice at her. My father heard this, came out of their bedroom, and flew into a rage.

"Don't you ever talk to your mother like that," he said.

"Fuck you," I said.

He raised his hand to hit me, and I wished he would have. When he did not, I called him a coward. He stared hard at me long enough to see I wanted to hurt. I wanted to die. Maybe he thought now was not the time to break an impressive streak, never having hit me with an open or closed hand before—only a black leather belt across my back, across my legs, across my ankles, steely in the truth that better him than cops. His part was never to nurture me, only to be Mama's heavy. He doled out the capital punishment, the psychological abuse, the money for Nise's and my activities. The way he showed us he loved us was by simply doing more than his own father had. In that moment in his living room, he lived up to that billing again. Rather than smacking me, as I wanted him to, as he surely wanted to, he spat at my feet and made himself content to ground me.

At school the following day, I was supposed to regurgitate how the Bolsheviks overthrew the monarchy; how the atom was split; how to conjugate verbs in Spanish. I'd drop out of the band after I was the only one still playing when the fight song ended during one football game. I was a full beat off, still learning to play the tenor drum I'd picked up just three months before, and I never properly learned to play it. My AP/IB classes I took with twenty-plus white faces and two or three Black ones like me became the hard classes, and I looked like failing in AP/IB History and eighth-hour Theory of Knowledge—a mandatory after-school class.

In November 2004, Mama found me in my room holding a knife, crying into my bed, trying to find the courage to kill myself. I was a coward. Mama was not. She willed my transfer to my neighborhood high school, Memorial Senior, two weeks before the semester ended. But not before she tried to make me talk about how I'd come to this course. She decided we needed to pray about it. She believed God could help me, could help us both.

We went to church, and there was no church like Higher Dimensions. Bishop Carlton Pearson was fresh off a failed mayoral run as "a conservative Afro-American," as he described his candidacy. "I happen to be a pastor and a bishop and . . . I'm running for mayor," he told the *Tulsa World* eighty years after the massacre, and my parents were on board.[14] "If I win," he said, "that is going to bring attention to the city from *People* magazine to *USA Today*. They're going to want to know what kind of city with a 60 percent Republican conservative voting bloc would put a [B]lack man in office." No, they wouldn't. Because he didn't win. Tulsa has never elected a Black mayoral candidate, though Pearson was not the first and far from the last to try.

But his popularity among Christian evangelicals, especially those who are Black like my folks, had peaked. His congregation was more than five thousand strong, and at forty-seven he was still a relatively young man in a profession littered with men twenty years older. He had the evangelical movement at his fingertips when he pivoted to what he called "The Gospel of Inclusion," a form of universalism. Pearson had come to believe that the fundamentalist faith was wrong, which counted as blasphemy among evangelicals.

Evangelicals believe a person must give their life to Jesus Christ to be saved from the fiery eternal damnation of hell, and that acceptance of Christ into their hearts was the only way to earn passage to heaven. In his public reframing of his belief, Pearson told us in his congregation that everybody was saved. That the threat of punishment was rudimentary and the best question to ask of those who are saved—all of us, according to him—was who were they saved from? God, Satan, or each other? None? All of the above? He told us, sitting before him, that he believed being kind and tolerant of all people and all walks through life was the way to peace on earth. That it was reasonable to believe Satan would be welcome into the kingdom of heaven. The evangelical community would have no part of this and labeled him a heretic.

Bishop Clifford L. Frazier, pastor at the City of Life Christian Church in St. Louis, did not hold back.[15] "He's crazy," Clifford said. "Even people who renounce Christianity but are familiar with the sacred text would realize that some fundamental problem exists here. For him to hold that view would mean that he is contra-biblical. To call what he has theology is really a malapropism. To espouse what he has is not theology, nor Christian. It is sheer, wild imagination."

Dr. Cheryl Sanders, a professor at Howard University of Divinity, explained how many Black folks felt about Pearson's new philosophy. "In the [B]lack church and community, we have some strong ideas about who goes to heaven and who goes to hell."

Tithes and offerings, the money that keeps churches going, plummeted at Higher Dimensions. Pearson's membership congregation dwindled so much and so quickly that he was forced to move out of his church, a facility so enormous that it is now home to a private Christian school. In the congregation, as he made his new direction known, I remember the church being stunned into silence. The Black faces I was so used to seeing jubilant, praising what God has done, fell slack-jawed.

In the van on the way to Delta Café, a favorite spot of my parents after church service on Sunday, my mother and my father laid into the man they'd once called their pastor. Mama believed the devil had gotten into Bishop Pearson, and my father began to talk about the man as if he'd never believed he was a man of God in the first place. Mama and my father continued on like this as we parked outside the restaurant, were seated, and placed our orders.

"Just goes to show if the devil can get to Bishop, he can get to us all," Mama said.

"That man has lost his damn mind," my father said.

"What if we just didn't go to church?" I said.

My sister immediately grasped what I was saying and recoiled.

"We won't, honey," Mama said. "We're gonna find a new church. Be sure of that."

"No, I mean," I said as my sister leaned away, "what if we just stopped going to church?"

My father leaned across the table and popped me upside my head. "You will not speak like that as long as you live in my house." I felt my fist clench and heard myself mutter the words. "What'd you say?" my father said.

I glared at him then like Black boys used to fighting for the rights to their father's lover do. "You're gonna get enough of hitting me."

He leaned forward, a lion longing for a taste of his cub. "You bad. Do something."

"Roy." Mama said it like a warning. Then I saw the warning wasn't for me. Our white server had arrived. She took our order. Later, my father mopped his plate with what was left of his cornbread.

As I ate my Delta's Famous Hamburger alongside my sister, I said nothing and listened to my parents begin a dialogue about other churches in the area. They wondered about what the congregation was like at Church on the Move and Rhema Bible Church, and I wondered just what loyalty meant when discussing men of God and His teachings.

I listened to Bishop Pearson, and my first reaction was how much I wanted to believe him; how much relief I felt at the prospect of not going to heaven but not being in danger of going to hell. After all, Christians backslide every day and lose the grace that comes with being in God's favor. Being saved was an important first step, but remaining in lockstep with the Lord was mandatory, autocratic, and impossible.

In that moment of relief, I was smiling. This was the world made clearer to me, and I became another heretic in it.

That was the last day I believed in God. That was the last day I believed in my parents' will to pray. I wondered how many more gave up God, refused to pray to him, after what happened to them in Greenwood, lived through the aftermath following, especially knowing a man of religion and son of a minister had stoked the flame that burned the community to ashes in 1921: Richard Lloyd Jones. Did those Black folks who still believed in King Jesus know that many of the people who tried to kill them believed they were serving God's purpose too?

Jones cofounded the church where Pearson preaches now, All Souls, founded in 1921. He claimed he was right to print the story titled "Nab Negro for Attacking Girl In an Elevator" that led to a mob convening outside the courthouse looking for a Black teenage boy so it might enjoy extrajudicial justice. Four days after the massacre, he published his thoughts in the paper he owned. In the June 4, 1921, edition of his *Tulsa Tribune*, he wrote: "Such a district as the old 'Niggertown' must never be allowed in Tulsa again. It was a cesspool of iniquity and corruption . . . In this old 'Niggertown' were a lot of bad niggers and a bad nigger is the lowest thing that walks on two feet. Give a bad nigger booze and his dope and a gun and he thinks he can shoot up the world. And all these things were to be found in 'Niggertown'—booze, dope, bad niggers and guns."

Only in the past decade has All Souls begun to reckon with its founder, even giving the granddaughter of Richard Lloyd Jones the "free pulpit" to speak her piece in defense of her grandfather at Humanist Hour at All Souls' Emerson Hall. I was there to hear her speak, and the ferocity with which she defended her grandfather elicited a chuckle from me. Then I looked around. I was one of a few specks in an ocean of vanilla. These were not my people; they were hers. They know what they took from us. They know what they did to us. They know what they owe, and they were all ashamed.

Still, I asked her out to coffee to talk about her grandfather and herself after she delivered her scathing speech culminating in her resignation of membership from the church. Outside Starbucks in Tulsa's Utica Square, she told me about her family. She told me about the house her cousin Frank Lloyd Wright built for her grandfather, a house so big that it had its own name, and her brother taking over the *Tribune* after her grandfather's death in 1963, and slowly it was dawning on me that she did not want to talk with me all. She simply wanted to be heard by me. She told me she was working on her family tree, and she had traced her lineage all the way back to twelfth-century Wales.

"Do you know where your ancestors are from?" she asked.

"They were slaves," I said.

THE WEEKEND BETWEEN MY LAST DAY AT BOOKER T. AND my first day at Memorial Senior High School began with a chilly Saturday, when the morning edges with the kind of cold that is bearable, like the freezing roof of your mouth when met with ice cream. Move around, grit your teeth, squinch your eyes shut, and move around until the piercing cold becomes something like a cool sheet your body swathes itself in. In a hoodie and shorts, I walked outside our duplex, beginning to jog toward the kind of body I'd wanted since I'd first seen Wesley Snipes fiercely shirtless as the original superhero of my childhood. Our neighbors, Fred and Edna, were a childless young couple who hosted Fred's best friend, Dave, a couple of weekends a month when he passed through selling software he always threw off as too complicated to explain to me when I saw him.

Fred and Dave were playing catch in the street with a football when I began to jog out of my parents' driveway. Dave called me.

"Catch!"

He launched the ball toward me, and I instinctively went off at full stride to catch it. As the ball flew over my head and out of reach, I cussed under my breath and ran after the ball still rolling down the street. When I threw it back from where I stood, perhaps thirty yards away, Dave acted surprised when he did not have to move as the ball found him like a dart in the center of his chest.

"Pretty good for a Black guy," he said.

I nodded, pleased to have pleased this white man. He threw to Fred, who caught me off guard when he threw the ball to me. The ball went around in this warped triangle, isosceles in color if not in length along two of its sides. We were quiet as the ball, small enough for adults to comfortably launch it to make themselves feel big, continued to move through air brisk but still. We could not have made more than three trips around the triangle when Dave decided to reverse course and throw the ball toward me again. The ball spiraled over the top of me, seeming to gain speed as it flew out of my reach and landed loudly on the pavement over the sound of my sneakers stomping against the street. I pulled up just short of the ball, cursing myself again for not having caught it and picked it up. As I turned to toss it back to Dave, he cupped his hands over his mouth, leaned back as if his body were a ruler with a spit wad attached to the end geared to flip, and shouted at me. "You gotta run like one of those Black people in Greenwood! You gotta want it!"

The coldness in the air was slowly being made to fade by rays of light sharpening through the clouds no longer able to hold day back from turning golden. I jogged my miles, jogged my weekend, pushing aside Dave's remark. As I grew older, Dave would float back into my conscious mind as I questioned why the world around me was quiet, peaceful even; as the white folks around me looked like they actually might want to help me for no other reason than pure altruism. You've gotta want it. Every Black man in Tulsa must want it. You've gotta want to survive. Because this world is designed to kill us.

*

The walls of Memorial were colored vanilla, decorated with a brick texture that made the hallways seem as clinical as a prison. Had they not been decorated with the red, white, and blue of the Charger mascot, it would not have been difficult to convince me the place was a juvenile delinquent complex. That was just after walking in through the front doors. The registrar's office and the principal's office were close by, but Mama told me my first stop needed to be my guidance counselor. I knocked on the windowed door above Mrs. Gaddis's title, and she opened with a smile that showed all her teeth. With hair curly blonde and shoulder length, glasses like tea-cup saucers over her eyes, and a loud, gold butterfly brooch on her red blouse, she looked like Angela Lansbury if she'd decided to rock her hair like Farrah Fawcett circa 1975. She took me by the arm and sat me in the chair in front of her desk while talking about how overwhelmed I must be; how brand-new this building, her presence, must feel; how committed she was to helping me feel at home in this, my new school, with just weeks to go in the fall semester.

One by one she listed the classes I'd been enrolled in at Booker T., apologizing for Memorial not having as many Advanced Placement classes—only AP English was an option for me—or any International Baccalaureate courses. She replaced my driver's ed class with weightlifting and told me she'd personally introduce me to the baseball coach and band director if those were activities I'd still like to pursue. She placed me in Mrs. Riddle's AP English class, Mrs. Berlin's European history class, Ms. Gilbert's Spanish 3 class, Mr. Burris's economics class, and Mrs. Donahue's pre-AP chemistry class and told me Ms. Smith's math class and Mrs. Matheson's physics class was the best she could do—the best classes they had for someone like me, she said.

"Someone like me?" I must've found it offensive. Like my question was leveled like an accusation.

"Someone from Booker T., dear. We're just not used to students as capable as you."

Shortly after printing out my new class schedule, Mrs. Gaddis took me by the arm once more and proceeded to walk me down the hallway. As we walked, she asked me about myself. Where did I want to go to college? What did I want to study in college? Had

I thought of running for student council at Booker T.? Could that change here? That my mother had mentioned I'd begun the process of trying to get into the U.S. Naval Academy and had already secured my appointment from our congressman. Could she help with that? She enrolled me in Memorial's new Engineering Academy, knowing that to attend the Naval Academy was to become an engineer. "I think it'll look good on your resume, don't you?" She asked these questions in succession, not slowly down enough for me to answer them fully as she knocked on doors to each of my classes and introduced me to my new teachers.

"Mrs. Riddle," she said, "this is RJ Young. He has transferred in from Booker T., and he will be one of our best and brightest. We're lucky to have him." My new teachers scarcely had more time to comment on Mrs. Gaddis's assertions before she'd whisked me away, right back through the classroom door and back into the conversation she was having privately with me inside this public school empty of denizens in the hall. I felt we'd must have walked more than half the school before we arrived back where we began, at her office.

She sat me back down in that chair, made eye contact with me, and asked me, with the most sincerity I'd ever felt in my life, if there was anything she could do for me. I shook my head, still marveling at this older white woman's charm.

After leaving her presence and encountering people, peers, who seemed much closer to regularly apprehensive and judgmental, I began to think Mrs. Gaddis was the exception she seemed to be. But Mrs. Riddle expressed happiness to see me the next day when school began and treated me warmly as she invited me to join them in reading *Macbeth*. Mrs. Berlin allowed me to tell her where I was in my IB World History class, and then offered to let me write a five-page paper on the Byzantine Empire for my semester grade. I told her I was earning a C in that class, which was the truth.

"I'm sure you were," she said. "But I plan to grade this paper, not your time at Booker T." In the rest of my classes, I found out that I was weeks ahead. In chemistry, I was beginning an orientation in organic chemistry only to find out Mrs. Donahue was still teaching Boyle's law. I was months ahead of my classmates in every class but English. Slowly, what became clear wasn't that I was going to be allowed to coast, but that I was going to be given the first chance I'd had since beginning high school to take a breath, to collect myself and orient myself as a person in high school without the stress of needing to be accomplished in high school, and I relished it.

When I stepped into the hallway, I didn't feel like one of many but one among a few. When class let out, I didn't feel I needed to rush to the next room. Five minutes to navigate the halls felt like fifteen. I stopped just outside Mrs. Riddle's classroom and closed my eyes. The walls didn't feel like they expanded when I walked in them, giving me room to inhale deeply. When I opened my eyes, my sister stood in front of me, scowling. "This is my school," she said. "This will never be your school. Your school is the Black school. You're not me."

Nise began her Tulsa Public School education at Byrd Junior High in seventh grade. While I discovered how much I didn't know and needed to learn just to catch up at Booker T., Nise flourished. At Memorial, she embraced the idea of becoming an engineer. She was determined to become a Black STEM graduate, and Mrs. Matheson made that her mission too. I knew this because Nise always had stories about what the robotics team might do, and Mama was a heavily involved parent with Nise, just as she was with me. Meant Mama and Mrs. Matheson talked frequently and openly not just about the Engineering Academy and the robotics club within it that competed and won championships, but about how they saw the world. Later I'd learn Nise's success at Memorial was one of the reasons Mama felt so comfortable with me transferring there.

Nise could see around corners. I envied her steeliness, her utter stubbornness. When Mama would try to rattle her, Nise refused to perform her kata, choreographed martial arts movements performed from memory to earn the next belt in rank to eventually become a black belt. Mama would yell at her to do it, that she wasn't going to waste her time with Nise if this was how she was going to act. Nise, like the revolutionaries I worshipped, simply sat down, her legs crossed, quietly defiant in the face of our military veteran parents. As Mama would threaten to give up on her, never to beat her, never to ground her, but to wash her hands of what I thought was the kind of care and personal tutoring every child must want from their parent, Nise stared off in the distance as if waiting for this hysterical and obtuse stranger our mother had become to disappear. That was Nise's superpower. She could will you to go away while displaying remarkable self-confidence and restraint. Often, I'd ask myself why I couldn't be more like her.

When the spring semester came, I'd made a list of things I'd like to try at Memorial. I'd never gone out for the football team. To his credit, Coach Adams didn't second-guess a rising senior asking if he might try out for the team without ever having played organized football before. I also ran, opposed, for parliamentarian on the school student council. I got a job at GNC and threw myself into bodybuilding, still pursuing my *Blade* ideal, and used the benefit of new testosterone roaring through my bloodstream to push my bench press ever closer to what I then thought was a mythical number. In that semester, I saved enough to buy my first vehicle, a 1980 Honda CMT. I still pulled the odd shift on weekends, at concession stands for youth baseball games and on the grill at public golf courses like LaFortune Park. But Nise refused to ride on the back of my motorcycle. My father would drive Nise to and from the parks while I rode.

On an afternoon leaving Mohawk Park on Tulsa's Northside, I put my Harvard hoodie over top of denim jeans and Doc Marten boots. I wore a full-face helmet when I rode, my mother's rule, and that helmet was what the nurse rubbing the road rash off my skin claimed saved my life. As my father pulled onto the highway in a brown Dodge Neon, he must've seen this was all wrong in front of him. He must've seen the handlebars shifting, jerking side to side in front of me. He must've seen me bulldog those handlebars to one side like I was chasing a world title at the PRCA National Finals. He must've seen my head bounce off the pavement one, two, three, four times as the bike and I skidded for the better part of a hundred yards after hitting seventy-five on the speedometer. He must've seen half my hoodie was gone, my jeans wore torn up, and he must've imagined I was dead. When I popped up, walking around full of adrenaline and anger, he must've believed in God the way I once believed in him.

My father has not hugged me so tightly since that day, and my sister has never shown me the least inkling that she loved me as much as she did that day when she burned herself on the exhaust pipe while moving my bike out of the road. She loved me so much she told my father to call our mother, to follow us to Saint Francis, a hospital, and that she would sit with me in the back of the ambulance. She was so kind to me that she let me yammer about totaling my bike, about $800 eaten in mere seconds by pavement and potholes, rather than telling me to shut up, that I could just as easily have been dead.

I missed a month of school, half the football season, and what I thought was a chance to make my senior year memorable when Mrs. Gaddis told me, through Nise, that I'd been one of the two boys selected to represent Memorial at Oklahoma Boys State.

Oklahoma Boys State began in the 1930s as a counter to anti-American activity. It was called citizenship training. Until my selection to Boys State, wrecking my motorcycle, surviving the crash, felt like the most pivotal event of my life. Indeed, being a Boys State representative felt like an anointing for the life I was meant to lead. Boys State was only for us most All-American boys in a state that is as rigorously Christian as it is jingoistic in its American identity. Ours is the state that loves servicemen and women as much as the black wealth that gushed from beneath our feet and the natural gas we fractured the earth to own. To stand for the flag, to pledge allegiance to it, is as solemn an act as the silence we allow for the memory of our dead. Only the pastor and the star football player own a position higher in the hierarchy of Oklahoma's vocational pyramid. To be a businessman who served in Oklahoma is to be a business that folks stand in line to patronize to demonstrate their patriotism. These Oklahomans know, in their marrow, that God blessed America and nowhere else. That they, as Americans in the Bible belt, are the most deserving of his favor and the righteous iron rod with which he acts. That they are masters of our fate, a country made primarily of the master race who mastered the Black race, and it is our will, like his, that will be done. I was going to the place where Skip Bayless said he learned to lead, where we, Oklahoma American Legion Boys, trained to form our government, learned to become leaders of our generation, and, most important to the many Legion members who sponsored and worked this weeklong intensive, exhibited patriotism.

When Mama dropped me off at Northeastern Oklahoma A&M College (NEO), my training began with my uniform. We were to wear jeans or khakis whenever we were not engaged in a strenuous physical exercise, and we were to wear matching white "delegate" T-shirts that all read the same across the front: OKLAHOMA BOYS STATE. With two boys selected from every high school in the state, we were separated into cities named after veterans. And our cities acted like platoons. We slept in the same pod, ate with each other, and competed as a unit. Each city elected a mayor, and each mayor wore a mustard-yellow T-shirt. When I ran for mayor and won, I felt righteous in my standing. I moved about the campus with a sense of resolve to stand in the world not as a Black boy first but as a boy becoming a man who happened to be Black. In this, the last vestiges of spring, the summer rising like heat to raise a cake, I was turning eighteen—a man in full before his final year of high school.

I took the measure of the campus like it was beneath me. The sidewalks showed cracks where I thought there shouldn't be. The classrooms held actual desks, like students admitted here were not so many college kids but kids still not ready for a four-year quality education, or so I believed. I couldn't stand to sit in those desks with their small cages to hold books beneath our chairs and their faux-wood trays for scribbling. In government class, I tried and probably failed to not roll my eyes as our counselor put us through the meaning of the American flag, what its red, white, and blue symbolized, its fifty stars signified. I threw myself into the work of a mayor at Boys State, keeping my city in line and tamping down any act that might escalate to riotous. In that function, I came to truly understand just how nefarious holding elected office could be, especially when struck with an arrogant self-righteousness for the physical space. I stared too often, too hard, at the green chalkboard where words like *duty*, *honor*, and *patriot* were written in a printed hand that matched the busted-down basics of Boys State. When we moved about the campus, we did so in a file. As mayor, I was responsible for either choosing to command and lead us like a drill sergeant alongside his charges, or delegating that responsibility to someone else. I chose to delegate, to exercise some of the wisdom I'd gleaned from reading biographies of CEOs and United States presidents. I was well into my thirties when I realized all those books I'd read by Walt Disney and Richard Branson or about Abraham Lincoln and John F. Kennedy were about white men. Even as I was reading more Black writers and about Black life, I'd go on sojourns in one direction, only to look and find I didn't know where I was in the literature.

In delegating the responsibility of leading the file to a white boy named Josh—everyone in my city was white—who had experience doing exactly that as a member of his high school's ROTC, I believed I'd made a good decision. Josh performed admirably, getting us to and from assemblies and activities without a mistake. When I was summoned with other mayors to go over the rest of the week so that we might be prepared for how some activities might work out, I returned to my city to find out most were angry I'd left Josh in this charge. He'd run them into a wall while I was away, and while no one was hurt, each of them was embarrassed. I heard out all who wanted to complain to me about Josh, and I kept track of how many people described a similar version of events. When I spoke to Josh, he'd told me that yes, he'd made a mistake, but that wasn't a reason to relieve him of this task he relished. As mayor, I sought out my primary counselor, Justin, for his wisdom in what I should do. Justin had just finished his first year in the Naval Academy, and as a former Boys Stater, he'd had the privilege of returning as a counselor. I'd spoken with him several times over the course of the first three days of camp, getting to understand not just what Boys State was about, but the role of a mayor inside of it—as he was once mayor of his city. I presented him with the facts I had, and I asked his opinion: What would he do?

"Relieve Josh of his duty," he said.

"It's that simple to you?"

"You need the men to trust you. They need to know you trust them. When this many of your platoon is upset with one man who clearly made a mistake, no matter how benign, you have to act, or you risk losing them."

"He's good at his job. He was careless this was one time."

"One careless mistake can get a man killed."

"But this is Boys State, right? Nobody is going to be in harm's way here."

"We're all in harm's way. That's what this place is supposed to be teaching you. America is constantly under attack."

I tried to change the subject. "Did you know our city isn't even named for an Oklahoman? It's named after Chuck Yeager."

"So?"

"So I thought it might be cool if they were named after our cities, or even our veterans," I said.

"People don't know enough about Tulsa already?"

"Maybe, but what about Broken Arrow or Tahlequah or Taft?"

"Taft?"

"You know, Taft, Oklahoma?" Justin shook his head. "Taft is one of the original Black towns of Oklahoma. There were a bunch of them. Taft, Boley, Rentiesville, Greenwood. Well, Greenwood isn't a town, but it was big enough to be one."

"Greenwood?" Justin said. "Isn't that the place you people burned down? Why would you want people to remember your crimes?"

I wished I could tell you I balled up my fists and punched Justin so hard that his jaw later needed to be wired shut. But I did nothing but take this white nineteen-year-old's words and let them fill air between us. I inhaled that air into my lungs like a sickness. Like the punch I wanted to deliver, the real of where I was, of whom I was among, smacked me. I relieved Josh of his duties. I didn't do it for the reason Justin identified; I did it for the opposite reason. The truth was that these boys trusted me because they did not feel threatened by me. The mark of the talented tenth is not my birthright. The plight of Black folks in America is. That the term "talented tenth" was created not by W. E. B. Du Bois but by white folks north of the Mason-Dixon Line reveals its true meaning and haunted me through the rest of high school. It was coined by a white minister from Stanford, New York, named Dr. Henry Lyman Morehouse. Begun as Augusta Institute in Augusta, Georgia, in 1867, the college moved to Atlanta in 1879 and was renamed Atlanta Baptist Seminary. The college moved to its current location in Atlanta in 1885 and underwent another name change, to Atlanta Baptist College, in 1897. Then in 1913, Dr. John Hope renamed the college for Morehouse after receiving a substantial monetary gift from Morehouse before his passing in 1917. In a short essay

Lyman published in the *Independent* in June 1896 called "The Talented Tenth," he defined the term years before Du Bois used it in his work.[16] "In the discussion concerning Negro education," Lyman wrote, "we should not forget the talented tenth man. An ordinary education may answer for the nine men of mediocrity; but if this is all we offer the talented tenth man, we make a prodigious mistake ... The tenth man, with superior natural endowments, symmetrically trained and highly developed, may become a mightier influence, a greater inspiration to others than all the other nine, or nine times nine like them."

Du Bois taught at Atlanta University—known today as Clark Atlanta University—from the fall of 1897 to 1910 and again from 1934 to 1944. In 1903, Du Bois published *The Souls of Black Folks*, a collection of fourteen essays including "Of the Training of Black Men," where he picked up Morehouse's term and put it to further use.

After my motorcycle accident, Mama took care of me for a week as I did nothing but move from my bed to the living room couch to watch movies and watch my body reveal how much healing hurt. Where skin once was, I was raw and exposed. Even after the nurse had scrubbed away most of the chunks of pavement embedded in my skin after the crash, I found tiny pebbles so large they bore into my skin and so small that the ignorant would dismiss them with a cursory glance. My father accused me of milking the situation. Nise asked how I felt only once after the crash. Only Mama believed me when I said my elbow was aflame or my skin felt like it was radiating. She seemed to experience my physical wounds as her own, still very much tied to me with an umbilical cord that, for her, did not transcend any attachment but one she refused to sever, especially when she knew I was in pain. As my body grew new skin along my forearms, my shoulders, my back, new ideas about what I wanted for my future sprouted.

When I returned to school, Mrs. Gaddis sought me out. She asked after my application to the Naval Academy. Had I heard back?

"I don't think I want to go anymore."

"Why not, dear?" This was the first time, the only time, I felt I'd disappointed Mrs. Gaddis, and her face could not hide that, though she tried.

"I think I want to do something different."

I'd taken to the idea that I could be a strength and conditioning coach at a university. I knew I loved sports, and I also knew I was not talented enough to continue playing them with an eye toward being a professional. I knew I liked to write, too, but at Memorial, that did not feel like the kind of thing I could do for money anymore. Mrs. Gaddis didn't ask to hear any of that. Didn't ask where I planned to go to college or where I wanted to be in life when I was thirty.

"Well, I really wish you'd reconsider," she said. She reminded me that I'd asked Congressman John Sullivan for an appointment. That not every person who wanted to attend the Academy got one, though it was a prerequisite for admission. That I could be the next Colin Powell—like he was the only Black man to ever achieve anything in the military, like my parents had never served. They were the people who took this decision not to go after the Academy for college the hardest.

At first, I thought this was because I'd let them down. That their dream was for me to serve as they had. Then, as I submitted my FAFSA for the first time in the spring of my senior year, I realized what they were afraid of. At the time, the loans didn't feel like money I'd have to pay back. At eighteen, the price of tuition was a number I was unable to contextualize—mostly because I did not have to immediately begin paying it out of my own pocket. But as those numbers began to show up, as I signed promissory note after promissory note, I began to realize, no, this money is not free. And my parents could not afford to send me to college. They were counting on my sister and me winning scholarships, another hallmark of the Talented Tenth, and paying our own way with our superior intellects. That was one of the reasons I settled on the University of Tulsa. It was billed to me as the city college, but also the university where the best and the brightest in the country chose to attend. It even called itself "the Harvard of the Midwest" in its literature, never once acknowledging that there is only one Harvard, and it ain't anywhere near Tulsa, Oklahoma.

Back at Booker T., during the first semester of my junior year of high school, a Black man in a blue suit and tie made it his business to recruit his alma mater. Earl, this Black man, had attended TU on a football scholarship and found his way back to the university. He'd risen to dean of admissions, and his mission was to recruit as many Black folks as he could to TU. In our meeting, one-on-one, in a room designated for such recruitment because Booker T. saw so many college recruiters, he told me about this place I thought I was familiar with and the advantages it bestowed on its students. He implored me to think about attending and told me I'd probably find out I'd won a scholarship to aid in funding my education. I thought scholarships were substantial, especially when they came from the universities themselves. After all, the stories that made the news were of National Merit Scholars and full-ride recipients of this or that Name Brand Scholarship.

When I walked across the stage at our final school assembly, where seniors headed to Tulsa Tech, Oklahoma State, the University of Oklahoma, and TU were announced as doing so, I watched as some but far from all of my classmates were announced as attending "with a scholarship." The cheers they heard filled the auditorium. Some of their loved ones even rose to give standing ovations. When my name was called, I heard similar cheers and gleefully took the envelope "with a scholarship" inside of it. For the first time, it felt real to me—college. After exiting the stage, I opened the envelope and saw the official University of Tulsa letterhead. I was going to TU "with a scholarship" of over $2,000. I was a sophomore before I finally looked up the price tag of one year's education at TU: $35,000. In my on-campus apartment, my stomach filled with a heavy pit made entirely of anxiety and fear. I vomited moments later when I realized how much money I owed this place and felt that fear grip me once more like shackles in a subterranean dungeon of my own creation. I'd never get out of here.

*

My parents offered to help me move into my dorm room at what was then called Twin South. The university was broken into four different dorm halls. Lottie Jane was for women only, John Mabee was for men only, and Twin South, Twin West, and LaFortune were coed. Proximity to women was enticing on paper, but in practice it proved rather ridiculous. LaFortune was almost always filled. It was the nicest dorm hall on campus, with a suite setup. It was filled with mostly athletes and honor students. But Jill wasn't one. She was the first person I met when I parked in the South parking lot. I'd just popped the trunk on my 1999 Oldsmobile Alero when she pulled up in a black Land Rover in the spot next to me. When she came around the back of the SUV to start unpacking, I introduced myself. This brunette, about five foot six and slender, looked at me like she was appraising me for sale—certainly not to buy. After learning her name, I asked her what she planned to major in.

"Business administration," she said. "My dad thinks it's good preparation for law school."

"So you want to go to law school?"

"That's what my dad wants, yeah."

"But you don't."

"Doesn't matter what I want. He's paying." She said it so coldly that I wanted to change the subject rather than risk upsetting her. She turned back to open the back seat of her SUV.

"Nice car," I said.

"Graduation present." She said it over her shoulder, showing me her back. I'd become a task she could bundle with others. "My dad bought it for me."

"For graduating high school?"

"That was the deal."

I didn't ask what the deal was. I was stuck. My parents loved me. I knew that. I also knew there wasn't a world in which they could've afforded to buy my $3,995 Oldsmobile, liability insurance, or gas money to fill it, let alone a Land Rover. After carrying my stuff up four flights of stairs to my dorm room, shutting the door, and wrestling with the security credentials that allowed me access to TU's internet, my first search on my Asus laptop was the price of a Land Rover. I was flabbergasted. Then I searched the price of a used Land Rover, and that felt almost as astonishing.

I came to understand that Twin South and Twin West were mixed bags when it came to the student body, but only with respect to IQ and academic achievement. Some of my classmates would win Fulbright scholarships and were studying for heady degrees in engineering: chemical, electrical, and petroleum. Some of us, like me, were studying Exercise and Sports Science with an eye toward becoming physical therapists or going into coaching. Some of us came from wealth, much of it right here in Tulsa. Some of my classmates were raised around people who answered to titles like executive, account manager, and chief of finance. I wanted to become a strength and conditioning coordinator at a major athletic department. Rarely did I meet a classmate with parents who did not already have a college diploma or a job that could afford to put them through school at TU. In this, I thought I lucked out with Daryl.

He was my first and only roommate in college. The more learned about him over the coming days and weeks, the more I grew to like him. He was quiet, reserved. Rather than immediately respond to a question, he chose to nod at it, acknowledge it, and consider it for a beat. Sometimes he'd follow up with something to say. But most of the time he was content to listen to me. He was from Des Moines, Iowa. He chose TU because Drake University didn't want to cough up enough tuition money to keep him in-state. On our first day together, I learned his parents were not that dissimilar from my own, though he and they were white. He was at TU on a full academic scholarship to study physics *and* electrical engineering. I told him I couldn't imagine how difficult that was.

"Maybe. Think you can, though."

"No way," I said.

"I don't mean school. I mean this." He gestured at the university.

"Nah, it's cool. I'm from here."

"That's what I mean." He paused for a moment. "I read about what happened here. Happened in Greenwood. My folks, they have friends who were Panthers back home. I"—he hesitated again—"I just mean to say I think you know what double-majoring is like."

Meanwhile, the truth bubbled beneath the comments I received on my papers in freshman English, and the barely passing grade I earned in Exercise Physiology in my second semester freshman year. The bubbles rolled to boil and left me fleshy and raw with a 2.75 grade point average. After four years of high school, I'd never finished worse than a 3.5 GPA. I wasn't built then to hide from my parents what I knew would be seen as a failing. My father took my GPA as a reason to chastise me, to motivate me with humiliation. Mama asked me what's wrong? What could she do to help? I told her nothing. I told her I'd be fine. That I'd take this as a learning experience, and I'd build toward the kind of GPA we'd all grown accustomed to for me. I moved out of the dorms as a sophomore. I moved into a one-bedroom apartment on campus believing that if I isolated myself, I'd force myself to study more, study harder. But it wasn't study habits I lacked.

My father lost his job during my freshman year of college. After more than fifteen years, he'd been fired for what he deemed a technicality. He wouldn't talk about what that specific technicality was, only that it wasn't fair to him. With my father jobless, both of my parents were listless, and I worried about them. I worried about my father, who decided to launch a landscaping business that he thought I'd help him with. When I told him no, he looked like I'd driven a stake through his dream, a dream I couldn't begin to understand.

Mama needed a job, needed income. It didn't surprise me that she enrolled in the paralegal program at TU. It did surprise me as to why. She watched me battle my sophomore year, picking up a job at Pep Boys as a mechanic to make extra money for food and other necessities in the apartment after giving up my meal plan. She watched me take on an $800 scholarship per semester to throw white girls in the air as a male cheerleader. I told her everything then.

I talked with her every day. I told her about how hard this was, how the only classes I liked taking didn't have anything to do with my major. Everything I told her I also journaled. After shifts at the garage, I'd walk into my apartment, drink NyQuil straight from the bottle, and type scribbles across the blue-lit screen of a laptop that was beginning to flicker like a lamp ready to give out. She'd come over a couple of times a week too. I imagine she saw these things I'd written. I imagine she saw them written across my face, quavering with my hands. I imagine she saw the tuition statements I'd piled into a drawer. I imagine she wondered where she'd gone wrong with me when I told her on one of her visits that I was going to fail a class called Philosophy of Art.

She set a meeting on my behalf with the chief financial aid officer at TU to ask how I might better afford my education. At his great wood desk, with the trimmings of an accomplished administrator about him, he stared back at my mother and me in the wooden chairs opposite his executive throne and told us there was nothing he could do for us.

"But what can we do?" Mama asked.

He sighed. He placed his elbows on the table and steepled his hands, fingertips touching like those of God in consideration. He looked at me and then cut his eyes back to Mama. "If he can't afford to be here, then perhaps he shouldn't be here."

Mama lifted me by the arm, walked me toward the door, and did not wait for her lead foot to hit the concrete outside the financial aid building before cussing his name. The next day she enrolled in the paralegal program. The move allowed her to receive financial aid while continuing her education. No one knew she used it to continue mine too, for the next two years. Mama cried that day she was told we were too poor for me to go to TU, and I have never forgotten just how angry seeing her cry made me. The jobs I had, the work I was willing to do, the joblessness in my family, these were all circumstances I believed the government was supposed to help us with. And no help came for me that Mama didn't finagle, didn't squeeze.

The world didn't seem so fit for me to be a strength coach anymore. The world felt wrong for me, not built for me, a Black child who grew to be a young Black man still believing in American meritocracy. When my mother had to go back to school to help me finish school, I could no longer shake what I knew. And so my life began to take on the shape of a Black man investigating exactly what I knew: the world is trying to kill people who look like me, and it has done so for a very long time. As I once had, as I once instinctively began asking better questions of my place in Tulsa, I kept journaling about it, and began to read with purpose about it. I read as much as I could around my schoolwork between my junior year of college and graduation.

Notes on biomechanics were reread before picking up *Notes of a Native Son*. I listened to Marvin Gaye, Al Green; dove into Duke Ellington's big band and studied Morrison's *Jazz*. I worked through Math with Applications coursework and then picked up *The Autobiography of Malcolm X*. I studied Sports Nutrition and then fed myself on Octavia Butler, Gloria Naylor, and Walter Mosley. And sports—always—I read about sports. I stalked ESPN.com, read my local sports section religiously, and was growing into the kind of fan who loved a mix of coolness and a precise angle toward history and politics over the general jocularity many sports fans lie about wanting in their coverage. It's the reason I picked *The Collegian*, the student paper at TU.

I read a bad piece about the happenings of the NFL off-season. The piece made me angry enough to send the sports editor of the paper a condescending email about how little knowledge they must have to possess about the sport to let this go to print. She emailed a response: "Put up or shut up."

I was not going to walk at my graduation. I no longer felt up for elaborate displays and ceremonies like that. I'd come to distrust many of the traditions and rituals we'd said we loved and needed. I told Mama this. She told me she didn't care what I believed. Graduation was for her.

"After what we did," she said, "you will walk across that stage."

I thought we resembled cattle in the practice gym at the Reynolds Center. We were tagged. We were undistinguished in our black matte caps and gowns sweeping across the hardwood floor. The gowns rustled as we spoke about nothing important while waiting to file through the tunnel chute before a handful of people we knew, but so many that we did not. One graduate's father was a perfect stranger to another. Mama was out there somewhere, though. She'd wanted this. She dressed for it. Made sure I wore a tie for it. She forced my sister and father to escort her. They sat together, three across. That was their task—to sit with Mama.

Mine was to walk out of that chute in the tunnel, smile up at them, and present a happiness I'd never felt as I shook the president's hand. The afternoon I spent sitting through commencement remains some of the most wasted hours of my life. The ordeal rattled. Sitting in the file with the rest of the College of Business only exacerbated how ridiculous graduating with a degree in Exercise and Sports Science was, underscored how little it mattered what I majored in to the rest of the world, and exemplified the confidence game that higher education actually is. I'd taken eighteen-hour course loads in back-to-back semesters to get here, and I still needed to finish three hours of Music Appreciation to pick up my degree. I'd failed Philosophy of Art as a sophomore, and I'd been denied—repeatedly—the chance to take twenty-one hours in a semester so I could get out of here. This also meant I needed to come up with nearly $1,000 to pay for a summer class. All this, while I'd gotten into a graduate program that had nothing to do with my major.

*

The Master of Professional Writing program at OU was one of the first of its kind, focusing on training writers in popular fiction and nonfiction. Like a master of fine arts degree, it was also a terminal degree. I thought at first I was going to pursue a master of journalism degree, but the more I looked into the MPW program, which offered a terminal degree, the more it felt like what I wanted for my life. I wanted to write magazine pieces, books, novels, screenplays. I wanted to make a living as a writer and not a writer who taught. This was the height of my hubris, of my naivete.

That was the biggest of several conscious decisions I made during my last semester of undergraduate work. I'd applied to three law schools, three master's programs for exercise physiology, and OU. When I learned I had earned scholarship aid, but that loan services were lining up to hand me a way to owe them between 4 and 9 percent interest on the money I'd need to attend graduate school, I narrowed my options to the places I could afford to move to. Only one school made the list. Only one program looked anything like allowing me to think about what some people call happiness. For me, it was the absence of sadness that equates for joy.

I wanted a job I didn't hate as much as I hated coaching people to eat leafy greens and exert themselves to stave off age, or coming home six nights a week with motor oil under my fingernails and replaying in my head the pained look of a customer who couldn't afford to repair their vehicle. The parts of self, the parts of the world I enjoyed most were in the story. The story of getting bigger, faster, stronger—my own journey into fitness—led to stories about super-heroes, myths, and legends. My tattoos, the first inked at nineteen, reflected that which I valued most in the world. From Aristeia to Anansi, my body was marked by them. That distance from ancient Greek to folklore Black is the way I experienced the world as an adult.

I knew so much about predominantly white culture, and not nearly enough about my own. Journalism and fiction were ways into learning more about me. Reading not widely but with purpose was my aim. Building a syllabus for myself within the MPW curriculum felt not only doable but necessary. I'd chosen professional writing as a graduate degree because I believed I could find a track to sports writing. That I'd grow into the kind of feature writer Ralph Wiley, Howard Bryant, and Wright Thompson demonstrated themselves to be. That I could write the kind of stories the *Best American Sports Writing* guest editors would pick. The stories I was drawn to had lit-tle to do with quarterback ratings, shooting percentage, or even the scoreboard at the end of games. The stories I loved to read, the ones I wanted to tell, were about the people who formed those statistics and scores and the origin stories of those people.

In the Bizzell Library on OU's campus, I'd walk in during the middle of a weekday afternoon, find an open computer, and punch up search terms in JSTOR and LexisNexis to supplement a Goo-gle search. My interests frequently bent to college football. People who aren't from Oklahoma might believe there is no pro football team here because the NFL has not established a franchise here, but there's been a pro football team in Oklahoma since 1895. Indeed, the Sooners football team predates the state of Oklahoma by nearly two decades, and you'd be hard-pressed not to find a person who has lived in the state for any length of time who does not know that. Our identity is tied to the win-loss record of that team. I'd wager there are more people from Oklahoma who could tell you the names of three OU football coaches before they could tell you the names of three governors. To earn anything like acclaim, to move up in the hyper-local sports media landscape here, is to become an expert and then an insider on that team. I was neither when I began writing stories about OU football in 2010 for the student paper, and the insular nature of covering the sport made becoming first an expert and then an insider seemingly impossible.

Even more awkward than trying to write stories that would make a hiring manager double-check the byline at the top was walking into media sessions as perhaps one of three Black sportswriters working the beat among thirty, and then the parade of mostly Black athletes brought in for us to pepper with questions about offense, defense, and which underclassmen were showing promise. Oklahoma Sooners head football coach Bob Stoops had a rule then, which was not completely uncommon around the country, that true freshmen couldn't talk to media. There was a certain amount of media training the athletic department media relations staff wanted the athletes to possess before they were allowed to answer questions. The benevolent view of this practice is that the university is preparing those players for a life of public speaking to come. The nefarious one is that the OU publicists viewed the media charged with covering the team as their adversaries, looking to trip up, con, or trick a player into divulging some information they wished he had not. This sort of atmosphere was made even more complicated when race was a part of the news or just mentioned as history. At the Bizzell, I immersed myself in the history of the program. I learned all of the stories white folks loved to tell about Bud Wilkinson, Barry Switzer, and Bob Stoops. I also learned about the history they chose to only mention during February, on Martin Luther King Day, or, later, when yet another unarmed Black man or boy was shot and killed by police. I once tried to ask a wide receiver what he thought about following in Prentice Gautt's legacy. The wideout answered the question, stumbling through it, edging around saying words like "racism" and "segregation" in a winding answer. I knew, almost as soon as he started speaking, that I wouldn't quote him for print. The wideout turned to answer another question. I expected one of the white folks on OU media relations staff to pull me aside. I was caught off guard when it was one of the white folks in the media corps.

"That was out of line," he said.

"What?"

"Asking him about Gautt. That was out of line."

I didn't argue. I didn't see how arguing with him then, there, would do me any good. But the admonishment stuck. I couldn't just ask a Black player what he thought about the first Black person ever to earn a scholarship and letter at OU without scrutiny, even if the university is loud about it on its website and in its literature. Something about *me* asking the question rattled at least one person with the power to keep me out of that room. It was clear I'd ventured into forbidden territory. Sports, for some, is where politics is not permitted. Sports, for me, is where society's values, its mores, and its prejudices are most visible. I became a sports writer because I wanted to meet, as often as I could, at the intersection of race, culture, politics, and sports. Something about this artificial harmony the university claimed would be exposed. This was the first time I'd tried to ask about race in what I thought would be my profession, and I didn't like the reaction. I walked back to my car thinking about how I was stupid to act on an instinct, asking another Black man about his Black experience. I drove back to my apartment thinking about how I'd taken Harry Edwards's *The Revolt of the Black Athlete* too literally and too far in one of the most conservative states in the country. "The plight of the [B]lack athlete has not received the public exposure and coverage that the situation warrants. And even when the subject has been taken up, the dehumanizing, demoralizing aspects of the [B]lack athlete's experiences rarely have been emphasized," Edwards wrote. "Instead, most reporters—white reporters in particular—have dwelled upon how meekly, how submissively [B]lack athletes have handled ugly situations or how gentlemanly they have been under explosive pressures. Humiliating incidents, if mentioned at all, usually are subordinated to issues such as the super-human qualities—on the field of play—of [B]lack athletes. Thus, most sports reporters have helped perpetuate the injustices that have been heaped upon [B]lack athletes." I thought about why I'd chosen this work, this profession, to get away from conversations about my experience, my history, my parents, the limits of this life because of my skin color. In this life, in Norman or Tulsa, not only did no one want to hear or read about the journey of the Black college football player in the state that wraps its identity in college football, but even asking a question about it could be construed as out of line.

Two days later I walked into the Gaylord College of Communications to meet a study group for our research method class. I took a seat at one of the tables in the lobby. The building was nearly brand-new. The place opened in 2004, just six years before I arrived, and was named for the family who dropped a $22 million gift on the university for the privilege. Glossy photos of journalists like Thomas Friedman adorned the halls. Friedman, Jim Lehrer, and Tom Brokaw would all be celebrity journalists awarded the Gaylord Prize for excellence in journalism—along with $25,000. This is where the MPW program was located too, with most of my classes taking place on the second floor. As I settled at one of the large conference tables made out of a dark and glossy wood that looked fit for a banquet, I heard my name. The wide receiver I'd asked about Gautt called out to me. He was a junior then.

"I didn't know you majored in journalism," I said.

"I don't. My girl does. I'm just meeting her here."

Good enough for me. "Well, thanks for saying hi." I made a move to turn away. He caught my arm.

"It what'nt," he said.

"What?"

"It wasn't out of line." Then he paused for a moment. "Thank you."

"Thank you for what?"

He looked around like the air around him circulated the words he was searching for and slipped through his grasp as strong as a breeze across the plains. "For acknowledging. For acknowledging us." He moved away quickly afterward like a soldier afraid of being accused of fraternization with an enemy. He moved closer to a door I ascertained as being the one his girlfriend must be behind. A few minutes later she walked out. I knew this because she hugged him when she saw him at the door and kissed him on the lips. As I got older, I wonder why I held on to that moment so closely and why it has been so clear to me. I was nearly thirty years old when that reason focused for me. His girlfriend was white.

From that moment, I spent more time being purposeful about knowing not just how many Black folks were in a room but which people were most likely to talk about, write about, be about Black issues. In college football, I'd swell each time I heard a sports media personality—white, Black, or Brown—even hint at a Black issue, whether it was the proliferation of Black quarterbacks and their intellect versus their white counterparts or the paltry number of Black head coaches to Black players or the seemingly unending labor issues that the NCAA, universities, and public at large continued to ignore. College football is a multi-billion-dollar business where the entire labor force goes unpaid in a barter system that most rational people agree is unfair. The more I heard folks talk about these issues with nuance and with little reporting, the more I felt a need to talk about them, and there was no way to do that without talking about history, our history, Black history. I sought out more books, more literature, on the Black athlete experience in the United States and found the cache overflowing. Scholars, journalists, and economists had been writing and talking about these issues since Reconstruction. Their work, though, was not spoken about, even on a campus that built a modern edifice to teach mass communication because the masses demonstrated little to no appetite for such truth. The history that makes us feel good is the history that proliferates into popular journalism, and the history that does not has little use to journalists and historians in a capitalist system like ours. We, as journalists, write about the people, places, and events that sell, and we do not raise up those stories that don't because we have to eat too. In this way, Americans get the news they want, and the news they want will never be ours. Black issues do not make most Americans feel good, and to find those issues in sports feels blasphemous to them. Of course, most Americans are white, though Black Americans dominate two of the three major sports in country—football and basketball. I brought this up at an OU men's basketball game with another white beat writer. He nodded, shrugging at points I made, like a kid in a required course patiently waiting for me to get to the end of my lecture so he could leave.

"Doesn't any of that make you want to do something?" I said it like an accusation.

"Like what?" He fired it back like a rebuttal. "I gotta focus on the game."

*

To understand how the nation feels at any moment, read the sports. To understand the nature of Black folks in sports, count the number of NBA players who are Black. Then count the number of NBA owners who are Black. Then count the number of NFL players who are Black. Then count the number of NFL owners who are Black. That nearly 70 percent of the NFL's labor is Black and male in a country where just 7 percent of citizens are Black and male is the story—not how many yards the league MVP rushes or throws for. Those numbers did not immediately present themselves to me. They were in the parts of literature and ephemera that I avoided. I didn't want to feel bad about the limits of this life, and I wanted to believe the world was open to me. Then George Zimmerman killed Trayvon Martin on a sidewalk because he could.

Heading into the summer of 2012, I had spent two years writing about Oklahoma Sooners football and men's basketball at the student newspaper, *The Oklahoma Daily*. I'd focused my time there on writing columns and features—when I could get access to players and coaches—to try to turn out the kind of clips that might land me a paid internship. It's the kind of thing I should've been doing in undergrad and following my first year of grad school. But I did not want to leave Oklahoma. I believed if I did, I would not return to finish my degree. As I learned just what was possible in sports media in the state, I also learned exactly what wasn't. My girlfriend was still finishing school, and I did not want to leave the only person I felt would look out for me other than myself. It felt like a betrayal. My girlfriend, who was white, had become the person I was most loyal to, especially as my parents disavowed me over my liberal politics and my being a more avid supporter of social democracy. As an adult, with the benefit of over one hundred miles of distance, I investigated the world through books and without the shadow of my parents for the first time in my life. My girlfriend supported this part of me, this part that was beginning to bloom intellectually and purposefully. I checked in with Mama daily during that first year away, but with distance, her snide comments about Obama, about race, about the white supremacist politics of our state had turned from the kind of remarks I chose to ignore to the kind I chose to challenge.

"He's a socialist, RJ," Mama said during a FaceTime call. "Obama's a lunatic socialist."

"He's not. But if he is, what the fuck is wrong with socialism?"

"I can't believe you just said that! Who is in your head? It's that girl, isn't it?"

"She's no more a girl than you are."

"I don't like her."

"So you've told me."

"And you don't care if I like her."

"No more than you care if I like your husband."

"Your *father*."

"As if I had a fucking choice in the matter?"

"But you picked *her*."

"She picked me too. I did—"

"To spite *me*."

I hesitated, thinking about her last emphatic word, and then I pressed my instinct. "You think I'm with her because she's white?"

This took her aback, if only for a second. "I don't care what color she is. But *that girl* is nothing like me. She just does what you want her to do—like some kind of blonde robot."

I gritted my teeth so that Mama could see my jaw tightened, clenched. She bared her teeth back at me, fangs shining in full glory. A moment when a complete stranger could recognize I am her son. We stopped talking daily after that fight. She kept calling, but I decided not to answer. When she called my girlfriend to try to get to me, that only served to renew my anger toward her. My girlfriend, trying to bridge-build, talked with Mama, tried to help her understand why I felt as I did, but those conversations became the ones that turned her into a puddle of tears.

"I think your mom hates me," she'd say.

"Mama ain't a hateful person."

"Then why does she beat me up so much?"

After that, I told her not to answer Mama's calls, Mama's texts.

I told her I, we, were going to take the air out of this conversation confrontation, suffocate it. My parents didn't pay for anything for me. Hadn't for years. Money was the language they understood. I didn't have any, but I didn't want or need theirs. This is how I fueled my estrangement. This is how I began to embrace my Blackness permanently. This is how I ended up in the Red Room at the University of Oklahoma's football facilities sitting next to wide receiver Kenny Stills in April 2012 with a microphone in front of his face, asking him how he felt about Trayvon's death.[17]

"I definitely saw it as a tragedy. I really couldn't believe it at first, that people would feel intimidated by a young African American male wearing a hood. Every time I have a sweatshirt that has a hood on, I have a hood on. What does that prove? Somebody has a hood on so you're intimidated by them? What is that? I felt like it hit home for a lot of people. I feel like a lot more people are conscious of it."

I asked him if he thought Black men should change the way we dressed in response to Martin's death. Stills was a liberal Black man in conservative Norman. He was fair-skinned, rocking a blond mohawk. His ears were decorated with diamond-studded earrings, and his sleeves were inky murals. His black Converse rounded out his black sheep persona. In thinking about his response to me, he let himself ponder the question.

"No. Not at all," he said. "I feel like a lot of it is stereotypes. It depends on the type of neighborhood that you live in. I don't know too much about this story, but it sounds like, from my teammates talking about it, that he was in a pretty nice neighborhood. They said that he had went to the store, and he had come back with a hood on. Someone was intimidated enough that they felt they had to shoot him. I feel it's unfair for people to be able to do that. If you see somebody else—not an African American male with a hood on—it's not a big deal. But you see him with one, and he's a threat. That's unfair, but that's the way the world works."

Stills was selected in the fifth round of the NFL draft after three years of football at OU, where he was consistently one of the team's best receivers. He's since led initiatives against police brutality and is one of the eighty-seven people arrested outside Kentucky Attorney General Daniel Cameron's house in July 2020 while demanding the prosecutor charge and see to the arrest of the cops who killed Breonna Taylor. But in 2012, when that article appeared in the state paper of record, he and I were vilified locally. I'd been freelancing for *The Oklahoman* for two years, driving to small towns around the state to report high school football games in places like Davis, Minco, Madill, and Cashion in the fall, and just that spring walking into the Red Room on the paper's credential to report a story or two. Through the Sports Journalism Institute and one of the paper's managers, Joe Hight, I'd received a paid internship at the paper for the upcoming summer, and they put me straight to work. The story was bold for the paper, bold in this community, but I didn't realize how bold until I checked Twitter and then later Facebook. People with "God first" and "Christian" in the bios wrote screeds about the story. Claimed Stills was race-baiting. Claimed the paper had a liberal agenda. A year later people I'd gone to high school with, college with, called neighbors, also claimed that the phrase "Black Lives Matter" insulted them following its circulation on Facebook in July 2013, when a jury acquitted Zimmerman of Trayvon's murder. That to say Black lives matter is supremacist rhetoric. One of those people was my mother. That was the day I unfriended her on Facebook. She'd seen me get married just a month earlier. We didn't speak again for three years.

The first full-time job I got in sports was writing about Oklahoma Sooners football, men's basketball, and recruiting for a website built on top of a message board. The site was a hub for people to post their comments, like a public email. The headline acted as the topic of conversation for each individual post, and the replies beneath were where the exchanges occurred. I have never met a person who posted on a message board under any name other than an assumed identity. Part of a message board's appeal, especially in sports, is anonymity. It provided protection for those who wanted to post sensitive information they believed the message board community would enjoy knowing. The counterbalance is that people use the privilege of anonymity to lie or give an opinion they might never under their real name.

For me, this was the first time I'd ever read a message board—let alone posted on one. But I was quickly made to understand by my boss that he expected me to post on the board, interact with sub-scribers on the board, and read it often. The main idea here was to know that the community, paying for the privilege of posting on the message board and learning inside information on the team from the staff writers as well as each other, was the lifeblood of not just my job but the entire industry around covering the Sooners. This was the first time I realized my job in sports journalism was not driven by my taste or reporting like a public servant. My job was to write about the topics and people the message board community most wanted to read about. But I didn't have sources inside the OU football program or men's basketball program, and my boss—who also reported on the team full-time—had developed sources within the OU athletic department over the course of more than a decade on the beat. Seemingly no time at all passed before I became aware of just how little I had to contribute to this site and its subscribers that they did not already know.

"You're here because you can write," my boss said. Saying it like writing was some kind of talent rather than punching at a keyboard.

But being able to write, to tell a story with detail, verve, and structure, was not a skill that was valued by the community I was writing for. Reading through their topics and replies, I found a large swath of people who were politically conservative in their language, even though talking about politics on the board was expressly against the rules and could result in a lifetime ban from the site. The players were written about as if they were property rather than people. Their abilities were constantly questioned based on nothing more than a feeling from something a poster had seen over a year ago. I once tried to insert myself into this sort of conversation and steer participation in the discourse to statistics, depth chart analysis, and the perspective of OU coaches who saw the player day to day.

"RJ's sticking up for the Black kid. Little early for that," one replied.

"It's not a race thing," another wrote.

"Come at us if we talk about the kid eating fried chicken or watermelon, OK, RJ?"

I replied that I hadn't mentioned the player was Black, and I was shouted down in the thread again. A couple of posters even pinged my boss to tell him they didn't like how I was "coming at them."

When I spoke to my boss about the exchanges, he made clear to me that the posters paid $10 a month for the privilege. "And they're only hazing you. They'll get over it. Just give it a minute."

Hazing me? Privilege to do what? Get their rocks off coming after me because I chose to participate in the discussion? I was the Black kid at the all-white lunch table. After all, none of my co-workers were Black, and none of them were women. All of them were white and male. I knew there were over three thousand paying subscribers to the site, and I guessed that most of them were white too. I tried a couple more times to talk with the community. Every now and again, one of them would tell me I wrote a decent article about a person they liked or didn't know much about. Two years after I was hired, I met my boss behind the bank where he paid me with a check once a month, and he told me that would be my last one. The site was losing money because the team hadn't played so well the previous year.

I believed him when he said that subscriber growth, and therefore revenue, was tied to how many games OU won in a season each year. I believed him when he told me I'd done a great job and worked hard for him. I believed him when he told me it wasn't personal. I took my check and sat in my truck for an hour, wondering what I was going to tell the woman I'd just married about losing our livelihood as she headed into her second year of law school. Later, I read congratulations on Twitter for a person my ex-boss hired to replace me. At that moment, I felt shame.

By then, my wife was in law school in Oklahoma City, just twenty minutes from the apartment we'd moved into so I could be close to my job. I'd applied for other jobs as a sportswriter and then news reporter at *The Oklahoman* and *Tulsa World*, but neither of the state's two largest papers nor my hometown paper wanted to interview me, let alone hire me. I'd put in applications at other papers across the country too. A few gave me an interview, and three offered me a job. But the money would not have been enough to take care of both of us, and we'd decided that she needed to finish law school. We'd done our homework before she set off on that path. The chances of a spouse finishing law school without support in the home were dismal. The divorce rates for those couples were also nearly 30 percent higher than the national average. We'd only been married for six months when I was fired, and the only thing I thought I had to offer her was physical support, emotional support, and the savings we'd scraped together.

I was listless then. I hardly saw my wife because school was that demanding. Plus, she'd managed to secure an internship at the Oklahoma Court of Appeals. Whenever possible, we trekked back to her parents' house in a suburb of Tulsa, went for walks, went to the dollar theater to see a movie. But this was one of the hardest periods of my life. I became an armed licensed private investigator for a while. I flirted with a career in bail enforcement, bowing out when I couldn't stomach chasing people down who I knew didn't have any money, for a system built to exploit them. I grew angrier, depressed, as Michael Brown, Walter Scott, Tamir Rice, and Laquan McDonald were all killed for looking and acting just like me. I found some measure of respite at the gym in Norman, tossing weights and climbing Mt. Everest eight times a day, seven days a week, over ninety-minute sessions. During one of those sessions, a former OU player saw me, waved, and walked over to me.

"Do you remember me?" he asked.

"I do. What're you doing here? Didn't you go to the league?"

He nodded as if he knew the question. He nodded as if he wished I hadn't asked. Just for a moment, I wished I hadn't. "The NFL is a tough work environment."

I knew the stats. Only the top 1.1 percent of college players across the FBS and FCS divisions each year get drafted to play in the NFL. Many of those don't make any of the thirty-two fifty-three-man rosters. Of those who do, careers last an average of three years. What's three years in the life of a man who lives seventy? What if all anyone remembers of you is those three years when you were the worst of the best in the world?

"I'm in school again, though," he said.

I bounded up the steps on the cardio mill, welcoming the change in subject. "What're you studying?"

"I'm getting my MBA. Then maybe law school. Maybe I can make it so these kids don't go through what I did."

"You're gonna be an agent?"

He chuckled. "Nah, I want to see them get paid while they here."

"Here like OU here?"

"Here like everywhere they play college ball. I'm like fuck a scholarship. We Rod Tidwell in this bitch."

"I feel you."

"I knew you would. Anyway, stay up, RJ. We all we got."

I step to that, to that thought he put in my head. The NCAA's a cartel that has profited almost exclusively from Black labor. The two highest revenue-generating sports in college are football and men's basketball. Both of those sports are dominated by Black men, yet we have seen no pay for their labor while white folks continue to profit largely from it. Most head coaches in both sports are white, and most of the workforce is Black. Even as legislation has been enacted on the state level and is being positioned at the federal level to allow college athletes to profit from their name, image, and likeness, there is no push, publicly or politically, for universities to pay their athletes out of their own coffers. Even now, white folks in charge have a problem with paying Black folks what they're worth and will allow them to make money only if it does not come directly from their pockets, which they've lined with money created from Black folks for over four hundred years. This despite name, image, and likeness becoming the largest issue to affect college football since integration, and those people who were early in it reaped the reward. There has always been wealth in backing Black talent, Black futures, especially in sports because it was the only avenue where we were allowed to prove we are worthwhile in the eyes of white folks because, for so long, white folks were the people who determined an American's worth.

To be a Black in America is to want some of what white folks have and to hate yourself for wanting it at all simultaneously. But a belief in the community that Black folks have fostered is not one that must be built on faith. Before, during, and after slavery, Black folks have found ways to push forward with invention and innovation so that we might survive. That is what Greenwood was. That is what Greenwood is: a Black community who banded together under segregation out of necessity because there simply was no place else to go in Tulsa. Out of that necessity came a measure of brilliance, sophistication, and prosperity that was so bright, so unheard of, that it has stretched to myth and legend at the height of the centennial anniversary of the night white folks decided they'd had enough of the luminous district many saw as a leprosy, and they aimed to kill it. That's what white folks have done throughout American history when Black folks have shown themselves to be not only equal but, in some respects—like football—superior. Black men partnering with white women continues to be taboo and is construed as a bludgeon against white masculinity.

Pointing out this hypocrisy, or that of segregation, or that of police brutality has often resulted in the blackballing of those first with courage to shout it, denounce it, and fight it. This was true of my Grandmomme. We moved back to Tulsa in the summer of 2016 because that's where my then wife had the best chance to begin preparation for passing the bar while following up with family friends and acquaintances she'd met during law school to try to secure a job. She did pass the bar, and she did get a job working with families and children in the state. Finishing law school had taken a piece from both of us, a part of the jigsaw that was awkward and left us incomplete by its end. It wasn't until her graduation that I realized one piece wasn't missing but several.

This was also the second straight year that I was doing freelance writing, turning wrenches, or performing the kind of investigative work that made me feel like a snitch to try to be anything other a deadbeat husband. When we moved to Tulsa, though, my then wife made clear she wanted me to try to find something like a career and not just enough part-time jobs to cobble money together. I didn't have the courage to fight her. I'd become so beaten down by the query process of book writing that I'd grown belligerently depressed. When my birthday came around that July, she asked me what I wanted. I cruelly told her a book deal. I'd decided then that I'd apply to grad school again because I didn't know what else I could do that would push us both toward contentment. I'd settled on pursuing a PhD in English at Oklahoma State University with an emphasis on creative nonfiction because that felt right, felt like something approaching the skill set I'd spent the last six years of my life developing and refining. That skill was sharpened with reading, the kind that led me to *The New Yorker*, but also to what's wrong with *The New Yorker*; the kind that led me into a tunnel reading about Paul Robeson the football player and dropped me off at an exit marked by communism, socialism, Marxism, and Black folks; the kind that began with Ida Wells-Barnett and dumped me into Black gun culture. I settled on the program, had begun the application process, and was already thinking of how I could ride the bus from Tulsa to Stillwater to complete the coursework necessary when my wife walked through the door. She dropped her purse on the counter, walked over to me on the couch, took my laptop out of my hands, and lay down in my lap.

"What're we watching?" she asked.

"Packers–49ers," I said.

"Preseason?"

"Uh-huh."

"On a Friday night?"

"Preseason."

"Why is that guy kneeling?"

"I don't know."

"Is he hurt?"

"I don't think so."

She made a noise like that was a good enough explanation for her, and I was grateful. That was the last time I watched an NFL game without thinking about what it costs to defend Black folks in America. That was the last time I watched an NFL game without worrying about how a Black boy might not make it home because he chose to walk down the street, jog through his neighborhood, or come across a police officer who might kill him for flinching at the sight of him. That was the last time I watched an NFL game without thinking about Colin Kaepernick taking a knee during the national anthem. That was the last time my wife rested her head on my lap.

THIRTY YEARS OLD, LYING ON THE CARPET WITH A MIND unable and a body unwilling to crawl into my bed inches away, I recounted all the reasons I wanted to die in my one-bedroom studio apartment on the south side of Tulsa.

I ate through what was left of the advance from my first book to pay for this apartment, to buy food to eat, to put gas in my truck. I'd been forced to trade in half of my books to a used bookstore because I could not accommodate my library in a space this small. I was going back to school in the fall to pursue a PhD in English that I did not finish. I was divorced and still unable to process my grief about that, even as I believed I had found another woman who loved me. I'd thrown away my belts when I first moved in two months earlier. The longest cord in the apartment was attached to an iron. I used to own a gun. I used to own two. I'd given them both to my best friend, Ron, who has continued to perform the kindness of keeping them out of sight when I visit him and never on his mind when we speak. He holds my sins against myself, and he's forgiven me over and over again, even as I could not forgive myself.

The first time I ever saw a therapist, I told her all of this. Her idea then is one I cling to even now. "Do what makes you," she said. Then, now, I read. I watch Marvel movies. I talk about college football. I couldn't write, even though writing made me, too. Writing is how I pay bills, how I find out what I know. In the excavation and introspection necessary to write my first memoir well, I hadn't liked what I found. I loathed me.

I did not feel worthy of Grandmomme's legacy, nor of that left by the Black folks who created Greenwood. I should've gone, left this city, Tulsa, but I couldn't do that either. The means to travel existed. I could have left Tulsa like most of my friends from high school and college. I could have found a city with a robust Black community, survived, gathered strength, and come back to this place that would never change and had done nothing but turn me against myself. In the summer of 2017, I felt stuck in Tulsa. I was itchy, tired, and sick, staring at the sickness in me drying into the carpet fibers. Before I fell asleep, I thought there was no worse place to be.

Selfishly, I felt there could be no worse place in the world for me, or any Black person, than Tulsa, this place nicknamed Magic City. *Is there magic here?* No, I did not die. I did not recover, either. I did not decide then, curled into myself, that I was wrong. I only decided my body was not. Then, my body finally let me sleep.

The next day, I stepped over my dry, crunchy carpet essence, flipped the hot water on, showered, and dressed to go to the gym. I picked up my backpack and walked downstairs to my truck. The gym was in a strip mall across from a Walmart and a tire shop. It shared the strip mall with an outdoor retailer, a long-closed dollar movie theater, another tire shop, and a Red Lobster. I tended to visit the gym when most people were at work and checking to see if it was socially acceptable for them to order a beer with their lunch.

I enjoyed this time because the gym was mostly empty, especially on weekdays. I scanned my keychain ID and made straight for a piece of cardio I'd prayed to every day for the last eight years, called a step mill. I needed to use a step mill because I'd torn the meniscus in my right knee playing catcher at Booker T., was too impatient to let it heal correctly, and had begun running sixty miles a week by the time I graduated TU. I loved to run then. I loved the fight then. I ran and I jumped rope. I ran and I hit the heavy bag. I ran and I flipped the speed bag. I ran and I danced with the sway bag. It was something to do with the rage, with the pain, a way to fight the world until *I* got tired; a way to pivot, shift my weight, and release the terror I felt into eighty pounds of sand, skinned in black, suspended helplessly from a chain, knowing this is what they think of me, this is what they'd do to me, this is what they did to us, the named and unnamed who survived the diaspora to learn a slower, tortuous way to die.

When my knee gave way while finishing a marathon, an orthopedist told me I couldn't run like I had any longer. He said I, a twenty-five-year-old with a resting heart rate of fifty-eight beats per minute, should expect to have pain in both of my knees when I turned thirty-five unless I "altered my habits." I couldn't tell him working out with such frequency and vigor kept me sane. I couldn't tell him if I don't have some way to expel this anger and bile I feel every day, it will fill me up until I explode. I couldn't tell him this was one I could survive a while longer. At the gym, a couple of days after my orthopedist's diagnosis, I asked the front desk attendant what the toughest piece of cardio in the gym was. She didn't hesitate. She told me the answer had to be the rowing machine or the step mill. There were two rowing machines and both were occupied that day, but the bank of six step mills wasn't occupied by anyone. At a gym, if there is a piece of equipment that doesn't get a lot of use, that's because people are afraid of it, like white folks have shown they're afraid of me. I climbed the step mill, and I haven't stopped.

I learned to extend my time on it from twenty minutes to an hour and half. I'd read fifty pages of a book while listening to Alan Silvestri, Bill Conti, and Hans Zimmer in my headphones. This morning it was all I could manage just to hit the start button. Twelve minutes had gone by before I heard my name.

"Excuse me, RJ? You're RJ, right?"

I scanned in front and, remembering I was on the step mill—I'm six-foot-five—looked down. A Black man with crispy waves, busting through his tank top and shorts, an Adonis of a man, was grinning back at me. "Yes, I'm RJ," I said.

"Man!" He bounced while saying it, like "man" had three syllables. "I *love* your show. I'm a subscriber. I *love* whatcha doing, how you representing for *us*, you feel me? You on your way. You gone do *it*, brother. You gone do it, and I'm gone tell everybody I knew it, and I met him way back *right here*. You keep going, all right? You keep going." He seemed to settle then, expectantly.

"Thank you," I said.

And then he was relieved again, like I'd said exactly the right thing. He nodded. "No, man, thank you. I appreciate you, brother." He raised a fist at me, turned, and walked toward the exit with his fist reaching to the sky.

*

The first therapist I ever hired cried within fifteen minutes of our meeting. We lasted just three sessions. In the second, she gave me an assignment. She wanted me to reach for an activity that was purely fun, purely for me. She was certain those activities could not be hobbies I'd walked through the door with, nor anything I might do as a vocation, or an occupation, like writing nonfiction. She wanted me to grab something in this life that was only meant to inspire joy. Now, I write late-night jokes. If the trend holds, I'll have a network late-night show in no time at all.

I'd made videos before. The process of planning, shooting, editing, and uploading were all-consuming to my mind. Making a video allowed me to line up my thoughts while they busily snapped open like flower blossoms speed-ramped times one hundred. First, I made videos with my then wife. Now, I made videos about going back to school, vlogging about earning a PhD in English. In refreshing my browser in YouTube's creator studio, I learned just how little people seemed to care. But I cared, and I loved them. I loved them so much that I thought incorporating aspects of this world I'd come to adore was worthwhile too. So, on a step mill, on a Sunday morning, I shot a video of myself reacting to a watershed win by Oklahoma at Ohio State. At the game's end, quarterback Baker Mayfield, who'd come to embody what OU football could be at its best—grinding, relentless, totally without fear in the face of what we feel meant to overcome—picked up an OU flag normally waved by cheerleaders, stormed to the fifty-yard line at the Shoe in Columbus, Ohio, waved the flag, and then planted it firmly in the ground. I was proud of OU's thirty-four-year-old head coach, a young man thrust into one of the biggest jobs in the sport with the seemingly abrupt retirement of his predecessor after eighteen years. Ohio State fans like to say "Ohio Against the World." The World could take a breather. Oklahoma did just fine. I said as much and uploaded the video.

People watched it, but more than that, people asked for more like it in the comment section. So I made more. First I did it just after games, and then during the week, and by October 2017, I was making a video about Oklahoma football every day. I was slowly creating a community that I very much wanted to be a part of and that crucially had nothing at all to do with the book project I was finishing. And that's what I believed it was. I didn't believe much would come of it, even as my Google AdSense account steadily hit the threshold each month with money made in the split between myself, a YouTube partner, and YouTube.

Within twelve hours, a video of me commenting on an egregious unsportsmanlike act with glee reached more than seven thousand views, a monster number for me, who was used to three to four hundred at the time. Then, I had just seventy-eight subscribers and very little money. In the creator studio, which is the back end of a YouTube channel, I saw that the video had even made me money. And it was fun. So I made more OU football videos. Talking about the Sooners, and the tedium and thrill of creating and editing video that would be consumed, let me smile. All of a sudden, I had more than a hobby. I had value—intrinsic and monetary. And the money is a big deal.

*

Despite what some have said and others have reported, uploading is a way to make a living. Strangers routinely donate money during live streams, not unlike some folks who tip strippers and cam girls, which makes me Magic Mike with a football. Sometimes I'd make $100 while rambling about OU football for an hour. Later, I'd make more than $700 a month in revenue with fewer than three thousand subscribers. This was enough to pay my rent and make groceries while I went to school, but it still wasn't what I thought of as my job. Writing my book was my job. Going to school was my job. Making videos kept me alive. Then a person dropped $800 in a donation with this line: "My husband loves OU football. He's got Parkinson's. He sets his watch by your videos. Please don't stop." Just three months later, Natural Light Beer awarded me $40,000 for a three-minute short film I made about why I was inspired to go to college. I had proof that I was good at it and the validation of people who said I was good at it. But it became less fun and more work, especially as the October deadline for my book became a February of the following year deadline. I nearly quit because I wanted to make something else. But I needed the money too. To plan, shoot, and edit a video can take me between one and three hours each day, and there have been days when I am not well. For days when I'm having a panic attack, filled with anxiety and unable to function, I have made five failsafe videos that I can schedule to go live at 6:00 p.m. with a few clicks.

Making a living on YouTube is not unlike making a living as a writer. In a market that's rich with ideas, techniques, and categories (read: genres), the best videos don't rise to the top. The most popular ones do. Videos that keep users clicking on more thumbnails get rewarded most, just like books that move the most units get rewarded most. YouTube doesn't care if your video is good. It only cares if it gets views and watch time and keeps folks on the channel. What I'm really saying is that Danielle Steele is no Lauren Groff. But guess whose house is bigger? Folks who have reached the minimum requirements—one thousand subscribers and four thousand hours of time users have spent watching your channel's videos—to enroll in YouTube's Partner Program make about $7.60 per one thousand views for a pre-roll ad—ads of thirty seconds or longer shown in front of a video—on a channel like mine. Pre-roll ads on popular brand channels like CBS and HBO can go for $20 per thousand views. For me, during a peak college football season, I'd make as much as $16.25 per one thousand views. Which means if you made one video, every day, for a month and those videos averaged five thousand views per upload, you'd make about $1,064 a month. Now what if those five thousand views were fifty thousand? Now your ad revenue income is six figures. Then there's merch. Then there's sponsorships. Then there's Patreon, and we're not even into developing a second channel yet. With a channel approaching fifty thousand subscribers, you can easily make more than $40,000 a year. In Oklahoma, that's enough to live—that is to say, stave off the wish to die—while perhaps paying back student loans that will plague you well into your golden years, such that those payments will feel like the indentured servitude that purchasing and pursuing a higher education has become. In the United States, let alone Tulsa, seeking a college degree is perilous and one of the most regrettable decisions we make as young adults because our society makes us pay for it for the rest of our lives. This never becomes clearer than when watching interest stack on federally subsidized loans month after month and wondering just where any person might find the funds to secure a down payment on a house while paying rent on, shall we say, a lesser abode. In talking with one of my professors at OSU, I learned I couldn't expect to make more than $50,000 if I managed to secure a job teaching with my PhD and a book.

The answer to my immediate adult life was becoming less ideal-istic and more pragmatic. Every video I uploaded was like a nonfic-tion piece I submitted for workshop. I don't see myself as a talented writer. I'm a working writer; always submitting, always freelancing, always manuscript writing, always magazine writing, always novel writing, always working on writing, always writing toward hoping to find talent enough to secure the next advance on working to-ward writing. Always banging at a stone tablet hoping to chisel out a phrase, a paragraph that might outlast, mostly coming up short with a sand-sketched sentence incapable of surviving a brisk breeze. But talking? In public? On a microphone? Into a camera? In this, I felt there was little effort at all. I'd simply present my thesis and support it. I could throw out a line and tell you a story, and I was getting paid a whole lot more to do that than to sit at my MacBook Pro and thrash about.

In Tulsa and in Oklahoma at large, we listen to the radio. Pod-casts are a natural evolution of the radio form, and while I'd first thought I was making a movie, like YouTuber Casey Neistat, I learned from the people on YouTube that they consumed what I was making like a simulcast radio show, a talking head delivering a strong opinion about the day's headlines in sports on demand, a video podcast. With my best friend Ron Taylor's help, believing in pragmatism, I adapted to their expectations rather than exclu-sively my own. In this, the AdSense revenue increased along with the amount of money dropped into my bank account each month. But it wasn't just Tulsa or Oklahoma who consumed me in this way, but every sports fan who chose to click a thumbnail with my face on it. I'd tried the more traditional way of being a sports journalist—writing—but the internet, with an emphasis on the most dominant social-sharing video platform in history, allowed me to leverage this thing—talking about college football—into a space where I not only made a living but built something like a following. Many high school football players face the same proposition. They want to play big-time college football but lack the physical traits necessary to compete. I felt that way—feel that way—in my professional writing life. Some artists are as talented as a six-foot-six, 260-pound edge rusher from Texas, drafted No. 1 overall in the NFL draft. Some outwork the six-foot-six, 260-pound specimen, but they can never have his gifts. You're either born with that frame or you're not. No amount of skill development will change that. We may only use what we've got, which is authentically Black. Three centuries of the United States' limitations on Black folks have forced innovation and genius in every discipline that is the envy of mankind. In music and in literature, in math and in science, there is an indelible imprint of Black ingenuity born from a legacy of lack. I had a laptop and a smartphone, and I created a show worthy of notice and attractive to companies wishing to advertise their wares because it was the pragmatic thing to do. Black folks are rarely afforded an option that is not rooted in practical survival. After all, that is our greatest talent and our greatest skill: we are the world's painfully anointed, remarkably genius social survivalists.

*

In 2018, the program director at a local sports talk radio station, a white man—they're all white men here—in Tulsa called me to ask if I'd be interested in talking about the Sooners once a week on one of their shows.

"How it works," he said, "is you'd be a guest on the show."

"How did you find me?" I asked.

"Well, I didn't," he said, "but I've seen your stuff on YouTube, and you're quite funny." He paused and then added "and informed," like he knew he'd should've led with that. "Anyway," he went on, "the owner of the station, he's the one who found you. He's a big OU fan, huge, and he told me to get in contact with you about this opportunity, and it turns out we know some of the same people."

The program director, like the station and the owner, they have names, just not here. I wasn't concerned about who had given the program director my phone number. That part was done. I wanted to know how much I would get paid to appear on this show once a week.

"Oh," he said, "we were thinking this would be good exposure for your site, your YouTube. You could promote your videos during your segment with our host." So no, he wasn't going to pay me. But I said yes anyway.

It was still just fun then, and I was still very much in my second semester of grad school at Oklahoma State. Talking about OU football then, especially in the spring, was a way to keep myself upright, sane, talking about a sport and a team I enjoyed even when it was not in season, and to buy groceries and pay the electric bill without further diminishing my advance on the book. When I was not making videos about OU football or doing (most) of the reading for classes and writing for courses, I spent time on YouTube, learning how to succeed on it and trying to find a way into it the way Neistat had. He had a video called "FILMMAKING IS A SPORT," and I felt he talked about, made short films about, making stuff the way I thought about writing. I dreamed of rebuilding my library, of sitting with the thoughts of Angela Davis, James Baldwin, Alice Walker, Colson Whitehead, and Ta-Nehisi Coates; flipping through Howard Bryant, Roxane Gay, Ralph Wiley, Octavia Butler, Zora Neale Hurston, and Toni Morrison. This is my literary family, aunties and uncs who allowed me my dream when I read theirs. They reminded me I am never alone. I imagined them walking out of a dimensional gateway, joyous and made proud, steady at my back, steeling it in tradition that stretches centuries back to the land dispossessed. Mine is the magic.

*

By the end of the 2018 football season, I was doing regular hits on radio shows in Oklahoma, Texas, and at Sirius XM, and I was learning from producers who booked me that I was good at it. A producer at Sirius asked when I planned to try to go into the business. I told him hadn't.

"RJ," he said, "you ever heard the phrase 'There's gold in them there hills'?"

I sat with that thought for a couple of days, and then I walked into the program director's office to ask his advice about what I needed to do to get a radio show.

"Would you like to do that here?" he asked.

I said I might, and he gave me a task. Find sponsors who would be willing to pay for the time on the station, and I could have my sports talk show. For an hour. On Sunday. At 10:00 a.m. Which means I was forced to sell my own show and then could only be hosted when anybody within range of the station signal was bound to be at church. I bargained for the air check—the record of everything aired on the station—for the time I was on-air to be mine and to be emailed to me the following morning, so I could upload the show as an audio podcast and on my channel. My friend Steve and a restaurateur agreed to back me, and I began hosting radio by myself on Sundays. I called the show *Fight Me with RJ Young*, and I learned I was good at it. I also learned that not everybody could host a radio show, and even fewer could host one by themselves. Talking for eight to twelve minutes at a time is not a skill we teach, nor is being cogent during that time. I've come to believe a person has to be terribly arrogant and courageous to occupy that chair, that microphone, by themselves, get in and out of breaks, tee up guests, call for sound, and still be entertaining. I've also come to believe no one on earth has skin so thick that the mean things people say about you, about your constitution, are not affecting.

I hosted *Fight Me* for an hour for a couple of months, then stretched that to two, leading into the day's NFL games. It was a nice part-time hustle I'd put together. Making videos during the week and hosting a radio show I flipped to a podcast on the weekend. I expected to finish school, though, and figure out whether I could be a full-time writer in Tulsa, though I'd have to entertain moving away if a job presented itself in academia. I met Jerry Ostroski in January 2019. Jerry hosted the *Coach and the Big O* show at the station where I hosted *Fight Me*. He's also a former All-American offensive lineman at TU and ten-year NFL veteran. But he got to know me because he grasped what I was doing before I did. He got my number from the program director and asked me to come up to the station one day after his show aired. So I did, and he took me to lunch. I didn't know he'd been listening to me for over a year on YouTube and on *Fight Me*.

I didn't know then, in just a month's time, that he'd get up from his chair and take another job. I didn't know that he'd pitch me to the program director as the person who should sit down in that chair still warm from his six-foot-four, three-hundred-pound behind. I didn't know I'd say yes to becoming the first Black person to host a daily sports talk show in Tulsa in June 2019. I didn't know that this white man, Jerry, originally from a small town in Pennsylvania, wanted to know me, got to know me, would care about me, check on me, when no one else like him would. I didn't know that his wife, Jayme, would come to trust me with her boys and girl; that his two oldest boys would come to call me "Uncle RJ"; that he would champion me, and would listen to me rage about this city, about its history, about this massacre, and never folded up, never quit the conversation when it felt hard. What I knew was that this friendship had come out of sports and sports talk.

I've loved sports as a writer, as a broadcaster, because I believe it is the truest lens of who we are as people. I know Americans love football most because eighty of the top one hundred shows on television every year are NFL games. That in Oklahoma, to know nothing about the Sooners is to be untrustworthy. My peers in class, who believe so much in the power of fiction, of criticism, of political journalism, did not know how to make sense of our history. I felt, in my community, that college football, coupled with the sobering knowledge of how these games we play affect us in our daily lives, was not just the best way to reach people in a manner that might bring my life purpose, but a purposeful occupation in this place I've made my home. My presence on YouTube allowed that opportunity to stay home, and for folks with jobs to find me. In October 2019, I purchased the first suit I had ever bought at Men's Wearhouse in Tulsa. It's navy blue, slim cut, tapered for my slender frame. Grand-momme would've loved it. She bought the first suit I ever owned and the next seven, every other Easter, out of the Sears catalog, because white folks in Hattiesburg saw us coming. We wear our affinity for God right on top of our skin, Black folks, and they'd trespass against us. I wore my new suit to New York City to be a guest on CBS Sports Network's *Time to Schein* as a college football analyst. I wore it again when I co-guest-hosted Adam Schein's show. In August 2020, I earned a job hosting national radio at ESPN on Saturday nights. It was then I knew I was going to be all right, after I'd dropped out of Oklahoma State and made my living from the radio station and YouTube, and that was enough for me until I got a phone call from FOX Sports offering me a job. I hesitated only once.

"Would I have to leave my home?" I asked.

"You're a Tulsa guy, right?" he asked.

"I'm a Tulsa guy."

"I say keep the magic in Tulsa."

The magic here is Black.

I'd built a company in the part of middle America that finds its tra-dition born in the South, and I'd built it so quickly and so well that one of the largest media and entertainment companies in the world wanted to partner with me. That I did this in Tulsa, a place where Black folks have been murdered, scorned, robbed, ostracized, since its beginning—the first law passed in the state was one to mandate

REQUIEM FOR THE MASSACRE   137

segregation—is not just something like a miracle but is born of my abject stubbornness. I loved Tulsa and I hated Tulsa, and I learned that both of those emotions came from the same place. When I first decided to go to grad school at OU, I did not choose to move just two hours away from the city I'd called home for the longest stretch of my life because it was my first choice. I did so because it was the pragmatic one. I couldn't afford to move to a coast where people meet people who are or become luminaries in media or publishing. I could afford to pack a U-Haul truck and ask my mother to drive my car behind me to help me move into a one-bedroom apartment across the street from the rugby pitch near campus. I'd fallen in love, gotten a job in Norman, gotten married, and had chosen to stay there for those reasons. When my then wife graduated law school in nearby Oklahoma City, she said she wanted to move back closer to home, where her parents and friends lived. By this time I was unemployed and counting triple-digit rejections on manuscripts and manuscript proposals for fiction and nonfiction alike. I was in no position to tell her I didn't want to return to Tulsa, and I certainly didn't want to return to Tulsa without a job, without wins to hoist aloft like national title banners, when I met her family and friends. Not long after we'd moved back, she all but begged me to recertify as a personal trainer, and I did. I was certified by the American College of Sports Medicine to personal train, and I hated it. I was good at it; I made the people in my charge better, pushed them toward expecting more from themselves. But I believed, as most with a college education believe, I had more to give, that there was more here for me.

I'm not so arrogant as to say I set out to prove I could become a national college football analyst, host, and writer at a place like the one where I worked without leaving Tulsa. But I did resolve to be loud about being from Tulsa if ever anyone cared what I thought about race and sports. I'd decided, should I succeed, that I would not hide that Tulsa had hurt me, has a history of hurting people who look like me, and that I relate to those who'd propagated prosperity in Greenwood not because they wanted to but because they had to. White Tulsa was closed to them, not unlike how most of Oklahoma is closed to the coasts. No one outside of this place much cares what happens to it, only what had once happened to it when white Tulsans murdered Black Tulsans. Those who stayed, and there weren't many who did, chose to be stubborn too. In investigating this place where I live, where I call home, I've learned that stubbornness defines we Black Southern writers, too.

Kiese Laymon left his native Mississippi to travel to Oberlin, Ohio, to teach in Poughkeepsie, New York, to make a stop in Bloomington, Indiana, only to find out he was needed back home. That he would always find his way back home. But he, like Jesmyn Ward, returned from Palo Alto, from New York City, with experience outside of these overtly anti-Black spaces, and that experience formed conviction. That conviction has enriched their work, steeled it, and instilled a belief in writers like me that not only is our work valuable—it is vital. Black folks are the vitality in the South, its most gorgeous and glorious offspring out of a grotesque and murderous struggle to survive, even now. As Laymon wrote in *Heavy: An American Memoir*, we are the Black abundance: "Everything about y'all is *erroneous*. Every. Thang. This that [B]lack *abundance*. Y'all don't even know." They don't, bruh. They only know we threaten them, and I'm tired of placating the insecurities of the uninformed and afraid by tamping down what the 13 percent have achieved and will achieve. In sports, in music, in literature, in science, in the disciplines and endeavors (white) Americans claim to hold dear, we have overachieved because we have to, using only what we've got. In the latest iteration of that overachieving Black abundance, Black creatives of my generation have leveraged the internet for our own means, for our stories. We've flipped blog posts into national award-winning books like Roxane Gay, told the truth in our criticism like Hanif Abdurraqib, and challenged each other.

We've flipped SoundCloud links into Billboard top 100 songs like Lil Nas X. We've taken a Twitter thread and created a must-see movie like *Zola*. We've taken jokes we threw out in 140 characters or fewer and turned those into a late-night premium cable TV show like *Desus & Mero*. "RJ," a Black student I tutored once said, "we stay making social media our bitch." MySpace popped because we created the ShadeRoom there. Clubhouse became valuable because Black folks gave it a valuation. Medium popped because Black writers deigned to gift our essays to the platform. All the *cool* this country creates has, at its bottom, a Black foundation. Jon Batiste stays loud about it in the song my intentional family will bury me at sea listening to: "We Are." Watch me float to sea as the St. Augustine High School Marching 100 and Gospel Soul Children Choir come through off that *one, two, ready and*—drums, horns, and the most gorgeous choir I've ever heard to send me home; a second line, trumpeting punchline, I will have earned some day when I am withered, tired some long-from-now year, when I was certain of ending things.

The 13 percent stays winning, even when the white majority locks us in prisons, floods our communities with drugs, refuses to financially repair us, and acts as if we are a problem it wishes to wipe away like the white folks who despised Greenwood. It's not a coincidence that Matt Ruff found the burning of Greenwood to be a critical jumping-off point for his novel, *Lovecraft Country*.

Lovecraft Country is a response to the cultural criticism that white people are the only people, the only race, respected in science fiction and fantasy writing. Ruff cited Pam Noles's essay "Shame," James W. Loewen's *Sundown Towns*, and Victor Green's *Negro Motorist Green Book* as inspiration for his work. The novel's chief thesis is inarguable: Black history reads like speculative fiction.

White Americans' physical and legislative brutality against Black folks is the engine that powers this writing. We, Black folks, were invaded. We were enslaved. We created our own magic. That Tulsa's race massacre runs adjacent to the plot is not coincidence.

That Tulsa's story becomes the backbone of hate, anger, and an intense mistrust of white folks for the protagonist's father, Montrose, demonstrates just how vile the massacre remains in the twenty-first century. Montrose fled Tulsa after white Tulsans killed *his* father in the massacre, and he hates Tulsa for it. To be of this place, from Tulsa, some one hundred years after the massacre is to know that in your bones. That is the Tulsa I know as well as I know my Black skin made me other before my Black skin made me proud.

"A kid can feel the loss from something taken away," Noles wrote, "even if they don't have the words to say exactly what it is or define the nature of this new pain. All a kid can do is try to find what caused it all, and blame." Knowing who to blame allows for a focused rage, a useful stubbornness—even though, on most days, I wish I was not that kid, even as I am an adult carrying that feeling today. As Brit Bennett noted in *The Vanishing Half*, Black folks always love their hometowns, even though we're almost always from the evilest places—like Tulsa—where white folks will kill us because we refused to die. "Only white folks got the freedom to hate home," Bennett wrote.

Mine, Tulsa, has always hated us, and that is the biggest reason I've decided to stay. To white Tulsans, I say I will not be moved anymore, because you haven't learned a fundamental truth about me and Black folks across this country: we're stubborn, and for us, to survive is to thrive. To punctuate the statement, I bought a home.

*

The comfort I felt walking into my home, wrapping myself in my mother's quilt on my couch and curling up in this place that belonged to me, brought me feelings of pride and utter vulnerability. My home is just over thirteen hundred square feet, with a front and backyard just big enough for me to enjoy a game of catch in each. It's a "wagon wheel" floorplan, a house designed to look like the wagon wheel on a covered wagon, with hardwood floors, zoned for a single-family in a high-density area.

The garage isn't big enough to fit my truck, as the house was built in 1959. The ceiling in the master bedroom fell through just three months after I bought it, and the air conditioner and furnace when out three months after that. When my friend Lee sought to replace it, he told me the unit was just two years younger than I was, and I was born in 1987. I had so little money left over after the down payment that I scarcely could afford to replace either the ceiling or the HVAC.

I still worked two jobs. I was a sports talk radio host and a sportswriter. If I had not held both jobs, I would not have been able to afford to save for a down payment, let alone pay the mortgage to follow. I'm grateful that the washer and dryer were included with the house, but I still needed to buy a refrigerator, and I don't pay for cable. This place, mine, was a dream I never believed I would achieve. My family moved to Tulsa when I was just thirteen. Our first home was in half of a duplex, and my sister and I were grateful to have rooms of our own. Since then my folks have rented a house once and moved into a three-bedroom apartment in South Tulsa, where they stay now. The proudest they have ever been of me was when they learned I'd closed on this home without their help. This was their dream for me too; a dream they never thought they'd live to see fulfilled so long after we left Panama City.

Own my house. Own my land. Secure my forty acres and mule. My existence and my embrace of being unapologetically Black in a city that would've just as soon shot me, killed me, and burned my house to ash—that is my resistance. In this, I am a full citizen of Tulsa. I graduated high school in Tulsa, graduated college in Tulsa, developed a scholarship program at a college in Tulsa, own a home in Tulsa. I am a single Black man from Tulsa with a stake in the ground and my name on the deed.

*

Since the 1921 massacre, there have been hundreds more race riots in the U.S.; 240 alone in 1943. But here in Tulsa, we haven't voted much since. In 2015, Chicago passed the Reparations Ordinance, which among other items provided $5.5 million for fifty-five families of Black suspects who were tortured during the reign of terror perpetrated by Jon Burge and the Chicago Police Department from 1972 to 1988. In Tulsa, we have seen no such reparations for the hundreds of families and victims of the massacre. So much ink has been splashed in the pages of every major metropolitan newspaper, alive and dead; academic journals from Long Island to Long Beach to demonstrate, illustrate, and argue their claims, and the city of Tulsa has said here's a sign on Greenwood and Archer, here's a sign outside Tulsa's Vernon Chapel AME Church, here's a city hall resolution that says we murdered you, Black folks, stole your wealth, mocked your grief, inspired your depression, and we owe you no apology and certainly not money.

So we Black Tulsans go on in this hot protesting summer of 2020, chanting our litanies, reciting our stories of how our family was burned, raped, and murdered, as the world continues to say how much it cares while performing little in the way of attempting to make us whole. That's what happens: racism becomes so ingrained, so utterly suffocating, so maddening that you are sure no one is listening. You become so apathetic that fighting out in the open feels pointless, foolish. In this, survival is elevated to an act of nobility, and Black homeownership the act of a guerrilla, a revolutionary. I've advocated for Black ownership for that reason and because I know that when we have chosen to fight back with armed resistance, Black folks have been overly policed, incarcerated, murdered, and then left in mass graves with no markings, no funeral, our stories nearly lost forever.

*

Take a half-assed look at Tulsa and you'll see that 1921 and 2021 are parallel. After Breonna Taylor was murdered in her own bed by police in March 2020, after George Floyd was murdered on the street in May 2020 by police, some Tulsans were gearing up for a celebration of Juneteenth in the midst of a pandemic, while the majority of Tulsans were going to attend a rally to celebrate the most racist U.S. president since Woodrow Wilson.

Yes, Donald Trump was coming here, and most Oklahomans couldn't wait to greet him. Never mind that none of us should've been outside, where the plague wafted through the air and feasted on our immune systems as we congregated in groups of tens to thousands. The plague no longer felt like the most dangerous viral outbreak of my life. Nope, that No. 1 spot in the Out to Kill RJ Power Rankings was once again held by capital-R Racism.

As MAGA supporters began to declare they'd be in Tulsa because my city was one of the only ones in the entire country that received both mayoral and gubernatorial support for holding such an event amid the plague, Trump announced plans to hold his Jonestown hoedown on Black folks' jubilee: June 19. Only after a loud nationwide rebuke did he and his sycophantic campaign staff deign to move the event by exactly one day.

So it was on June 20, 2020, that I left my partner Laurel's home in South Tulsa with a notebook, a pen, and my phone. I wasn't going to protest. I don't believe my protesting would've or could've changed a damn thing. I protested after Trayvon Martin was killed. I protested after Mike Brown was killed. And Eric Harris and Eric Garner and Terence Crutcher, and then I quit. Laurel was the first person to tell me about protests erupting across the country after Floyd's murder. She was optimistic that this was more than a moment and white folks were finally going to make the change to end racism in America. I looked at the TV, watching folks shout from the streets and Minnesota, and thought how hopeless that was and how hopeless this all is. "We did that after Trayvon," I said.

Many white folks don't care about our protesting. They care about what makes them feel good or bad. A Black person telling a white person just how unfair, unequal, and impossible this country is for us makes them feel bad. A Black person telling them about their bootstraps and how he or she rose from obscurity to Be Somebody makes them feel good. That's what Trump did so well. He made white folks feel not just good but self-righteous in their racism and hatred of Black folks, of me. He knew, before any of his opponents for the presidency in 2016, what Black folks have always known. People don't vote based on what is rational or right. They vote based on what makes them feel good or bad. And there have always been more white folks with access to voting booths than Black, Brown, green, blue, or orange. We are the minority, and it behooves us all to see that as a number more than we do as skin color.

Check the voting tallies. Then check the prison populations. That's where you'll find my country 'tis of thee. The year Trump was elected, my state, Oklahoma, led the nation in incarceration. In fact, if Oklahoma was a country unto itself, it would've led the world. Oklahoma imprisoned nearly eleven hundred (1,079) people for every hundred thousand residents. That year, 2016, every county in Oklahoma went red for Trump, and I live in the second-largest county in the state, where little pushback was made to keep Trump from holding his event. Perhaps if that weren't the case, the George Kaiser Family Foundation wouldn't have begun funding the Tulsa Remote Program, which offers a $10,000 bounty to people just for moving down the street from me.

This city where my mayor, G. T. Bynum, who earlier that year was lauded by *The New York Times* for aggressively locking down the city in March 2020 to mitigate the plague, offered a flaccid response to Trump's rally on Facebook: "Was the nation's first large campaign rally after the arrival of COVID-19 my idea? No. I didn't even know the invitation had been extended until BOK Center management contacted the City regarding Police support for the event."

And when he found out, did he rebuke this event? No. Did he attend this event? Yes. Was he reelected later that year? Of course he was. This man who said with a straight face: "Tulsa, the racial and economic disparities that still exist today can be traced to the 1921 race massacre."

Jesus Christ, (white) Tulsa. You're doing it again. That's what I thought. Three weeks past the ninety-ninth anniversary of white Tulsans murdering Black Tulsans, you're doing this again. You've learned nothing, and you've heard nothing. Through a World War, an actual civil rights movement, and into a brand-new millennium, you're still advocating, voting for, and encouraging the subjugation, humiliation, and termination of Black folks. Nothing's changed since Oklahoma was a territory, since it was a state, and since a group of white men picked up guns, knives, and bats and congregated at the Tulsa County Courthouse on June 1, 1921. I was angry about and angry with Trump, about my city hosting Trump, but not stupid.

The violence that we thought might await anyone who traveled to the BOK Center wasn't just real; it was frightening. I don't carry a gun—not anymore. A gun still more likely to get me killed than to prevent my being killed, especially with any police presence nearby. And even with a racist in office—and maybe because—there's going to be a heavy police presence. Besides, this is America. Anybody can get a gun in America, and a person with a police badge is always going to be more intimidating, deadlier than a gun. What's one gun when cops kill Black boys with impunity? When you ask what power is, ask who and what is holding the gun. Seven months after his rally in Tulsa, Trump showed us once again what power looks like. He incited a coup and propagated the first insurrection at the capitol since 1812, and I knew one Trump supporter who wished she had been there. She is my mother. It's not as complicated as you think. It's actually straightforward to her.

"I don't think any MAGA supporter actually intended to get caught up in the breaking of the windows and barging in," she said.

She contends that the folks who showed up for the rally on January 6, 2021, had no intention of staging a coup and, further still, that the Capitol Police was excited to let them in. She also wishes she could have been there because she believes the election was stolen from Trump and ergo, from her. "And the evidence bears out that the election was stolen," she said. "And so I would have wanted to have been there to protest that."

When Rush Limbaugh passed weeks later, my mother mourned.

"He should be allowed to lie in state at the rotunda at the Capitol," she said on the day of his passing, "but he won't be allowed to do that. I hate that."

Couple my mother's deep admiration for Trump, Limbaugh, and the political right with this: She was one of just five children to integrate Jefferson Davis Elementary in 1965 and was the first person to graduate from college—Southern Miss—in my family. She boasts a terminal degree in marriage and family therapy, worked as a drug rehabilitation counselor at Pine Grove Behavioral Health, and raised me and my sister alongside my father.

When she learned that I was going to the Trump rally in Tulsa, she was upset. Not for me and not because she worried about my well-being, but because she couldn't convince my father to go with her. But afraid for me?

"No," she said, "not at all. Because Oklahomans are different than most of the people that were there." She described them as interlopers who simply wanted to promote violence. "Most of the people that were there were people who could make it from the East and West Coast. Oklahoma is as the king or queen of conservatives right now . . . Right now we are the reddest of the red states and Tulsa County is the reddest county inside the reddest state."

*

But I wasn't planning to be in harm's way any more than I needed to be to write down what I saw, to take pictures of what was done, and to talk with people who were attending or around the rally at the BOK for whatever reason. Laurel still didn't like it, and she told me so at her kitchen table.

Laurel is a single mom with two daughters who had just started elementary school. I call the oldest Weapon X and the youngest Brave. They were seven and five, respectively. When she learned I would go against her wishes anyway, she decided the girls could come with us.

"I remember entertaining the thought," Laurel said, "that what if the girls saw it, but from a distance? Are they at an age where they can understand Black Lives Matter versus not? And I still don't know the answer to that question. But the concern over you getting hurt was something I thought maybe the girls and I could mitigate. If a white woman and two little white girls were with you, and we could circle around you, like some sacred tree that nobody's allowed to cut down, then you would be alright."

I said no to that. Then she told me she could leave the girls with her mom and go with me. I said no to that too. I couldn't stand the idea of what might happen to the girls if something happened to Laurel. As her partner and their godfather, I felt sound in my decision. After all, if something happened to Laurel while she was at the rally, at least three lives would be impacted. If something happened to me, I would be all that was lost. This was perhaps the only time in my life when I felt, even wrongly, that my life did not matter as much as those lives of the people I love most. I told her that this was where I knew she'd be safe. But there was still reason to believe I wouldn't be. While the three of them would be safe in predominantly white South Tulsa, there was an increasing concern that violence would break out in downtown Tulsa—just down the street from Greenwood. In this, I shirked my responsibility to them.

Laurel is the parent who stops a movie more than a dozen times to answer the questions of her seven-year-old about the first Tobey Maguire *Spider-Man* movie; a movie that doesn't hold up nearly twenty years later. I told Laurel I thought so. Later she asked me what I meant by that. I told her I had this same thought about a movie I love called *The Last Dragon*.

The movie is not good, but its not being Oscar-worthy does not change that I love it. She accepted that. "I have become my big dork dad in that way," she said. I told her she's a really great dad; a responsibility that I neglect behind the convenient excuse that the girls have a father, and I am not him. Their father loves them very much; he sees them for half of every week and every other weekend; he has reinvented himself so he can remain in Tulsa and love them. I'm just the godfather, and I'm the only Black person in this odd mix of family. Then I would I wrap myself in that knowledge, so I don't have to be responsible with my life. I can put myself in harm's way and claim solitude in matters of race that are so important to me but can negatively affect the people who love me. Makes it easier to be selfish in the pursuit of a cause, a way of life, that has eluded Black folks for so long and rears its head in my face and Laurel's most days. That idea is the one Laurel holds closely, gracefully, when discussing me. "The closest way that a white person can come to understanding racism is loving a non-white person," she said. "Having someone that you'd literally share your life with, and you are planning a future with, who faces racism, is not a reality you can outrun. You're in it. You have to be. White people can and do live a life where they can choose to ignore racism. Being with you means it's with me every minute of every day. All I can do is support you."

The kindling incident for the fires in Tulsa on June 1, 1921, was a Black man accused of raping a white woman. Had Rowland been white and Page been Black, none of us would know their names.

Had I lived in 1921, I am certain white men would've tried to lynch me rather than acknowledge my humanity. In 2020, there are Black Tulsans I know and had called friends that believed a Black man in love with a white woman must hate himself. They're wrong. I find myself in Black culture and the oppressive politics of the state and the people who protect the white power structure. Acknowledging that structure is acknowledging the privilege of being white and the disadvantage Black folks face inside it. That also means acknowledging that the least enlightened among us would still see me brutalized and killed and see Laurel as damaged and deranged. Nearly fifty years after the massacre, Black men and white women were still taboo not only in white communities but in Black ones as well. *Loving v. Virginia* overturned miscegenation law in 1967, but at the center of that case is a white man professing his love for a Black woman. Had the inverse been true, I have doubts about the verdict being the same. Even now, as an interracial couple, the narrative does not braid neatly in the minds of most. I refuse to display this precious us, Laurel and me, to people I believe to be racist—white or otherwise.

We'd read and seen across the internet and TV reports about people coming from across the country, in the midst of the plague, to show support for Trump. We'd seen the rhetoric from those people too. They felt safe voicing their racist beliefs here, in my hometown, because this place had not only tolerated but promulgated many of those beliefs over the course of the city's history. As I pulled onto the highway, I thought about how this city, known for its evangelical Christian faith, often lacks a fundamental grace in how it treats its non-white citizens. I live here still because I've learned to navigate that gracelessness and because my parents choose to call this place home. If something happens to them, I am all that is near to help. But on this day, I decided the best way for me to voice my displeasure was to contribute using the tools I possess. In learning about the massacre, I found myself constantly asking after firsthand accounts—primary sources. I learned how those sources, those stories, those people, had been suppressed or erased. I learned there are people who had and have names on buildings, schools, across Tulsa who benefited directly and indirectly from the violence shed and the livelihoods wrecked by the perpetrators of the massacre. I needed to go to the rally to record what I saw, what I felt, and what happened. If the lions don't tell their stories, then the hunters will be sure to take all the credit.

When I neared downtown, neared Greenwood, I saw businesses boarded up like violence was certain, though the streets were mostly vacant of people when I parked at the Guthrie Green. I expected to see more people, to see signs of aggression, of discontent. I didn't see any of that, and I saw just a handful of people until I reached the bridge. Then, like an angry red patch of herpes, there they were: Trump's people in all their unrefined and deplorable glory, descending upon the biggest venue in the city. Their TRUMP 2020 flags were anchored in their truck beds. At least three blasted Lee Greenwood's "God Bless the U.S.A." out of lowered windows as they waited their turns to find parking. The jingoistic nature of the event hit me with a force that felt as oppressive as triple-digit Oklahoma heat. As much as I detested it, I accepted it. Many of those folks might be from out of town, but they are perfectly Tulsan: the kind of people who will claim that they'll bleed on the flag to make sure the stripes remain red; the kind of people who see a protest as an act of treason unless it's they who are protesting, then will commit the act of treason anyway and call it patriotism.

In learning all that I have about the massacre and what that singular event has done to me and Black Tulsans like me, I've found myself mounting a lawsuit of my own. Building a case. Gathering evidence. Planning my opening statement—this—and my closing statement toward the end of this journey that pushes through the centennial anniversary of the most horrific attempt at ethnic cleansing since the founding of this state. I have treated each of these facts as if they could change a mind. I have treated the writing of this book, the pages of journal entries and the hundreds of conversations I've had with sources, friends, family, and myself about the massacre, as if they could change a mind. That they could persuade someone to see the injustice for what it was and it continues to be. That the white person who claimed to not know, not care, or not believe the past is the past might see the error of that thinking, put it down, and begin anew with a sense that Black folks live. When I first learned I might have the opportunity to write this story, to tell it from the vantage of a Black Tulsa native who owns property in the place where so many descendants of citizens would've burned my house down, I turned to a man named Howard. He'd never heard from me before, and he had no reason to take my call. But after a plea in private message over Instagram, he took my call and let me tell him the burden of it all. Howard had written books about race, according to white folks. Howard wrote about Black folks for Black folks, according to him, and he'd diagnosed my problem right away. I still cared to change the minds of white people. I'd written my first book with that intent, even going so far as calling the working title of that book *How to Be a Better White Person*. He told me that was fine, but to be clear about what that meant. "Not all of them are going to see your humanity," he said. "You have to decide if you still need them to."

Howard had decided long ago that he did not need affirmation of his humanity from someone who did not already recognize his. Just a couple of blocks from the BOK Center, I felt alien again in a group of people who never see me. BLM ARE RACIST PIGS one sign read, and that was the most offensive one I saw that day. Still, more and more of Trump's people never went away. At Seventy-First and Memorial, just a mile north of where Laurel lives, a van remained parked on the corner for nearly a year selling Trump 2020 merchandise. The wares were more exotic outside the rally, but the beats were the same. Hate for Obama and the left. Lots of gun paraphernalia and idolatry of Trump on the right. Transactions were being made in cash for the most part, and I chuckled at the thought of how little of that money would ever make it back to local, state, or federal government.

I moved through the street, looking at this awkward bust-ass bazaar. The items for sale and the way these folks wore their pride in Trump in Tulsa recalled that of the white folks who took trophies from the bodies of the Black men they lynched; the full-grown urchins who ravaged the pockets of a murdered man; the evil men who broke into the houses of Tulsans under siege and took what they wanted carnally, materially. At McNellie's, a group of white men in a frat uniform of polos, khaki shorts, and Sperrys flew a blue flag that read TRUMP 2020 FUCK YOUR FEELINGS in white letters.

Seeing your humanity questioned so often, so thoughtlessly, and so superficially, I let myself breathe in the idea that it is not up to me to make white people feel better about the spiritual violence done to me against laws white men like them first drafted. There it is again—me arguing with my oppressor, a defense attorney representing himself at trial in front of a jury who looks nothing like me and see anything but what I do. I won't do it again. Our history has often been written with an appreciation for how white people feel about the facts of racism in America. Facts here being two: The first one is the chief problem to solve for racism in America: that white people have never politically believed Black folks are their equal, and the second is that the Constitution of the United States was written to reflect this. I am, to them, three-fifths of a person.

The invention of police further illustrates this point. There was no such thing as police when Anglo-Saxons and Africans came to this land. But along with the Europeans enslaving Africans, indentured and otherwise, white folks formed their own groups and militias to enforce slavery. These groups led to the formation of slave codes, one of which was that a white person could stop an African-looking person in the street and demand identification. At the beginning of the seventeenth century, nothing like slave patrols existed. The task of disciplining and controlling slaves fell to the white majority at large: Every white person was responsible for the discipline and enforcement of slavery in the United States. But with slaves continuing to run away and incite and participate in slave rebellions, plantation owners formed those slave patrols. Some patrols worked in concert with the state and indeed became a part of the state, as the slave patrol in New Orleans became the New Orleans Police Department in 1853. The Ku Klux Klan became a slave patrol following the Civil War and was a willing vehicle for white supremacy and violent hatred meted out on Black folks. During the massacre, white Tulsans were deputized locally for the express purpose of violating Black Tulsans. No Black person was deputized during the massacre. No wonder the grand jury blamed the massacre on Black folks. To them, every white person was a cop, and cops operate with immunity and impunity in times of great scrutiny. Many white folks did nothing at all during this period from the seventeenth century, and even until now. For this, they are all implicated, and nowhere near the number of them that claimed they'd show up to the rally were there.

Outside the bazaar, there was no crush of white folks, even though Trump's campaign staffers claimed that twice as many people as the city counts as residents, 800,000, were estimated to be on hand. The ten days leading up to this one had been filled with such bravado and threats that I felt let down by the flaccid nature of this event as some of those outside the BOK Center began filing into the building. I watched a stream of the event on my phone just a block away on the steps outside the Tulsa Performing Arts Center—alone. The reliably red state had not shown up in a pandemic for the president, a man who had spoken for over a week about how he wanted and expected a full crowd at the BOK Center. I thought that surely when his plane landed at 5:00 p.m. local time that he'd be inundated with followers. Yet there, on those steps, I was smirking at the absurdity of being surrounded by boarded-up buildings for a man who walked onto stage in front of a few thousand to a Linkin Park song. As Trump spoke with both of us just blocks from the epicenter of the massacre, I remembered that Oklahoma governor Kevin Stitt had encouraged him to visit Greenwood Avenue, to walk under the overpass the city built to cut through the neighborhood and visit the memorial just outside the Greenwood Cultural Center. Trump sent his vice president, Mike Pence, instead. But what would he have seen but a Black Wall Street monument topped with a tarp because we expected white folks to do what they had done in 1921 once again: vandalize, tear down, and rape us of our property, our stories? Along with him were visits from Jesse Jackson and Al Sharpton. Around this time LeBron James and Russell Westbrook had also decided it was time for their names to be lent to producing documentaries about the massacre for the following summer.

As the rally was ending, I decided to walk to the let-out because, if there was to be violence, I expected to find it there. Mayor Bynum certainly did. He enacted a city curfew for the weekend, believing that this would discourage Trump supporters and protesters from squaring off. Then, because he felt it was a bad look or because Trump came down on him or because he's a coward—all can be true—Bynum lifted the curfew just over twenty-four hours before the rally was scheduled to begin. He said the Secret Service had told him there was no need for a curfew, yet Trump's people placed the curfew idea at Bynum's feet, claiming that hundreds of thousands of people stayed home not because the pandemic was in full effect but because of the curfew order.

Cops are positively thought of in Tulsa by most, and most are white folks. But even Tulsa Police managed to look awful when officers arrested protester Sheila Buck, who was occupying a space outside the rally, had a ticket to the rally, but was also wearing a T-shirt that said I CAN'T BREATHE. Buck, a Catholic school art teacher, was kicked out of the rally for her shirt. But on my walk toward the let-out I saw National Guardsmen and state police at the ready with firearms out in plain sight and riot vehicles on the bottom floor of a parking garage, just as Black Tulsans had seen National Guardsmen and police ready to harangue, harass, injure, and kill them during the massacre nearly one hundred years ago. I felt myself typing even more furiously into my phone, marking with ever more pressure on my notepad to disseminate the rage I felt at this sight. Earlier that day protesters and Trump supporters had met, shouted, but did not turn violent. For less than an hour, TPD closed an entry point to the BOK when Trumpers and protesters met.

Later that night, the phrase tossed around was that of emotions running high, but not so high that rioting began. Still, TPD fired those pepper balls into the crowd as they reached each other at Fourth Street and Boulder Avenue. By midnight, most folks had gone, after just 6,200 people attended the rally at the BOK, according to the Tulsa Fire Department. What was once thought would incite violence and foster fear, a rally in Trump country, had only demonstrated just how unwilling many were to be seen and to participate for a man they'd ultimately vote(d) for. The tepid rally was a relief in the interim. My city was not on fire. My neighbors were not dead. But Tulsa had forgotten her history again. Tulsa had become an embarrassment again. In this, we mirror our country for the world. Following fear and threats of violence, we look the fool. Perhaps that's where the so-called racial progress lies, though. This time we just looked like clowns. One hundred years ago we were killed by such clowns, and the scars have still not healed here—or there. Tulsa is real America, and real America still doesn't want Black folks here. When I pulled into my driveway, I sat for a moment trying to be grateful for what did not happen and still dreading what might happen next. The racists didn't just come to town. They haven't left, and they're still trying to kick us out.

Months later, I stood outside of ONEOK Field, which abuts Greenwood Avenue, waiting to cast my vote in the 2020 U.S. presidential election. The pro baseball stadium is in the Greenwood District, owns an address on North Elgin. The park is home to the Tulsa Drillers, whose parent club—the Los Angeles Dodgers—won the World Series just one day before ONEOK became the only polling place in Tulsa County for the next three days during Oklahoma's early voting period for the November 3, 2020, election.

Laurel and I were among the first Tulsans to travel to the ballpark on that Thursday, the first day early voting commenced. As soon as we found ourselves at the end of the line, I found the clock app on my phone and started the stopwatch, and, with that, the wait. We were among the hundreds of Tulsans snaked inside and outside of the fence to the ballpark who had congregated to vote.

The weather was cold. The temperature did not rise above thirty-eight degrees before noon on that Thursday set for early voting. The umbrellas we Tulsans held above our heads did little to stop the cold and wet from chilling us further as the raindrops slipped, slid, to the concrete sidewalk and crashed down. The rain splashed and soaked our shoes, our socks, our pants legs. Laurel and I had begun the day somewhat boisterous. We took her car and parked just north of ONEOK at the Tulsa satellite campus for Oklahoma State University early that morning. We walked a couple of blocks south toward the line of voters that had already formed before voting began as one man walked the other way. He shouted to us that the line was long; like that was reason enough to give up and go home. A white man passed by us in line. "Over there you can vote in five minutes," he said. "You'll stand in line here for two hours."

As the line had only begun to move just after polling opened, he couldn't know how long we'd wait. I suspected voting is not a (birth)right he ever had to fight for. Voting is not a legacy he left.

I suspected, for him, voting was a nuisance, and he was eager to leave. I couldn't leave. Waiting was the least I could do, especially because this day, October 29, is Grandmomme's birthday. I am resolved. This is my city. This is my family's legacy. After standing, waiting, freezing, drenched in frustration, I stopped the timer on my watch three hours, thirty-two minutes after I had started the timer, I cast my ballot. I voted just down the street from where Black Tulsans lost their lives, homes, and livelihoods nearly a century ago.

100 Years Later . . .

I N SPRING 2021, DURING THE WEEKS LEADING UP TO THE centennial of the Tulsa Race Massacre, messaging proliferates. The remnants of Tulsans' participation in last year's protests have compounded, though the ferocity with which we took the streets has waned. Greenwood Avenue is marked with varying signs of graffiti, murals on buildings, and new tenants moving in just in time to take advantage of tourists expected to come to Tulsa to mark the centennial. "BLM" is spray-painted red, blue, and yellow on the overpass stretching across train tracks and along the fence at ONEOK Field. There are flyers claiming BLACK LIVES MATTER alongside ones reminding me I'm in what is known to many as Black Wall Street. That BLM and Black Wall Street are antithetical ideas is not a subject I find Black or white people are willing to address. Most people I've met want to keep the discussion simple. Ideas about capitalism versus socialism, individualism versus collectivism, are not welcome when the central theme is Black violence at the hands of mostly white people of the past. Tulsans could find nothing more nuanced to say because nuance muddies an otherwise simple slogan that's easy to disseminate. It's the reason I stood in front of the overpass looking south at the gorgeous mural painted across it.

In large block letters, the mural reads BLACK WALL ST. Inside each one of the letters creating the phrase are beautiful depictions of Greenwood before and idealized after the massacre. In the "B," Dreamland Theatre is painted green with purple signage above the marquee. The "L" depicts the marquee cross at Vernon AME. Musicians are featured inside the "A"; the intersection of Greenwood and Archer beside a man, woman, and two children illuminate the "C" in gold, pink, yellow, and white shadows. The GAP Band takes over the second "L" in "WALL," and the Hornet mascot for Booker T. Washington High School is represented in the "T" just before the period.

The flourish isn't lost on me. Booker T. Washington is the person most cited for billing Greenwood as Black Wall Street, and the moniker features all over Tulsa and especially in Greenwood. T-shirts, cups, hats, and monuments to those people killed and businesses razed during the massacre are adorned with the phrase BLACK WALL STREET. Indeed, nationally, "Black Wall Street" is the first term associated with Tulsa in reference to the massacre by most, and this mural I'm standing in front of features in brochures, magazines, and websites promoting the city in the lead-up to the centennial commemoration. When I read articles, stories, books about the massacre, Black Wall Street never fails to earn a mention—nor does Washington being given credit for inventing the phrase. But I wonder, looking at this mural, when did Washington first say "Black Wall Street"? To what person? In what piece of writing? Under what circumstances? What bothers me even more than the provenance of "Black Wall Street" is the idea that few other people have thought to ask.

*

Booker T. Washington's concept of compromise likely carried into Greenwood's perception of itself, and certainly into the modern recreation of Greenwood's cultural history as "Black Wall Street." But Washington calling Greenwood "Black Wall Street" is apocryphal, perhaps perpetuated to mythologize an all-Black district that needed no such falsehood to secure its place in history. The phrase was originally coined as "Negro's Wall Street." The possessive is as noteworthy as the word "Negro": This belonged to *us*. And *us* was birthed by a Black woman, as are all things born good, grand, and gorgeous in this world. If Eve was the first woman and Africa the birthplace of man, we all are born of a Black woman.

Amen.

*

In July 2021, *The New York Times* recounts that "white rioters" "descended on the city's Greenwood District, a Black community considered so affluent that Booker T. Washington, the author and orator, had called it 'Black Wall Street.'"[18] In May 2021, Paul Gardullo, a historian and curator at the Smithsonian's National Museum of African American History and Culture, tells the *Washington Post* that "Booker T. Washington called it 'Negro Wall Street.' We call it 'Black Wall Street.' Black Wall Street was not just about wealth . . . It's about community, churches, schools, businesses, homes, social clubs, people pulling together to demonstrate Black power in a Black community in a world that was denying them Black power and a sense of authority."[19]

This phrase, "Negro Wall Street," bothers me for the creative license it asserts—there was no stock market exchange in Greenwood, no banks, never have been—and because no one can point to a newspaper clipping, an essay, a bit of scholarship, or even anywhere in Washington's own writings where he explicitly called Greenwood the "Negro Wall Street of America," which has become Black Wall Street and the first phrase that comes to many minds, both in and out of Tulsa, when Tulsa's name is summoned. Few point out the obvious fact that Black folks—particularly contemporaries of Washington—did not begin referring to themselves as Black for at least forty years after the massacre occurred and fifty years after Washington's death. Indeed, we were even called colored before we called ourselves Black (Power). But I can't venture around a corner in the district without seeing that phrase, "Black Wall Street," on storefronts, in graffiti, on T-shirts. I find this odd.

I want to know when Washington first said the phrase "Negro Wall Street," and what drove him to compare an all-Black district, hardly the only one in the U.S., to New York City's Wall Street, home to the most influential financial market in the world. I start with the Wikipedia page about Greenwood. In the part of the entry titled "History" and subtitled "Roots," there's a sentence that read "The success of Black-owned businesses there led Booker T. Washington to visit in 1905." I immediately check the note that substantiated that sentence as fact. The reference leads to a book called *Booker T. Washington and the Struggle Against White Supremacy* by David H. Jackson Jr., a work that calls attention to educational tours Washington traveled on throughout the South. In his book, Jackson wrote: "Washington began these particular statewide tours by traveling through Arkansas and the Oklahoma and Indian territories in 1905, and these tours won him much support for his agenda." However, Jackson did not write that Washington visited Tulsa, and his only reference to Tulsa in his book is with respect to the massacre and "how white fury and vengeance could result in total destruction of [B]lack communities." The Tuskegee Institute National Historic Site made a similar claim on its Facebook page in June 2020.[20] "In 1905 Booker T. Washington visited Tulsa, Oklahoma and dubbed the city the 'Negro Wall Street,'" the Tuskegee account posted. "On that visit he encouraged the residents of Greenwood to continue to build and cooperate among each other." But the Tuskegee Institute Historical Site account did not cite a reference for the claim of Washington visiting Tulsa, talking to Tulsans, or calling Greenwood "Negro Wall Street." Another book cited on the page, *Booker T. Washington: Builder of a Civilization*, written by Emmett J. Scott and Lyman Beecher Stowe and with a preface by

President Theodore Roosevelt, referred to a speech Washington gave at Muskogee, but nowhere else in Oklahoma.

In searching newspaper archives and academic journal databases, I find Washington visited Oklahoma on November 20, 1905, and in August 1914. In 1905, he arrived by train at 4:47 p.m. and was "royally received," according to the *Muskogee Cimiter*.[21] He delivered a speech at the corner of Okmulgee and Second Street on what was dubbed "Booker T. Washington Day" in front of "7,000 souls." He attended a banquet in his honor at the local Elks Lodge before taking a train out at 7:30 a.m. the next morning to Fort Smith, Arkansas. "I have but one object in coming into the territories," Washington said, "and that is to see for myself, as far as a short visit will permit, the condition and progress of my race, who have come here from all sections of the country, and to say a word that shall be designed to promote their interest."[22] He didn't mention or refer to Tulsa or Greenwood even once in his speech. But he did implore Black folks to continue living as second-class citizens.

These Oklahoma visits from Washington are important because they're evidence that Washington thought that Northeastern Oklahoma, in particular, was a good example of his mission furthered: racial progress through industrial application and political conciliation. He thought the only way forward for Black folks was to acquiesce to white folks' separate-but-equal doctrine and to not push against second-class citizenship. The December 1, 1905, edition of the *Bixby Bulletin*, a newspaper in a suburb of Tulsa, published a story where Washington's name appears under the headline after refusing to insert himself into Oklahoma politics. The headline read: "Negroes Disappointed: Booker T. Washington Refuses To Discuss the Quay Amendment." The Quay amendment would've given Black folks the right to vote under state law. "He refused positively to discuss the matter," the *Bulletin* reported. "His advice to negroes has always been to leave politics alone, and rely for their advancement on industrial pursuits, and he would not change that policy, even for the sake of a consummation which he presumably regarded as of great importance."

Still, in Oklahoma Territory and then the state of Oklahoma, his message found admiration until the massacre occurred. When Greenwood's Dunbar School outgrew its home for the second time after just eight years of operation, principal Ellis Walker Woods enlisted the help of architect Leon B. Senter to design a four-room building at 507 E. Easton Street at Elgin Avenue as a stand-alone high school while the old Dunbar School remained in place for elementary and junior high studies. In his book *The Victory of Greenwood*, ironically published by Jenkins Lloyd Jones Press, author Carlos Moreno, the grandson of Richard Lloyd Jones, noted the "new building was named the Separate School for Coloreds." Greenwood's community, not lacking in self-respect, decided to name the high school after Booker T. Washington, though no reference to a public vote was noted in Moreno's work. As one of the only buildings spared in the massacre, Booker T. Washington High School and its building took on an outsized meaning for Black Tulsa. I always found this odd. Washington was the "Great Compromiser." He settled for less and asked Black folks to do the same. But Booker T. Washington High School's reputation became and remains one of uncompromising excellence. The school is North Tulsa's most prominent and endearing mascot, a symbol of the Black excellence Black Tulsans desire to remember and aspire to for generations.

In 1925, the Greenwood District hosted the annual National Negro Business League, an organization first founded by Booker T. Washington, ten years after his death in 1915. Washington founded the NNBL in 1900 in Boston. By 1915, the NNBL claimed more than six hundred chapters in thirty-four states, and Washington tried to speak at many of those chapters. With that spirit of business before and after the massacre, Greenwood was home to over two hundred Black-owned businesses by 1942. Still, when he visited, Washington made no mention of Greenwood or Tulsa in 1905 or 1914. Indeed, during his 1914 visit to Muskogee, Washington put more of an emphasis on what Black folks might accomplish across the country rather than focusing on Oklahoma or Muskogee—let alone Tulsa. In a special edition published by the *Tulsa Star* on August 19, 1914, citing Washington as "World's Greatest Living Negro," Washington is quoted as saying, "If there is any place where the Negro has a chance to show his mettle it is right here in the United States." To be sure, many Black folks thought highly of Booker T. Washington at this time. In 1920, 99 percent of people named "Booker" in the U.S. were Black, according to a July 2014 paper published in *Explorations in Economic History*.

In perhaps the most well-known book about the massacre, Scott Ellsworth's *Death in a Promised Land: The Tulsa Race Riot of 1921*, he makes no reference at all to Booker T. Washington as a person, though there are multiple references to the eponymous high school. He makes no reference to Booker T. Washington stating that Greenwood was "Negro Wall Street," or the man's visit to Tulsa. In *Riot and Remembrance: America's Worst Race Riot and Its Legacy*, James S. Hirsch wrote, "Booker T. Washington visited the most famous [B]lack town, Boley, and believed it was 'another chance in the long struggle of the Negro for moral, industrial, and political freedom." But he made no mention of Washington calling Greenwood "Negro Wall Street."

In his book *The Burning: Massacre, Destruction, and the Tulsa Race Riot of 1921*, Tim Madigan revealed that Richard Lloyd Jones, perhaps the person most responsible for the massacre, had broken bread with Washington. "Among the stories proudly passed down through the decades by the Jones's descendants was the one from his years in Madison [Wisconsin], in which Jones invited Booker T. Washington to stay as his honored guest because the famous Negro had been turned away by white hotels in the Midwestern city." But there was no mention of Washington visiting Tulsa or labeling the Greenwood District "Negro Wall Street" in Madigan's book either.

In 2014, attorney, playwright, and historian Hannibal B. Johnson wrote a short pictorial history of Greenwood called *Tulsa's Historic Greenwood District* as a portion of Arcadia Publishing's Images of America series. In the first chapter, he noted, "Dubbed the 'Negro Wall Street' by Booker T. Washington, it became the talk of the nation." However, Johnson failed to cite where, when, or to whom Washington said that the Greenwood District was "Negro Wall Street" in his book on the subject—let alone "the talk of the nation."

In his book *Tulsa, 1921*, journalist Randy Krehbiel's exhaustively cited historical account of the massacre, he wrote, "The 'Black Wall Street of America,' the name given Greenwood by Booker T. Washington during a 1913 visit, was a bit of a misnomer. Greenwood had no formal financial institutions, no banks, no brokerage houses. In a sense, 'Black Main Street of America' might have been more accurate, for Greenwood was alive with an enterprising spirit of commerce remarkable given [B]lack Americans' limited access to capital and markets in the early twentieth century." Krehbiel cited another work by Hannibal Johnson as his source for "The Black Wall Street of America" moniker being bestowed on Greenwood by Washington, and he did not provide a location or newspaper of where Washington said those words attributed to him in 1913. I followed his citation note to another work by Johnson called *Black Wall Street: From Riot to Renaissance in Tulsa's Historic Greenwood District*.

In that book, Johnson wrote, "Legend has it that famed African American educator and author Booker T. Washington bestowed this moniker on Tulsa's vibrant [B]lack business district." He cited journalist Jonathan Z. Larsen as the source of that legend for a piece he wrote for *Civilization: The Magazine of the Library of Congress*, called "Tulsa Burning," in winter 1997.[23]

When I find the article Larsen wrote, I read the portion Johnson cited: "The Greenwood section of Tulsa bristled with such energy, prosperity, and promise, that Booker T. Washington himself—so the legend goes—dubbed Greenwood Avenue 'the Black Wall Street,'" Larsen wrote. But Larsen did not cite a source for this quote attributed to Washington, either, and made no reference to when Washington was in Tulsa, if ever, or to when or where he'd called Greenwood "the Black Wall Street."

Still unsatisfied, I consult Robert J. Norrell's biography on the life of Booker T. Washington, *Up from History*, and find no reference to Greenwood in Tulsa, Oklahoma, or even Indian Territory. It would not have made sense for Washington to write about Greenwood, Tulsa, or Oklahoma in his autobiography, *Up from Slavery*, because it was published in 1901, four years before his first visit to the territory. There's no mention of Greenwood or Tulsa and scant mentions of Oklahoma in his book-length works before or after his trips to Oklahoma. His longest work about any portion of Oklahoma he visited is about the all-Black town of Boley—sixty-five miles south of Tulsa. He wrote autobiographical pieces for *The Outlook*, a magazine that began in 1870 under the name *The Christian Union*, folded up by 1935, and was best known for publishing Washington's pieces and counting President Roosevelt as an associate editor. One piece, published on January 4, 1908, recounted his time in Boley and opinion of the town a year after Oklahoma achieved statehood.[24] "Boley, like the other negro towns that have sprung up in other parts of the country, represents a dawning race consciousness, a wholesome desire to do something to make the race respected; something which shall demonstrate the right of the negro, not merely as an individual, but as a race, to have a worthy and permanent place in the civilization that the American people are creating," Washington wrote. "In short, Boley is another chapter in the long struggle of the negro for moral, industrial, and political freedom." Yet again, he made no reference to a "Negro Wall Street," Greenwood, or Tulsa in his piece for *The Outlook*.

In his latest work, *The Ground Breaking: An American City*

and Its Search for Justice, Ellsworth noted that Don Ross began writing a series of columns in 1968 about the race massacre for the *Oklahoma Eagle*. "Tulsans have been trained generally to sacrifice truth and realism, to suppress their history," Ross wrote, "for the sake of keeping superficial harmony in relations." He retold the stories of the massacre using two primary, and then little-known, sources.

One of them was Loren Gill's 1946 University of Tulsa master's thesis on the massacre. The other was a firsthand account by a Black woman, Mary E. Jones Parrish, of the massacre called *Events of the Tulsa Disaster*. I consult both, and I believe Parrish is the first person to call the Greenwood District "Negro Wall Street" in print and perhaps ever.

Parrish traveled to Tulsa for the first time in 1918 to see her brother. She returned to her home in Rochester, New York, after her visit. She stayed in Rochester for just five months before moving to McAlester, Oklahoma, to take care of her mother, who died six months after Parrish arrived. She moved to Tulsa shortly after her mother's death, and she lived through the massacre. Her book is the most well-known firsthand account of the massacre, and it was published in 1923. "Going East on Archer Street for two or more blocks there you would behold Greenwood Avenue, the Negro's Wall Street . . ." She did not attribute the phrase to Booker T. Washington at all. Parrish coined the phrase, and she coined it as belonging to Black folks—the Negro's Wall Street. It was theirs. It is ours.

Since Black Tulsans will swaddle themselves in a phrase that is false and that I patently reject as inaccurate in reality and spirit, the recasting of this moniker of Black Wall Street needs to be reconsidered. Greenwood was simply a closed-circuit community where Black folks patronized each other *for no other reason than that they had to*. Tulsa was segregated by law. For a Black person, to attempt to patronize a white-owned establishment was to court disaster.

Indeed, Dick Rowland used the bathroom at a white-owned establishment, and the result was the worst act of domestic terrorism in American history.

There is no record of Booker T. Washington visiting Tulsa, let alone Greenwood, nor did he call Greenwood "Negro Wall Street" or "Negro Wall Street of America" or "Black Wall Street." Mary Parrish did. "Negro Wall Street," and its evolutionary eponymous "Black Wall Street," is the invention of a Black woman, who claimed Tulsa as her home and refused to let people forget her people were robbed, terrorized, massacred, and dumped into unmarked mass graves. I share all those characteristics save one: I am not as strong as the weakest Black woman. That Black Tulsa—that Greenwood— has latched on to this phrase with such ferocity speaks to what it has always wanted for itself: to be elite. The birthright of my community, its sanctioning of that moniker, is an expression of who we believe we are, but also who I believe we still could become. That white folks allow the name, but not the rebuilding that must happen to honor it, also harkens back to the days before 1921, when all was well if we Black folks didn't outperform our white counterparts lest they kill us. But the spring of 1921 was the heyday of O. W. Gurley, a follower of Washington, and he would soon learn just how fragile a mere sixteen-year run of prosperity in Tulsa could be. There was a time when I thought Tulsa would've been better served to follow Du Bois's philosophies, though, especially since he did not believe in Washington's philosophy of compromise, second-class citizenship, and segregation. In fact, Du Bois not only believed Black folks are the equals of white folks but that a talented few Black people needed to be put on pedestals among us. To this end, I find it odd that Tulsa's Booker T. Washington High School is not W. E. B. Du Bois High School, precisely because that school is marked not just for excellence but specifically for Black excellence.

Standing in line to vote in November 2020, I met a Black Tulsan named Eric. He was layered up, wearing a Dallas Cowboys hoodie tucked inside a black parka. There was a gray wool hat on his head. He looked like he had expected to wait. Eric told me he'd lived in Tulsa most of his life and was happy about the upcoming events planned for the centennial. I told him I hoped the centennial commission would decide to do something at Booker T.

"Many of us know or have known people who went to school there," I said. "And it's one of the few institutions that has survived and thrived. I'd like to see us all included in that way."

He nodded, shifting in line just a bit. His movement reminded me I was freezing, and it was raining. "I hope so too," he said, rubbing and breathing into his hands. "But I'm grateful that someone is going to recognize what Black Wall Street was."

"Paying respect to Greenwood only feels right," I said.

Eric stopped his hands for a moment like he'd heard something a little off. And then leaned in. "You mean *Black Wall Street*," he said, saying it like I'd made mistake. "Paying respect to Black Wall Street, Black excellence, reminding these peckerwoods we got brains and guns too."

I shut up, fell back. I couldn't risk continuing. I didn't want to argue with Eric, this Black man who looked twice my age, standing in line to vote. I didn't want to challenge Eric at this place we were standing in, at ONEOK Field, a block south from where white Tulsans sat up on Standpipe Hill and watched their friends kill us and burn our homes down. I didn't want to tell Eric that this was never anybody's Wall Street.

I was even more bothered with Eric equating Greenwood, his Black Wall Street, to Black excellence. To argue with him, to give him concrete examples about how his viewpoint was inaccurate or flat wrong felt like I'd be crushing him, a Black man who has seen Tulsa take so much and omit even more about us and our ancestors. That equating this place to Black excellence, Black exceptionalism, normalizes the systemic racism we still face as Black Tulsans. That Black excellence centers cishet Black men and that Brittney Cooper was right to point out in her book *Eloquent Rage*: "Black men grow up believing and moving through the world politically as though they have it the toughest, as though their pain matters most, as though Black women cannot possibly be feeling anything similar to the dehumanization and disrespect that they felt." That Black excellence spotlights Washington and O. W. Gurley and omits or denies other forms of Black life and experience, notably women like Parrish who coined the phrase so associated with Washington. That normalizing Black excellence makes being ordinary impossible for Black folks. That the idea of Black excellence is used by white folks as a way of justifying our humanity. That I don't want to have to be excellent to survive Tulsa because I'm Black, and yet that is exactly what I've had to become. I wondered how we Black Tulsans came to believe such an idea was worth exalting in Tulsa, and I was forced to ask where I first heard about Black excellence. I found myself re-reading Du Bois's *The Talented Tenth* as the centennial approached.

*

Through the first quarter century of the twentieth century, W. E. B. Du Bois had risen to become the most conscious Black voice in America. As the first Black person in history to earn a PhD at Harvard and a cofounder of the National Association for the Advancement of Colored People, he planted a seed of Black radical tradition in Greenwood with a speech he delivered in 1926.

Following his visit to Tulsa, Du Bois wrote in *The Crisis*, a magazine he founded: "Black Tulsa is happy," referring to Greenwood just five years after the massacre. "It has new clothes. It is young and gay and strong. Five little years ago fire and blood and robbery leveled it to the ground, flat, raw, smoking. It knew murder and arson and wild, bitter hatred. Yet it lived. It never died. It reeled to its feet blindly . . . Scars are there, but the city is imprudent and noisy. It believes in itself. Thank God for the Grit of Tulsa."

Du Bois spoke and wrote then through a Black nationalist's lens of what Black folks should do. I can see Greenwood in his words too when, in June 1933, he celebrated the forty-fifth anniversary of his graduation from Fisk University in Nashville in an address to the alumni association called "The Field Function of the American Negro College." He believed "no college for Negroes which is not a Negro college . . . While an American Negro university, just like a German or Swiss university, might rightly aspire to a universal culture unhampered by limitations of race and culture, yet must start on the earth where we sit and not in the skies whither we aspire."

Du Bois, though, believed in the nefarious ideals of eugenics—his "Talented Tenth"—and championed the equality of Black women while enjoying his stance in the patriarchy. "The Talented Tenth rises and pulls all that are worth the saving up to their vantage ground," Du Bois wrote. "This is the history of human progress; and the two historic mistakes which have hindered that progress were the thinking first that no more could ever rise save the few already risen; or second, that it would better the unrisen to pull the risen down."

No man or woman has a right to curtail humanity, no matter how noble he or she claims their mission to be, because that leads to a total disrespect for humanity, especially Black folks' humanity, at large and an arrogance that is dangerous to the idea of an interdependence on each other for the sake of each other. Humanity must simply live, and we, as Black folks, must be for that task and that task alone: to take care of those who are here today rather than cast our eye toward those who have yet been born alone. I realize such a thought can strike some as incendiary, but that is not my aim. However, birth control as a means of genocide is not a new idea, and it frequently is one perpetuated by those who fancy themselves neoliberal in this capitalist economy. Black folks recognize that immediately in many instances, and so did journalist Joshua Prager in his book *The Family Roe: An American Story*, when he delved into the story of Black folks' mistreatment in medicine and reproductive rights:

> Of course, medical mistreatment of [B]lack Americans extended back at least a century, from the experimental surgeries of Dr. James Marion Sims on enslaved women to the appropriation of [B]lack bodies for use in medical training. And in 1932, five years after *Buck v. Bell*, the Public Health Service began its notorious study of syphilis in Tuskegee, Alabama, knowingly withholding treatment from [B]lack men for decades until they died. Mindful that the [B]lack community had reason to distrust the white medical establishment—and not long after a federal court rules, in 1936, that doctors could provide contraception for medical purposes—[founder of the birth control movement Margaret] Sanger formed what she called the Negro Project, enlisting [B]lack minsters to speak well for her clinics.

"We do not want word to go out that we want to exterminate the Negro population," Sanger wrote in 1939, "and the minister is the man who can straighten out that idea if it ever occurs to any of their more rebellious members."

Sanger also enlisted to her cause [B]lack intellectual leaders, among them W. E. B. Du Bois, founder of the National Association for the Advancement of Colored People. Like Sanger, he believed in eugenics (if not sterilization). "The mass of ignorant Negroes still breeds carelessly and disastrously," wrote Du Bois, "so that the increase among Negroes, even more than the increase among whites, is from the portion of the population least intelligent to fit, and least able to rear their children properly."

Du Bois wrote those words in a June 1932 essay called "Black Folks and Birth Control" that was published in the *Birth Control*

Review, more than three decades after the death of his firstborn. He went on, speaking of Black folks, "Like most people with middle-class standards of morality, they think that birth control is inherently immoral. Moreover, they are quite led away by the fallacy of numbers. They are cheered by a census return of increasing numbers and a high rise of increase. They must learn that among human races and groups, as among vegetables, quality and not quantity really counts."

It's clear he thought little of many of the people of his race, whom he chose to lead, but from throwing in his lot with Sanger I'm led to believe he also believed many of us Black folks did not belong on this earth alongside him. Indeed, Sanger saw birth control as a means not just to empower but to cull, especially among Black folks. As Prager notes, Sanger, being a white lady, complicated a sentiment that some Black folks supported and others utterly disavowed:

> And as the clinics that Sanger planted in [B]lack neighborhoods took root—and her American Birth Control League became in 1942 Planned Parenthood—the [B]lack community came to distrust not only birth control but its white purveyors. Come 1954, a [B]lack pathologist in Chicago named Julian Lewis wrote that birth control, and Planned Parenthood in particular, was leading the [B]lack community toward "race suicide."

The charge took, echoed by all from Langston Hughes to Dick Gregory to a group of [B]lack nationalist organizations that in 1967 passed a resolution calling birth control "[B]lack genocide." Five years later, a social worker in Minneapolis named Erma Craven asserted in a much-cited essay "that the unborn Black is the real object of many abortionists." She added: "The whole mess adds up to blatant genocide." Much of the [B]lack community agreed; a poll conducted in 1973 by two [B]lack professors in Massachusetts found that 39 percent of [B]lack Americans believed that "birth control programs are a plot to eliminate [B]lacks."

The Brooklyn-based congresswoman Shirley Chisholm dismissed such talk as "male rhetoric, for male ears." The great majority of [B]lack women approved of birth control—80 percent of [B]lack women in Chicago, for example in 1970. Still, a conspiracy had entered the zeitgeist. And for good reason. "Negroes don't want children they can't take care of," explained a Black social worker in upstate New York named Urelia Brown, "but we are afraid to trust you when your offered help has so often turned out to be exploitation."

I outline Sanger's point and those Black arguments against it because Du Bois supported her mission, and that is terrifying to me, as he was one of the best of us by any measure, and here he refused to fight for the weakest among us.

"Society," President Theodore Roosevelt said, "has no business to permit degenerates to reproduce their kind." Roosevelt wrote that in 1913, and six years afterward Indiana passed the first law in the country mandating sterilization for "criminals, idiots, imbeciles and rapists." As scary as that is, the scariest representation of how the U.S. embraced eugenics was the Supreme Court's 8–1 decision to legalize sterilization and call it constitutional in *Buck v. Bell*. Writing for the majority, Justice Oliver Wendell Holmes said, "It is better for all the world if, instead of waiting to execute degenerate offspring for crime or to let them starve for their imbecility, society can prevent those who are manifestly unfit from continuing their kind. The principle that sustains compulsory vaccination is broad enough to cover cutting the Fallopian tubes."

Holmes's reasoning belies a world where sterilization is not just law but one of our valued social mores. Among Black folks, a reluctance to take advice from a predominantly white medical establishment is ingrained, and in many cases for good reason. (Though the Tuskegee Syphilis Study is a misconstrued one and is evil in a different way. The withholding of a cure is not the same as injecting what one is told is a cure and turns out to be disease.) We do not trust this institution called the United States, and it has done little to win our trust. However, I did not expect Du Bois to play a part in the skepticism, though that's more about my own naivete than his. He was among the first generation removed from slaves; he endured and witnessed atrocities against Black folks for tame acts like a Black man looking at a white woman for too long or not stepping off the sidewalk to make way for a white man quickly enough. While I read and change my opinion of what's best for me, what I think is best for most, I keep believing the rest of the world does the same, and I am frequently wrong and ridiculed. Even suggesting Du Bois is a eugenicist is met with derision among Black and white folks alike, though I don't know what else you might call a person who believed in limiting the number of people allowed to procreate. Limiting the number of people on earth also goes against one of Du Bois's core beliefs about growing the number of elite Black people in the world. If there are fewer people, then there are fewer Black people and even fewer genius Black people. Violence against any population leads to unforeseen outcomes, just as does limiting a woman's right to choose if she wants to have an abortion or not. The best we can do, as a society, is to allow people as much choice as we can without those choices causing others undue hardship or pain. That's difficult because it requires trust in those individuals and the institutions who purport to serve them. It's too easy and too dangerous to look to one person to make a decision that affects many. But we do it, and sometimes we look to those long dead and gone for their wisdom cultivated in a time long past for what we should do to protect our future. I got here by asking Du Bois questions about what I should do at a pivotal juncture in my life, as a Black man approaching middle age with life looking very different than how I thought it would look for me when I was eighteen. I've since learned it says more about me that I looked to Du Bois and others for answers than perhaps what they had to say that I could take with me. In questioning Du Bois's politics and motives, I learned more about my own. My worry now is would I have had a chance to become the man I am in the world Du Bois envisioned? I don't know, but I have my doubts. At best, perhaps I would've had a chance to go to school until I was needed in some field somewhere in the South. At worst, Du Bois might've seen me killed in the womb or my parents unfit to procreate. My Black hero would've killed me and said it was for the greater good of the race. I submit to you there is no such thing. The actions of an individual might not diminish the achievements that individual has given the world, but it's impossible to say that learning the facts of the life of a Black radical like Du Bois has not changed me.

John Hope Franklin saw Du Bois for the first time when Du Bois visited Tulsa in February 1926, when the most important Black intellectual in history spoke before the Oklahoma Negro State Teachers Association, allowing for not one but two instances when Du Bois visited Tulsa to none by Washington, because yes, I'm keeping score. Ever modest, forthright, and remarkably honest, Franklin wrote in an article in *The Massachusetts Review*[25] titled "W. E. B. Du Bois: A Personal Memoir" how much he appreciated the man: "I recall quite vividly, however, his coming on the stage, dressed in white tie and tails with a ribbon draped across his chest, on which was pinned some large medallion, the kind I later learned was presented by governments to persons who had made some outstanding contribution to the government or even to humankind. I had never seen anyone dressed in such finery; the image I had was more of dukes and princes than an editor, scholar and civil rights leader. I can also remember that voice, resonant and well-modulated, speaking in line he had written on note cards with a precision and cadence that was most pleasant to the ear. If only I could remember what he said! No matter, perhaps, because the impression he made on me was tremendous, and I would make every effort to hear him in the future wherever and whenever our paths crossed." It's no coincidence that Franklin chose to attend Fisk, as Du Bois had, and he would later become a valued colleague and friend to Du Bois, even asking his advice and help in completing his encyclopedia of African people and the diaspora.

As the leader of a peace group, the Peace Information Center, Du Bois was indicted by a federal grand jury on February 8, 1951, for "failure to register as agent of a foreign principal" during the height of McCarthyism, when "communism" and "socialism" were synonyms for "evil" in America. The charges were eventually dismissed, but not before Du Bois suffered the humiliation of being handcuffed and jailed, his reputation sullied among white folks and Black folks alike. Having gotten married for the second time just six days after being indicted, he was arraigned on February 16, 1951, and his new wife, Shirley Graham, saw firsthand how Black folks turned on her new husband and how much that hurt him.

In his autobiography, Du Bois noted that *The Chicago Defender*, the Blackest newspaper of them all, wrote, "Dr. Du Bois has earned many honors and it is a supreme tragedy that he should have become embroiled in activities that have been exposed as subversive in the twilight of his years." Du Bois described other instances of Black folks leaving him when he needed them most. "The intelligentsia, the 'Talented Tenth,'" he wrote in *The Autobiography of W. E. B. Du Bois*, "the successful business and professional men, were not, for the most part, outspoken in my defense." The fraternity he had helped found forty-five years prior, Alpha Phi Alpha, was full of a bunch of brothers who turned their back on theirs. "Today it contains in its membership a large number of leading business and professional Negroes in the United States," Du Bois wrote in *Autobiography*. "Yet of its 30 or more chapters covering the nation, only one expressed any sympathy with me, and none offered aid. It is probable that individual members of the fraternity gave my cause support, but no official action was taken save in one case. In my own New York chapter I was bitterly criticized."

On May 24, 1960, Du Bois told the Oral History Project of Columbia University: "I never had the slightest doubt but that we were going to gain our equality here in America."

Just two months later another Black jewel, representing our best, the most talented of Du Bois's Talented Tenth and a frat brother to Du Bois, found his way to Tulsa in service of equality on behalf of the diaspora. On July 28, 1960, a Thursday, Dr. Martin Luther King Jr. stepped in front of a crowd of fifteen hundred mostly Black faces at First Baptist Church in North Tulsa to tell them that the recent decision to overturn the law of separate but equal, just six years prior, was not enough, that they must continue to believe in this country, the white folks in it, that they had the capacity to be better than they could ever know. The event was called the "Freedom Rally" and is the high point of Tulsa's nascent attempt to join the fight for civil rights.

Neither the *Tulsa World* nor the *Tulsa Tribune* covered King's visit to Tulsa in its time. Only Black Tulsans remember him; only Black Tulsans carry so much of this city's history where state law prevents it being taught in schools.

Thirty-one then, King directed Black Tulsans to embrace his tenets of nonviolence and voting. "We must learn to live together as brothers, or we'll die together as fools," he said.

Tulsan Princetta Newman, sixteen then, remembered King being shorter than she thought he'd be, expecting a physical giant of a man to match his reputation as the most important and perhaps the finest Black man this country has ever produced. "He was not what I expected. He was too short," she told the *World* in 2020. "I thought, 'It can't be him.'" She wasn't actually sure it was him until he spoke, and his distinctive conviction rang true. What shocked her still was that the voice he used to publicly speak was the one he used to speak with her. As the daughter of John Cloman, the president of the Tulsa Colored Voters Chapter of America, the organization that arranged for King to speak in Tulsa along with cosponsor the *Oklahoma Eagle*, and an alpha like King and Du Bois, Newman was among the first to greet King. "Even in everyday conversation, he boomed," she said. "That's just how he talked." She keeps a signed typewritten letter of reply from King to Cloman, about choosing to come to Oklahoma, as an heirloom. Jim Goodwin, a senior at Notre Dame then and later publisher of the *Eagle*, received the honor of introducing Vernon AME pastor Ben Hill, who introduced King to the audience.

Just fourteen then, Patricia Boxley made sure to shake his hand, to get his autograph, to receive his message. "It was such a message of hope," she told the *World*. "You were just in awe in his presence."

Eight years later, a white man shot King in the neck, killing him as he stood on a hotel balcony.

Even the threat of change, however incremental, the threat of equality, even as trivial as casting a ballot into a box, has led to white folks killing our best, our brightest. How can we ever hope to live as equals among a people who enslaved our ancestors and have taught their children to hate us for generations? Where yelling out "Black power!" and "Black lives matter!" aren't heard as affirmations but as fighting words? To white folks, our lives do not matter. And they prove it every day, as they proved to Du Bois more than four decades after the massacre and in the sixty years since.

In 1961, the Supreme Court's affirmation of the McCarran Act, banning passports for "communists and communist sympathizers," led Du Bois to believe he was still in the nation's political crosshairs. In a letter to a friend dated September 13, 1961, referenced in a 1993 essay titled "On Du Bois' Move to Africa"[26] by Herbert Aptheker in the *Monthly Review*,[27] Du Bois said he could not "take any more of this country's treatment." In this same letter, he also suggested it was "time to leave" the U.S. because "American Negroes can't win." But even in this statement I see Du Bois wanted to be an American. After all, he does not just call us *Negroes* but *American Negroes*, his way of asking white folks to see some Black folks as worthy of being called Black American. His Talented Tenth was meant to help Black folks as well as white folks see Black folks as American, and he was not alone in that thinking. In her article for the *Journal of American Physicians and Surgeons* titled "The 'Science' of Eugenics: America's Detour," doctor and lawyer Marilyn M. Singleton noted, "Dr. Thomas Wyatt Turner, a charter member of the NAACP, and many [B]lack academics at Tuskegee, Howard, and Hampton universities promoted 'Assimilationist Eugenics.' They proposed that 'The Talented Tenth' of all races should mix, as the best [B]lacks were as good as the best whites. These folks were a bit more evolved in that they believed genetics was co-equal with environment." If this is the price for becoming a Black American—debasing ourselves and leaving our perceived lesser brothers and sisters behind—I am not willing to pay it. Even Du Bois found out that his citizenship was not contingent upon how talented he was but whether or not his papers were in order.

In his book *The Color Line: Legacy of the Twenty-First Century*, John Hope Franklin also suggested that in the final years of his life, Du Bois had come to believe finding a way for Black folks to exist as full citizens of the United States was an "intractable" problem and that he had "given up on it." It's little wonder that when Kwame Nkrumah, president of socialist Ghana, asked Du Bois to write and edit *Encyclopedia Africana*, he welcomed the opportunity and left on October 5, 1961. He and his wife arrived in Accra in July 1960. The researching and writing of that encyclopedia, which he joked would take ten volumes and ten years per volume, consumed the last years of his life. Still, upon arriving, Du Bois told Nkrumah that he and his wife would like to keep and renew their American passports. At the U.S. Embassy in Ghana, he was told he and his wife had been barred from passport renewal, their passports made invalid, and was urged to return to the United States at once. Shirley Graham was so angry that Du Bois needed to physically restrain his wife from injuring the clerk. Following this seismic event in their life, Du Bois asked President Nkrumah if he and his wife might become Ghanaian citizens. "Ghana would be honored," Nkrumah said.

I doubt Du Bois loved the country of his birth, even as he acknowledged that he had never been fully welcomed into it and never would be. "For this is a beautiful world; this wonderful America," he wrote in *Autobiography*, "which the founding fathers dreamed until their sons drowned it in the blood of slavery and devoured it in greed. Our children rebuilt it. Let then the Dreams of the Dead rebuke the Blind who think that what is will be forever and teach them that what was worth living for must live again and that which merited death must stay dead. Teach us, Forever Dead, there is no Dream but Deed, there is no Deed but Memory." Du Bois likely died with that lasting thought. The day after Du Bois was born, February 23, 1868, and the same year O. W. Gurley was born, Andrew Johnson was impeached. The day after he died, August 27, 1963, Martin Luther King Jr. led the March on Washington for Jobs and Freedom. Black folks are still marching, still begging for a fair wage and the freedoms white folks enjoy in a country they designed for themselves, where they were the commodity and the capital to build their kingdom. As the United States refuses to make the changes necessary to create a more just society for non-white folks, and especially Black folks, Black folks still believe there is somewhere else to go. There is not. There is nowhere but here.

The 1921 Tulsa Race Massacre Centennial Commission's ten-day event begins on May 26, 2021, lasts through June 6, 2021, and claims to commemorate the worst act of domestic terrorism in U.S. history. The Black Wall Street Legacy Festival begins on May 28,

2021, and lasts through June 19, 2021, with events daring to demand reparations for the three living survivors of that atrocity that we know about and descendants of those victims we don't.

I drive to Oaklawn Cemetery at Eleventh Street and Peoria Avenue. I park across the street at the tennis court, step out of my truck, check both ways for traffic, and stop. I can't force myself to jaywalk. I was, I am, that afraid. I walk back east, the way I'd come, to the crosswalk at the intersection to take the path across the street to the cemetery. I stop short of the gate.

Born on New Year's Day 1911, Clyde Eddy was the first person of some prominence to get into the public record that the bodies of massacre victims were at the Oaklawn Cemetery. "In the spring of 1999," a report by the Oklahoma Commission to Study the Tulsa Race Riot of 1921 wrote, "an eyewitness was found to the digging of a mass grave at Oaklawn Cemetery. Mr. Clyde Eddy, who was a child of ten at the time of the riot, witnessed white laborers at Oaklawn digging a 'trench.' There also were a number of [B]lack riot victims present in several wooden crates. While Mr. Eddy did not directly see the victims being placed in this trench-like area, it is reasonable to assume that its purpose was for a mass grave. Mr. Eddy recalls this area being within the white section of the 'Old Potters Field' and was able to point out the area in a visit to Oaklawn during the spring, 1999."

Eddy knew where the bodies lay, yet the city refused to dig. I clutch the fence, thinking about how many people he must've had tell him that he was crazy. Eddy helped start Tulsa's first Black Boy Scouts of America troop and was an Eagle Scout, like me. The first words to the Scout Oath are *On my honor I will do my best to do my duty to God and my country and to obey the Scout Law to help other people at all times; to keep myself physically strong, mentally awake, and morally straight.* I believe Eddy internalized those words, as I did, when he was a boy. Why else stand in the truth he knew when so many about him called him a fabulist, a liar, behind his back? No white person I've spoken to in Tulsa has ever told me they believed Eddy, only that the city—always the city, never white Tulsans—would never do such a thing. That even in Tulsa, where the worst act of U.S. domestic terrorism ever occurred, white Tulsans could not be so cruel as to dump Black bodies into ground and conspire it all up for more generations.

Tulsa mayor G. T. Bynum used his position to launch an excavation to find out, once and for all, if there were mass graves at Oaklawn. On October 19, 2020, archaeologists discovered twelve bodies in coffins in the Black Potters field at Oaklawn after just five months of digging.[28] On June 8, 2021 that number rose to twenty-seven. According to a city document, there could be at least thirty people buried in the space they've chosen to excavate.[29] At the fence, I feel tears welling up.

I feel such pain striking my chest then. I feel myself crumble to my knees, an enormous heavy chain pulling me to the ground. Those tears stream down my cheeks. An entire century passed as Black folks were told over and over again that these mass graves were nothing more than myths. I let my arms hang while I weep for those families of Black folks buried in the ground, lost in location. Lost to those who want to mourn them, plant their grief in the soil alongside flowers annually, and remember. I weep for the families of those people we've found, who will get to see their relatives reburied, given a proper homegoing, and allowed what I've come to know is the privilege, not the right, to a peaceful grieving of the people who made way for them, for this life we live, for the better life we want our children to live.

*

I climb into my truck, wondering if it was this hot, this oppressively humid, on May 25, 2020, when Derek Chauvin dropped his weight into his knee like an anvil crushing life from George Floyd. How must the road have felt against his left cheek as he felt himself losing consciousness? Did he believe this was hell? Did he believe this was how his life would end? I ask myself all these questions and more as I drive to the Gathering Place just off Riverside Drive, site of the first centennial event created by the commission, a display of art from the Kinsey African American Collection.

The parking lot is full of cars and vans and trucks and white folks—so, so many white folks. As I navigate up and down the full lot, trying to find a space, I spot license plates from Indiana, Texas, California, Colorado, New Jersey, New York, and Michigan. People bustle on the sidewalk and through the middle of the street as if daring a vehicle to hit them, as if they were not tourists but Tulsans—like they live here. I look at them all as trespassers, as folks gawking at the spectacle of an entire city on its bullshit, touring a park I never thought was built for my benefit, nor that of any other tax-paying Tulsan.

The Gathering Place is the crown jewel project of the George Kaiser Family Foundation. The park is over sixty-six acres, with an adventure playground, a climbing playground, cradle swings, a river for canoeing, several grass spaces for concerts that could be held simultaneously, a reading tree large enough for several families to picnic underneath, a picnic lawn, a water mountain, several walking paths, a restaurant, three basketball courts, a street hockey court, a street soccer court, and a volleyball court. There is also the fifty-thousand-square-foot Discovery Lab, a hands-on museum for kids with a three-hundred-seat amphitheater, café, and plaza. With an initial investment from Kaiser of $350 million over the first five years of its construction, the Gathering Place was finished and opened on September 8, 2018, at a total cost of $465 million. The park maintains a $100 million endowment for event programming and maintenance. With an estimated net worth of $7.9 billion, Kaiser sought to create a public space out of private wealth in the city of his birth. In his book, *The Great Oklahoma Swindle: Race, Religion, and Lies in America's Weirdest State*, Russell Cobb explored how an elaborate agreement between GKFF and the city of Tulsa made such a park possible: "Kaiser's foundation created a GKFF Park Conservancy, an LLC that essentially loaned the park to the [Tulsa] River Parks Authority for one hundred years. The LLC remains in charge of the maintenance and programming of the park. This arrangement gets trickier because the River Parks Authority is not technically part of the city or county government but rather another public-private partnership created in 1974 during Tulsa's last monumental attempt to transform the nature of the Arkansas River, the prairie river that runs through it. Gathering Place, then, is a public-private partnership whose public partner is a public-private partner whose public partner is Tulsa and whose private side is a subsidiary of a foundation known for its public-private partnerships."

An example of how this public-private partnership park runs aground with state law is its attempt to enforce a policy prohibiting open or concealed-carry guns, knives, or other weapons. Oklahoma law allows for openly carrying firearms in public spaces, and Tulsa Police has decided not to enforce the Gathering Place policy on firearms to ward off a legal fight with Second Amendment rights groups, leaving the private security at the Gathering Place responsible for enforcing its policy.

While that part always made me smile, I frown when I think of the same effort being put into treating the massacre as if it did not occur for seventy-five years and then changing the narrative into one of Black excellence rather than that white folks—many of whom are descendants of the neighbors living around the Gathering Place—burned Greenwood down and killed dozens of its residents for the crime of getting by.

How many of these white folks knew our history? How many of these white folks would do something other than gawk at our failings? How many had not heard of the massacre until they watched a television show that ripped off our history for entertainment and didn't even have the decency to film even part of the show here and exercise some of that economic development they claim to be about? How many of these white folks couldn't care less about my hometown until Trump brought his circus to us in the summer of that plague-addled year? I wondered how many of them would forget the massacre almost as soon as the centennial came and went.

"We are committed to creating a gathering space that is a recreational, civic and cultural destination for all walks of life to enjoy, promoting inclusivity in our city," according to the Kaiser Family Foundation's website in a section called "Our Commitment."[30] "We are committed to enhancing the River Parks system while preserving the area's natural ambiance and integrating the new space into the greater surrounding area. We are committed to Tulsa, to all who live here and to all who visit, that they may be positively inspired to play, learn, interact, relax and gather together."

Most Black Tulsans cannot gather at the Gathering Place without effort, however, because they live in North Tulsa, a section of the city still so segregated from other parts of the city—South Tulsa, Midtown, West Tulsa, and East Tulsa—that the streets are marked with an "N" in front of them, like Hester Prynne's scarlet "A." The closest major intersection to the park is Thirty-First Street and Riverside. To get to that intersection from Thirty-First Street North in Tulsa is a drive of about twenty minutes, nearly ten miles north of the park and through downtown. The Gathering Place does not have dedicated public transit running to or away from it throughout the city. In March 2020, eighteen months after its opening, the Gathering Place announced a partnership with Tulsa Transit for a spring shuttle program that was to run through May, but only on weekends. It's this kind of half measure that leads me to believe Gathering Place simply exists for the people with the means to find their way there without the help of the park itself and, in doing so, lets down a large group of the people it claims to serve before they even step into the park proper. There are acres of parking spaces to reinforce this feeling. If you have access to a car, you can have access to the park. Tulsa is a city for drivers, and there are many Black Tulsans without access to vehicles.

*

A couple of days before my trip to the Gathering Place, Rico, the owner of the barbershop where I get my edge-up, asked me what I thought about all these folks coming to town over the next week. I sat in Armond's chair getting my line-up, diagonally across from Chris's chair, and directly across from Rico's chair. This is Rico's shop, and he's not shy about acting that way.

"Stacey Abrams, John Legend—all the cool-ass Black folks coming through," Rico said.

"I ain't mad at a *Coming 2 America* performance from John Legend," I said. "Hit Tulsa with that shit, and you got me. If he fucks around and bangs out 'The Fire,' I might levitate."

"Jay gone be out there in centerfield with a raised fist and shit scaring the hell out of these white folks," Rico said, laughing, the only man in the world who would shorten my name from two letters to one.

"How?" I said. "It's sold out."

"Hey." Chris pulled his clippers off his client's head and pointed the sharp end at me. "Don't give that man 'The Fire.' That's the Roots. That's Black Thought. Johnny Fairytales or whatever ain't got it like that. Put his Black ass behind a piano somewhere talm-bout conversations in the dark or somethin'."

Rico was laughing so hard he stopped cutting his client's hair. "That's cold, Chris."

The white person sitting in Chris's chair had a look about him like he didn't know whether to laugh. Chris kept his face solid.

"What's cold?" Chris said. "That's his whole get-down. He ain't fend to turn Tulsa into Freaknik or whatever. Just take your girl, let him wind her up, and enjoy the after-party cause you know damn well John Legend ain't for the fellas."

"Yeah, and him and Stacey only coming through when we're on our bullshit," I said, pulling the conversation back to local politics. "Why the fuck Stacey gotta show up when we suck the most?"

"I hear you," Rico said. He shrugged. "But at least they showing up, you know, Jay? At least, right now, feel like white folks want to come here."

I felt a burning in my chest then. I wanted to erupt. But I didn't. I couldn't. I didn't want to challenge Rico. I didn't want to challenge his optimism anymore. There are not enough of us to survive. We are rare. We are endangered.

"I'm not satisfied with showing up," I said.

"Yeah, well, you wouldn't be, *N'Jobu*," Chris said.

Armond pulled out the razor to edge me up. He stopped for a moment and then laughed. "He's right." He leaned over. Put that razor to my scalp. "You kinda are N'Jobu." I felt the razor slowly taking hair off my scalp, knowing I wanted to say something and couldn't. The man was literally holding a knife to my head. At that moment, I had to do what I do most often in front of white folks: be quiet, lest they find some way to injure me in my zeal to attack their flawed thinking. This was not just the room where Black men give you the nickname of the father of the man who infiltrated Wakanda, defeated its monarch and greatest warrior in ritual combat, and then jacked him for his chain. This was the room where you wilt, where you are told to stand down, and a small part of you dies. You trust these negroes, more than you trust any white man you've ever met in your life, to put a straight razor to your neck, and because of that trust, you will always have to hear these niggas call you N'Jobu because these niggas are your people, and there simply are not enough of your people left to quit them. But you're still pissy and annoyed in this chair when Armond gently taps you and says, "Relax, nigger. It's all love."

*

At the Gathering Place, though, I challenge the thought. Yes, the cool-ass Black folks and all matter of white folks are coming to Tulsa. But what are they showing up for? Which part of this do they think is important? Because this is a circus, created by people who claim to have the best interest of the massacre's requiem in mind.

The Kinsey Collection on display at the Gathering Place is the first event under Tulsa's big top, inside the boathouse tucked deep in the park. According to the Gathering Place website, "The Kinsey African American Art & History Collection is a traveling exhibition with a wide range of art and artifacts, including books, documents, photography, paintings, fine art, and personal belongings that tell the story of African American triumphs and accomplishments from 1595 to present day. The collection is composed of more than 700 rare primary source historical objects and artifacts."

I find a place to park, step out, and furiously pound out steps toward the boathouse as this humidity manifests in sweat beads across my brow. I'm inherently suspicious of white strangers showing up on behalf of a Black cause, and here they are watching their kids play on state-of-the-art playground equipment and enjoying $5.89 hamburgers while Tulsa Public Schools beg for money enough to feed our kids at lunch. I can't blame them for that. I blame us for that, and I'm angry all over again. I hate this place because it's so welcoming to strangers and so cruel to us, to me, to Black folk. Only after we tell you about our Black pain does a magnificent curation like the Kinsey Collection show up. That's the math: Black pain for a little bit of stardom; Black tragedy for a little national media attention; Black death for a brief acknowledgment of lives and property loss that generations will never recover.

As I walk toward the boathouse, I ruminate about the music, art, and entertainment about to be displayed. I'm hot and unreasonably angry at the sheer number of white folks traipsing through this park, and now that I recognize it, I have to call Laurel. She has to talk me down. She has seen me shouting at the television, cursing during reading yet another story in *The New York Times*, in the *Washington Post*, in the *Tulsa World*, about this place no one cared to acknowledge before a television show aired on HBO. She tells me she's proud of me. She asks me to tell her what I see, to bathe myself in manicured grass, the smiling children chasing each other on giant toys suited to their developing motor skills as they learn to fall. The walk from my space near the entrance to the boathouse where the collection is on display must be a half mile long. Even in shape, it's a trudge, I tell her.

"I know this walk is hard for you for a different reason," she says. The reason is hurt, pain, the ever-present feeling that is all wrong.

I tell her I love her, and she asks me to call her when it's done. I hang up without saying goodbye and feel myself weighed down, dizzy. I grab the fence closest to me, steeling myself. I count backward from ten. Then I count from zero. I feel my heartbeat slow as I open the door to the boathouse, to a high ceiling and a room that feels like it's as large as my house. A white woman, blonde hair buzzed short, with a mask over her face, sits like a happy sentry behind a table filled with books.

I glance at the books and then force myself to appreciate this exhibit—what was on display, anyway. I read about Shirley and Bernard Kinsey, who set a goal after their marriage in 1967 of visiting one hundred countries, collecting artifacts from their journeys, only to realize they had not really collected any from their own people. They sought to change that, and in the process collected some of the finest and most important Black American artifacts ever produced. What is on display inside the boathouse is a fraction of their collection, but a fraction that might've never found its way to Tulsa under different circumstances. The city demonstrated what it does to its own Black finery and importance one hundred years ago:

it burns it to the ground. But here, now, there is an original copy of Victor Green's *The Negro Motorist Green Book* published in 1941, like the one in the glove compartment of my '08 Dodge, grayed out and stamped "complimentary" just above the title. There's a typescript of the landmark U.S. Supreme Court case, *Brown v. Board of Education*, the foundation of Booker T. Washington High School's becoming a magnet school. There's a photo of U.S. Army Lieutenant Benedict Mosley, who was awarded the French Croix de Guerre for his role in the Battle of Argonne in 1918. I wonder if Mosley would've been one of those Black veterans who picked up a gun on that Memorial Day weekend in 1921 and descended upon the courthouse to make certain Dick Rowland didn't hang like Roy Belton did. Mosley was a Harlem Hell-Fighter. Tulsa was a hell, and there were Black men who were fighters.

On either side of these artifacts, encased in a glass desk remembering the triumphs of Ida Wells-Barnett, Green, and Mosley, there are photos of splendid-looking Black men and women. They look ready for church. A note written on the wall has the title: "Posing African-American Progress in the Midst of Racial Injustice."

"With the development of the cabinet card as a more affordable means of creating photographic images during the 1870s," the info card reads, "photo studios sprang up in virtually every main street in America. This included Greenwood Avenue, aptly referred to as 'Black Wallstreet of America,' the main thoroughfare of the Greenwood District of Tulsa, Oklahoma, where A. S. Newkirk photography studio was located. Before the massacre, Greenwood District of Tulsa was one of several affluent Black communities located throughout the United States in the early 20th century. The segregated Greenwood District thrived as the epicenter of African American business and culture in Tulsa. Scores of African Americans fleeing racial oppression from less racially hospitable locations in the United States began relocating to Oklahoma during the post-Reconstruction period in search of a better life."

Put that way, you might believe Tulsa was this haven of racial progress. You might forget white Tulsans killed their Black neighbors. Telling the full truth is hard. Half-truths feel better, sell better. You're not going to move units telling people how awful the world is with a history lesson. History, often, is written to make us feel as if we're doing just fine, when most of the time, we're all fighting angry. I gaze at the bust of a slave boy, encased in glass, and imagine myself. I see his features, his round nose, soft cheeks, full lips, wooly hair, and see myself being torn away from Mama, sold at auction, tortured for loving not one but two white women in my life, jailed or killed for refusing to know my place in the caste system created by colonizers.

*

I move on to Ava Cosey's work. The piece is called *Ancestor's Torch*, a gorgeous oil painting of a Black woman in a green dress, with golden handcuffs on her wrists, gold earrings on her ears. Her hair is curly, without product, and a beautiful braid wraps across the top of her head like a crown. "We didn't come to America because it was a better place," Cosey has written above her creation's head. "We came and made it a better place." The dress holds phrases like "traffic lights," "bicycle frame," "super soaker," "rolling pin," "hair straightener," and "thermostat control." These are the names of inventions by Black people in America, and a Black woman held them all. Next to her is another Black woman, created out of whole cloth. In June 2012, economist and Michigan State professor Dr. Lisa Cook studied patents granted to Black inventors from 1870 to 1940. She called the study "Violence and Economic Activity: Evidence from African American Patents, 1870 to 1940."[31] She found 726 patents issued to Black folks during that time. Some inventions included a flying machine, a roller mechanism for player pianos, and a telephone system. She found that Black inventors were awarded patents on par with white ones through the 1870s and 1880s. Between 1884 and 1889, Black patents skyrocketed. But they fell off in the 1890s, due in part to *Plessy v. Ferguson* becoming law. She then added analysis to her research to account for the rise in lynchings of Black folks in the 1890s. When lynchings slowed in 1899, Black patents awarded began climbing again. But in 1921 the number of lynchings had decreased, as had Black patents awarded—corresponding with the race massacre. "Accounts of the Tulsa riot suggest that many at the time believed that government failed at all levels," Cook wrote, "and that this was a turning point in federal policy and national practice related to property-rights protection, and that the country was likely headed toward racial warfare." Following the massacre, whites were awarded patents at 2.2 times the rate Black folks were, and we have not closed the gap since. The year with the most patents awarded to Black inventors was 1899. In this, the Tulsa Race Massacre changed the country for the worse. Along with people, business, and economic wealth, generations of inventors, creativity, and intelligence were lost too.

*

Sea Island Woman, quilted from cotton, silk, wool, and applique, balances a bowl on her head, her hat in her hand. She is clothed in an intricately patterned red gown, a mix of flowers, leaves, and paisleys. A black jacket keeps her warm and a head scarf protects her from the sun. Bisa Butler's *Sea Island Woman* is so fine that, at first glance, this quilt looks like an oil painting. I marvel at Butler's genius. She put textiles to work in examining her subject's unique detail and forcing the observer to recognize each stitch of a marginalized people.

A bust of Frederick Douglass sculpted by Tina Allen is on display just behind me, and I realize there is not one piece in the boathouse that is polemic in nature. All of these pieces are meant to make us feel good—and, more to the point, make white folks feel less afraid, less intimidated, by our Blackness. Here, in these works at the Gathering Place, I see the Black history white folks don't really mind. There's no room for Emory Douglas, renowned artist and member of the Black Panthers, in this collection. There's no place for a piece that challenges whiteness, white supremacy, or presents a truly Black experience apart from a white one. Yet I find myself leaning forward, wanting this to be enough and wanting it to be all ours and none of theirs. There's still hope for that. Perhaps the truly great Black works in the collection are waiting for me at the Greenwood Cultural Center.

I walk to the table again, seeing the attendant. I ask if this room is all there is on display.

"This is it," she says matter-of-factly.

I am surprised at how deflated I feel. I want more, even of this tamed collection of us. I see the books, thick hardbacks, titled *The Kinsey African American Art & History Collection* in front of the art sentry. Some are simply stacked atop each other, and others are enclosed in a sleek black box.

"How much are the books?" I ask.

"These"—she points to the gray matte finished copies—"are $65, and those"—she points to the enclosed boxes—"are $95."

"What's the difference?"

"The box, I think," she said.

Even through her mask I can make out how sheepish she feels saying the words aloud. $30 for a box? Nah. I buy the $65 one. The circus gets my money. I bury my head in the book as I walk back to my truck.

Nearly a week after my visit to the Gathering Place, the John Hope Franklin Center for Reconciliation holds its first event as a part of its 12th Annual Reconciliation in America National Symposium. "The Future of Tulsa's Past: The Centennial of the Tulsa Race Massacre and Beyond" is an outdoor event featuring sculptor Ed Dwight on Thursday afternoon, at the start of the Memorial Day weekend. The event is described as a tour of the outdoor museum, John Hope Franklin Reconciliation Park. I'd been there several times before, though not for years, and I want to know what Dwight has to say about the memorial he created, how he thinks about it.

I drive to the cultural center first, though, to view the rest of the Kinsey Collection on display there, four days before the marquee event put on by the centennial commission at ONEOK Field, with a list of speakers and performers that includes Stacey Abrams, John Legend, and actor and author Hill Harper. People are already coming from out of town to be a part of a commemoration that feels like a dark, bizarre spectacle. I am delighted to find a parking space in the cultural center parking lot. But where the Gathering Place was mostly white, this place, Greenwood, is filled with mostly Black folks. I walk into the cultural center and am greeted by a Black Tulsa Police officer working as security for the exhibit.

"Is this where I can see the collection?" I ask.

"Yeah, it's here," he says, gesturing to a room just behind him, "and just a little bit that way," gesturing northward, "in the office area."

"Thank you," I say. I take two steps toward the door and then stop. Those first two steps were me getting away from a cop. But I stop because he is a Black man. I turn around.

"What do you think about all of this?" I ask the cop.

"Oh, it's a nice exhibit," he says.

"No," I say, "I mean all the white folks coming in and the pomp and circumstance this weekend."

He chuckles. "They ain't been in here."

I chuckle too. "But you know what I meant, right?"

He nods solemnly. "I think it's time it got out."

"But it's been out for the better part of thirty years," I said. "Twenty if we're just gonna start with the first commission report."

"Tell you a story," he says.

One day, he was going through the McDonald's at Pine Street and Peoria, just off Highway 75. He drove a truck then. On the back of that truck, he had a license plate-holder that said, simply, BLACK WALL STREET. A white person saw that plate as he was rolling through the first stop in the drive-thru at McDonald's, where the cashier takes your order. When Black Cop came to a stop at the drive-thru window, that white man got out of his car and started walking toward the driver's side of Black Cop's truck.

"Now, you see me," Black Cop says. "You know what I do. I've done it for forty years, and you don't roll up on a man like that." He says when he saw this white man rolling up on him at the drive-thru, he put his hand on his gun. The white man had the audacity to knock on his window. Black Cop said "What?" to this white man, like he was ready for this white man to start something.

"I just want to know what your plateholder means," the white man said.

Back at the cultural center, looking at me, Black Cop lets out a sigh of relief, reliving the moment. "Man, I thought he wanted trouble. But he didn't want trouble. He wanted a *history lesson*." Black Cop laughs at that. "So I gave it to him." Black Cop says he saw that white man a few years later, and he'd asked his parents about the massacre. "Turns out his great-grandma was hiding Black folks in her basement during the fighting," Black Cop says. "Imagine that."

"I've heard stories like that," I said.

I tell Black Cop the man most responsible for inciting the massacre, Richard Lloyd Jones, claimed even he hid his Black servant staff in his basement during the burning and the killing.

"The thing is," I say, "I never run into any white folks whose ancestors were doing any of the shooting, setting fires, the looting. Don't you find that suspicious?"

"Hey, young blood," Black Cop says, sounding exasperated,

"with that kind of attitude, how're we supposed to heal? I see from your face that you got all this aggression." He points to his heart. "You got to let that go."

I feel stuck between wanting to vent at this Black man and saying something I know might make a cop angry. I want to tell him we were never made whole, have never been financially repaired, so how can we heal? How can you not feel angry? I want to tell him we lost lives, futures, whole families to ruin. I want to tell him none of the white folks who perpetrated these crimes were tried and convicted, let alone arrested, by people who wear a badge just like his. But I take too long, and he fills the air with another story, a story about how he'd tried to help young Black men once in the 1980s.

"They were probably just like you," he says. Black Cop tells me he was one of the original members of TPD's gang task force then.

"But we didn't go busting heads," Black Cop says. "We got to know the kids." He used to work All-City, a late summer football tournament between Tulsa Public high schools. He and his partner would be tasked with roaming through the crowd during the games. "And I can't tell you how many times we were able to de-escalate a disagreement or a fight from being something way worse because we knew the kids. We were doing good."

One of the ways he and his partner did good during those years was by putting on what he called "side-by-sides." They'd go to TPS schools, ask the teachers and principals to bring them "all the problem children, the bangers," and sit them down in desks. He and his partner would mount pictures of young men, teenagers, on the blackboard. He'd put up photos of those boys who went to school in the area who were alive six months ago. Then, next to those, he'd put up photos of all the boys who used to go to school in the area who weren't. Most of the time he mounted pictures of the same boys.

"See," Black Cop says, "I was showing them what's waiting for them if they keep going down this path. Well, one of those boys' mama saw our deal one time, and she got us shut down. I'm like, 'Hey, I'm not the reason your child got killed.'"

Another Black man comes up to him then. Black Cop introduces me to him. He is an off-duty Black cop. I shake his hand, then shake Black Cop's hand and made some excuse about running low on time.

"Make sure you take this in, young blood," Black Cop says. "Remember, wherever you are in life and wherever you're going, this history is what made all of that possible."

I dash into the room, hoping this history will save me from saying any of the things rising in my throat like bile.

The exhibit at the cultural center is broken into two rooms. The one I bolt into features a painted portrait of Bernard and Shirley Kinsey. They look proud and oddly decadent among these artifacts they've spent decades collecting. It dawns on me then that another portrait of them was on display back at the Gathering Place. It's as if they want me to know they are the reason all of this is here, every bit of our history on display. It is not enough that their name precedes the word "collection." I need to walk past the portrait to see our history, and I am greeted with a large term on the south wall: ROOTS.

Below ROOTS is a four-paragraph report summarizing how Africans were forcibly trafficked to Europe and the Americas beginning in 1450. It explains how our value to colonizers lay almost exclusively in planting and harvesting crops—sugar, tobacco, cotton, rum, molasses, timber—and manufacturing metals. There is not one word written about how African nations sold our descendants into slavery. European slavers, and later American slavers, kept detailed, first-person accounts, notes, diaries, documents, and ledgers outlining their human criminality. The report notes that Olaudah Equiano has the dubious distinction of being the first person captured and sold into slavery from near his home on the Niger River.

He was bought by a British naval officer and later sold to a Quaker, who allowed him to purchase his freedom. Equiano learned the language of his captors and slavers so well that he later wrote *The Interesting Life of Olaudah Equiano*. The book was the first personal account of the life of a slave along the transatlantic slave route. His story, like that of those who survived the massacre, has become one of the most precious heirlooms Black people own. I turn to look at the west wall, where I see another tremendous feat of scholarship and personal accounting: *Narrative of the Life and Travels of Mrs. Nancy Prince*, by Nancy Gardner Prince, published in 1853. A first edition of her memoir sits encased in a glass box. She'd married a free Black man from Boston in 1824 and they traveled together to St. Petersburg, Russia, where they lived for nearly a decade. I think about Paul Robeson and how hospitable he found Russia a century later. The Princes lived as servants in the Czar's court, became multilingual, owned a boardinghouse and a clothing business where Nancy sewed and sold fine attire. When she returned to the United States in 1850, she was overwhelmed by American racism, particularly in the South. After nearly a decade abroad, she found this country foreign and vicious in its hate of her and her people.

From Prince's autobiography, I move to a first edition of the second autobiography of Frederick Douglass, *My Bondage and My Freedom*. In the information card about the book, it notes Douglass wrote a letter to one of his former slave masters, a ship captain named Thomas Auld. Like many who live with extreme trauma as a part of their lives, he had more to say. Next to Douglass's book is *Letters of the Late Ignatius Sancho*, an African, published in 1782. Described as "an extraordinary negro," Sancho was the first African person to vote in a British election. He wrote music and poetry and became an abolitionist in the eighteenth century.

"Son? You OK?"

I turn around, a bit frightened, and see the off-duty Black cop has walked into the room.

"Son?" he says again.

"I'm fine!" I snap at him.

He put up his hands like he didn't mean to offend me.

"I'm sorry," I say.

"It's OK that it hurts," he says. "Means something to you if it hurts."

I nod, hesitate, and then I ask, "Does it ever not?"

"No. All you can do is be grateful."

"Grateful for what?"

"That they existed," he says.

I don't want to nod to that any more than I want to nod to the progress made in the struggle for Black folks in America. I do, though, my body forcing genuflection.

That they existed. That they cut a way. That I am because we are.

I moved on to a printed copy of a proclamation first posted in 1798: "Any Person May Kill and Destroy Said Slaves." The info card notes that President George Washington signed the Fugitive Slave Act into law in 1793. Until the Thirteenth Amendment was passed by Congress in 1865, white Americans derived this as a mandate to capture escaped Black men. This action helped spawn the slave patrol, which is foundational to the invention of police in America. This 1798 proclamation was issued in response to just two slaves who'd managed to escape a North Carolina plantation. Paul Robeson's father, William Drew Robeson, escaped the Roberson Plantation in Marin County, North Carolina, in 1860. Because it was not an infrequent act, slaves escaping, the Albemarle Insurance Company sold slave insurance with rates as high as $130 for an eight-year-old Black boy. The flyer posting their rates is mounted next to the 1798 proclamation.

Stepping around the old head who dropped *That they existed* on me, I nearly walk past Henry Butler's letter mounted on the left side of the south wall, "extremely important to the Kinseys, because it shows the compassion of the female slave owner." I could see how

Mary Ann Graham selling Butler's wife and children to him "for a nominal price" can be viewed as humane during an inhumane time—if you're white. Graham set a price. Butler paid it. It was a transaction of the kind she was raised with and used to. I refuse to feel grateful for that. I turn from that artifact to what looks like a Rorschach Test on the wall in a golden frame. Peering closer, I can see it is handwriting, but I can barely make out just two words written in the middle of the ink splatter: "Marriage, 1598." I read the info card of what has transformed from an ink blot into a document of tremendous pride and importance to me in an instant. The info card says it is a copy of the EARLIEST KNOWN BLACK MARRIAGE RECORD and is on display with special permission from the Catholic Archdiocese of St. Augustine, Florida. I gasp, a slight thrill.

The first record of racially based organized slavery in America took place in St. Augustine, Florida, in 1565, when Africans were trafficked there by the Spanish. The info card notes: "Augustin & Francisca were married on the third Sunday before Lent of 1598, in St. Augustine Catholic Diocese, by Father Richard Arthur. This is the earliest known African American marriage record in what later becomes the present-day United States, establishing the existence of African Americans twelve years before the founding of Jamestown."

I leave the room. I'd spent perhaps no more than a half hour in that room, sweeping along with the emotional current of my history laid before me, wrapped in the commemoration of a massacre. I am tired. I walk out, turn immediately the other direction when I see Black Cop still sitting guard at the table. I put my hands on my knees. I take a breath, then another, and see there is still another room to walk into; still another room of great triumphs and haunts. I think about leaving. I think about giving up for the day. Then I think about how quickly all this history will be swept away to some other city, some other town, suddenly out of sight, just like I am sure this week of centennial events will be forgotten by the world at large by the Fourth of July. I walk into the next room.

The first piece I spot in the next room is a first edition of Booker T. Washington's *Up from Slavery*, an autobiography of the man whose name was on my first high school; who was born into slavery and helped usher in an unprecedented age of education among Black folks, or so we've told ourselves for the better part of one hundred years.

I tear up, wanting to touch Booker T. Washington's autobiography, wanting to feel past the glass to the soul of this man who cared so much for Black folks, who asked us not to antagonize white folks. Perhaps he knew intimately that they were capable of this massacre and wanted to save us. He knew it because he'd seen it his entire life.

The next piece I see, on the west wall, is framed Confederate currency. The state of Missouri, a slave state, had its own. So did the Confederate States of America. The first CSA dollar was put into circulation in April 1861, just two months after the CSA was founded. As there were more and more losses on the battlefield, the dollar lost all value as a medium of exchange with Confederate General Robert E. Lee's surrender to Union General Ulysses S. Grant at Appomattox.

Across the room, on the east wall, I see how Black folks rose immediately following the Civil War: a lithograph on the wall of "The First Colored Senator and Representatives in the 41st and 42nd Congress." I read on the info card that twenty-two Black men served in Congress between 1870 and 1901. Thirteen of them were born into slavery. I can't hold it anymore. I cry. I can't stand it any longer. I trot out of that room, do not return the goodbye from Black Cop on the way out of the glass doors, and speed-walk around the corner. I sit down in front of the Black Wall Street monument on the east of the cultural center and across from Vernon AME where I cry until I don't need to cry anymore.

GATHER MY EMOTIONS AND BEGIN WALKING TOWARD JOHN
Hope Franklin Reconciliation Park to hear Ed Dwight talk about
how he designed the park. I head south, making a horseshoe loop
around ONEOK Field on this, the last day before the Black Wall
Street Festival and centennial commission's events wouldn't overlap.
The streets are buzzy, though not full. There are Black folks with
fanny packs and sunglasses staring up at the street signs on the east
side of Archer Street and Greenwood Avenue. A Black family of five
takes a picture just across the street from the Greenwood Rising
Black Wall Street History Center that will be unveiled at its dedication a week later. It's odd to see that family posing near a space
that had once been left undeveloped and mysterious. For years, I
wondered who owned the land on what I knew had become a lucra-
tive piece of property across the street from the two brick buildings
acting as the last vestiges of Black Tulsa in 1921. Those buildings,
spanning the 100 block of Greenwood Avenue, had not been renovated since the 1980s, and here is a brand-new center, not there this
time last year, staring back at me with a brand-new smugness.

The Greenwood Chamber of Commerce asked the city to take
responsibility for keeping those brick buildings on the 100 block
upright and the block clean when streets across the country were
on fire in 2020 and Tulsa was gaining national renown for hosting

Trump's rally. In June 2020, the Chamber sent the city a letter. "The responsibility of maintaining 100-146 North Greenwood Avenue should not fall upon the Greenwood Chamber of Commerce, Inc., a private entity," according to the document obtained by the *Journal Record*. "The City of Tulsa is obligated to maintain public safety, repair public sidewalks, and provide adequate street lighting, pursuant to the City of Tulsa Code of Ordinances, Title 11, Chapter 1, Section 101, Public Works Department." After mulling whether to ask the family of five why they'd come and were taking pictures, a Black woman calls out to me from across the street.

"Sir, sir!" she says.

She and a little girl, Black, two afro puffs mounted on either side of her head, flag me down as if I might fly away. They finish jogging across Archer Street, the adult dragging the child behind her by the hand. "Thank you," she says, catching her breath. "We're from out of town."

"It's OK."

"Are you from here?" she asks.

"Yes, ma'am."

"Thank God. Do you know where the Greenwood Cultural Center is?"

I turn around and point north. "Just head toward that overpass, and it's on the other side."

She looks north, over my shoulder, through the baseball stadium. "They put it next to a highway?"

I nod.

"White folks," she says, and beckons her child.

As they walk away, the little girl throws a look back at me like she has no idea what they are doing there. For a moment, I wonder too. What *are* we doing here? I continue on my way. A Black man, shirt off, do-rag on, in charcoal shorts, runs around the block in circles at the corner of Elgin Avenue and Archer.

I turn the corner north at Elgin and Archer. I stop just before reaching John Hope Franklin Reconciliation Park to look up at the street sign and let myself have another slight chortle. The intersection at Elgin and Reconciliation Way is still funny to me. It was not always called Reconciliation Way—it's only been that for less than a decade. Until 2013, it was named for one of the founding members of Tulsa, Wyatt Tate Brady. His signature is on the 1898 charter. He was a member of both the Tulsa chapter of the Ku Klux Klan and the Sons of the Confederate Veterans.

In 2011, a story in *This Land Press* revealed Brady's racist past and acknowledged his name on the streets of Tulsa. Black Tulsans and other activists protested the street being named after him. Tulsans who wanted the Brady Street sign left alone argued that changing the name would lead to revisionist history, as if there is any other kind. The issue was put before the city council, and they voted 7–1 on what it believed was a compromise: to rename the street for M. B. Brady, a Civil War photographer with no ties to Tulsa, but it would keep the name Brady on the street sign. In the same city council meeting on August 15, 2013, the council voted to give Inner Dispersal Loop the honorary name of Reconciliation Way, after the John Hope Franklin Center for Reconciliation. The Inner Dispersal Loop is the largest physical impediment to business and residential growth in Greenwood. Later, the city council, acknowledging its Black citizens, finally changed the Brady street name to Reconciliation Way, too.

A bit farther up Elgin Street, cement blocks form a wall just before reaching John Hope Franklin Reconciliation Park. On the wall, I find a flyer with a dashing Black man wearing a suit and tie standing next to a handsome white woman wearing a dress, corsage, and hat looking back at me. Below their photo is a three-paragraph story describing the legend of how Dick Rowland and Sarah Page were the kindling for the massacre. The story the flyer tells is one of love.

December 1920 and snow was falling softly on the streets of Tulsa as Diamond Dicky Rowland skipped across the muddy streets dodging mud puddles and horseshit. His shoes stayed just as shiny as his new diamond ring, bought with a ten-dollar tip given by a newly-minted oilfield millionaire. Flashing a wallet full of big bills to impress the other white men, the millionaire wasn't necessarily being generous to the shoeshine boy. Not being of equal worth to use the whites only bathroom, Diamond Dicky Rowland was obliged to cross the street that winter night to use the colored bathroom at the top of the building across the street. The elevator door opened and there was a new operator, a seventeen-year-old girl named Sarah Page. She already knew what floor Dicky wanted just by looking at him. They rode in silence to the fifth floor where Dicky exited quietly, soon to return and depart in the same manner, relieved.

He crossed the street and rode that elevator at least once a day every day he worked. Sometimes it was just the two of them in the elevator and eventually he knew Sarah's name, and she knew his. They weren't friends, but they came from something similar. She was a young divorcee, a child bride at the age of 15 left lonesome by her no-good husband after just six months. She took the only work available to her just as Dicky did. They knew it wasn't acceptable to fall in love, but life as they knew it wasn't acceptable anyway. Sarah liked the way Dicky was polite to her unlike the businessmen and their secretaries, always demanding her service without so much as a please or thank you.

It was as hot as summer already, but it was only the end of May, 1921. The sweaty elevator made everyone eager to get out. Sarah had been quietly keeping a secret. She had been waiting for days until finally it was just the two of them in the elevator. Soon Dicky found out that he was going to be a father. The news was as disturbing to him as it was for her to deliver. Unknowingly, the emotional reaction of these two young lovers ignited a firestorm of racist destruction.

As the elevator door opened, she cried. He ran. Tulsa burned.

I marvel how easy that story is. How easy it is to tell. How easy it is to believe. How badly so many of us want to make the relationship between Dick Rowland and Sarah Page into one of romance and all its interracial taboos. That's the one that people want to believe most, even though it's difficult to prove. That it's almost impossible to disprove is its appeal.

When I arrive at the park to hear Dwight, I am not surprised to find out the event is running late. The sun bears down with ferocity in the mid-afternoon, and I am pouring with sweat, happy to find shade beneath one of the awnings set up around the park. From there, I take in the park again. I try to count the number of times I've come here in the decade since it opened and get as far as six times, seven now, and not since last year. This park is gorgeous. The waterfall behind the Hope Plaza still flows as it did eleven years ago, and the flowers alongside the hedges protecting the walkways look like they've been freshly planted. I choose not to walk the labyrinth in the middle of the park pavilion called "Healing Walkway." Once had been enough. I watch others do it, though, stopping solemnly to read the plaques, as Dwight has tried to mix our local history with national history throughout his work. I remember the only sign of Buck Colbert Franklin at the park is a quote attributed to him across from the Tower of Reconciliation, which is built right in the middle of the park. "Lift as we climb, the eternal verities shall prevail," Buck Franklin's quote reads.

The Tower was built with the idea that you might start looking at its bottom, seeing the foundation of racial strife, then rise up with historical events toward reconciliation. I've never made it past the bottom. Though I've tried, I can't see past a foundation for society built on racism and violence. When I see the event is about to get started, I move closer to where I know Dwight will speak.

Several news crews set up cameras in front of a microphone where Dwight is to talk. He stands in the corner, a diminutive man, glad-handing folks dressed in their Sunday best like him. I think about introducing myself to him and then notice how I am dressed— gray cutoff-sleeved T-shirt, gray sweat shorts, and red Vans on my feet. I better not.

A crowd of about fifty begin taking seats on the grass and long benches inside the park. I keep seeing that word "reconciliation," and it vexes me. I put the word into the Google app search bar on my phone. It returns two definitions for the noun. "1. The restoration of friendly relationships. 2. The action of making one view or belief compatible with the other." That does not sound to me like it's what we are doing, not here, not this week, not in Tulsa. An older white woman sits down next to me. She looks strained with urgency.

"Did you see the poster on the way here?" she asks.

"Poster?"

"The Dick Rowland–Sarah Page poster? Flyer? On the sidewalk?"

"Oh, yeah. I saw it."

"Do you believe it? Do you think that's how it happened?"

Before I can answer, a voice booms from the speakers, filled with feedback. We cover our ears. Startled, a short Black woman backs away from the mic, waits for the sound techs to tell her they'll fix the problem, composes herself, and then addresses the audience once more. After speaking about how gorgeous the park is, she tells us about the remarkable Black man who's designed it. The park gets its name from one of America's foremost historians, John Hope Franklin, who might not have lived such a full life if not for his father and attorney, Buck Franklin.

Buck was born in Homer, Oklahoma, in the Chickasaw Nation of Indian Territory on May 6, 1879. His parents were David and Milley Franklin. In his book, *My Life and an Era: The Autobiography of Buck Colbert Franklin*, edited by John Hope and John Whittington Franklin, he said he "wanted to preserve for my children and posterity the fact that I had the greatest parents that ever lived in any age." He was named for his grandfather, a slave, who, as "property of a full-blood Chickasaw Indian family, the Birneys," saved for and bought his and his wife's and his ten kids' freedom.

Buck attended Roger Williams University and Morehouse College, back when it was still called Atlanta Baptist College. Though he didn't graduate from either, he found a mentor that he followed from RWU to ABC, and he named his son after him. Buck believed "[p]ossibly the greatest president and leader the school [Morehouse] ever produced was Dr. John Hope." After returning home following an illness that strickened his father, Buck applied for a permit to represent a woman, Eliza Harris, in gaining enrollment into the Chickasaw Nation. After helping her secure enrollment, he believed he'd found his calling.

"Awaiting the outcome of Mrs. Harris' case settled forever the question of my returning to college," Buck wrote. "The experience had done something to me: it had awakened and aroused something that had been asleep in me since that late evening when I had driven Colonel Stokes back home and he had said, dryly, 'The experience will help you when you become a lawyer.' Then, too, I've always been stubborn. I've never liked to see little people being picked on by big people." He studied law by mail using a correspondence course delivered from the Sprague Law School of Detroit, Michigan, in 1906. He sat for the bar exam in Oklahoma in November 1907 and received his passing grade—second highest among test takers—in August 1908.

In 1911, Buck was in court in Shreveport, Louisiana, for a client's case. When the judge called for Buck's client's case, Buck stood as his client's lawyer to show he represented the defense. The presiding judge's face turned quizzical, and he asked Buck why he was standing up. Buck told the judge that he was his client's attorney. The judge was aghast. He told Buck a "nigger" wouldn't act as a lawyer for any person in his courtroom. After handing down this admonishment, the judge forced Buck to leave the courtroom. Four years after this experience, his fourth and final child, John Hope Franklin, was born.

When John Hope was just six years old, his mother, Mollie Franklin, was packing up to take her family to Tulsa to join their father and her husband. But she received a telegram, just one day before the massacre began, telling her to stay in Rentiesville. The telegram told her the massacre would likely be ongoing by the time his message reached her and not to leave until she heard from Buck. He wanted his family safe while he performed the work of taking on Black clients who'd lost their businesses and homes and sought financial repairs and of collecting on their insurance claims immediately following the massacre. "While the ashes were still hot from the holocaust," Buck wrote, "certain questionable real-estate men influenced the mayor and city commissioners to enact an ordinance with an emergency clause prohibiting owners of lots in the burned area from rebuilding unless they erected fireproof roofs and buildings. At the time, I had formed a law firm consisting of attorneys I. H. Spears, T. O. Chappelle, and myself. We erected a tent as an office at 605 East Archer and employed Mrs. Effie Thompson as temporary secretary, since she and her husband had lost their drugstore in the fire. We immediately filed an injunction action against the city to enjoin and prohibit it from enforcing the ordinance. Among other things, we alleged that the fire was not the fault of our client, Joe Lockard; that to enforce such an ordinance would be equivalent to confiscation of property without due process; and further, that for all practical purposes, it would make the city a party to a conspiracy against the plaintiff and others similarly situated to despoil them of their property; it would be using the city for the selfish purpose of arraying citizens against each other; and such acts were outside the legitimate police power of the city. In the end, our client prevailed, but while the case was pending, a friend of ours was arrested a dozen times because he persisted in rebuilding his home and place of business." Buck and his firm "instituted dozens of lawsuits against certain fire insurance companies who had insured properties of families and firms in the destroyed area, but in all cases where the policies did not insure against 'riot, civil commotion,' and the like, no recovery was possible—fully 95 percent of cases."

Buck sued the city for passing the ordinance that banned Black Tulsans from rebuilding in Greenwood, and he won that suit in the Oklahoma Supreme Court. He worked as a civil rights attorney in Tulsa for more than fifty years, until his death on September 24, 1960. It was his life's work. He's buried in Tulsa at what was once called Booker T. Washington Cemetery and is now called Rolling Oaks Memorial Gardens.

When John Hope was born, his mother, Mollie, took maternity leave from her job as a schoolteacher just long enough for John Hope, the youngest of her four children, to learn to walk. She returned to the classroom with her son in tow because there was no such thing as a daycare center, and no family or friends to care for her child during the day. She gave her three-year-old a piece of paper, a pencil, and an order to be quiet or there would be consequences. Taking a look at her students' penmanship one day, she noticed John Hope had written something too. He'd copied the entire blackboard letter for letter, just as she had written it down. When she quizzed him about what he'd done, she learned her son could read and write at age four.

Buck moved from Rentiesville to Tulsa in February 1921. Mollie, who'd given birth to their third child by then, raised her children as a single mom for the next four years, which did not come without its challenges and abject racism. Living in Rentiesville then, it was not unusual for would-be passengers to take the Katy to and from Checotah. The train stopped and began moving again before Mollie, John Hope, and his sister, Anne, were seated. When the conductor walked into the car where they sat, he told them they'd have to move: that car was for whites only. Mollie refused on the grounds that it was too dangerous to take her children from one car to another while the train was in motion. She also took pains to point out the train had not stopped where she and her children could board the so-called Negro-only car. Having heard this, the conductor stopped the train. He forced Mollie and her two small children off the train to "teach them a lesson." They walked home through the woods. John Hope was six.

When John Hope was twelve, in 1927, he became a Boy Scout in Tulsa. He was in downtown Tulsa when he spotted an old white lady cautiously trying to cross the street. He saw right away that she could not see clearly. He tried to perform a good deed that day, as is required of every Boy Scout, and took it upon himself to escort her across the street. While in the middle of the intersection, the old, near-blind white lady asked John Hope if he was white or Black. He told her he was Black. She snatched her arm away from his grasp and demanded he keep his "filthy hands off her," he wrote in his autobiography. "Realizing that for her my race defined my cleanliness as well as my ability to guide her safely across a busy intersection, I left her stranded in the middle of traffic."

As a teenager, John Hope fondly remembered walking to his father's law office to talk, to investigate, to see Tulsa as the city was and as it still could be. John Hope plainly saw Black Tulsa,

Greenwood, for what the district was, and he wrote as much in his autobiography: "On the way to the modest two-story building that housed my father's office, I could view all of those small businesses that have recently—and inaccurately—been touted as 'Black Wall Street.' There were no banks or insurance companies as those in Richmond, Virginia, and Durham, North Carolina."

In the summer of 1928, John Hope worked a paper route without having his own paper route. As a team agent, he worked with a white man, D. Rippetoe, to deliver the *Tulsa Tribune* because the *Tribune* "did not permit African American boys to have their own paper routes." He worked with Rippetoe, taking the stacks from him after school and on weekends, hocking the editions in all-Black Greenwood. His reward for this was his pay and, sometimes, he could be the only Black paperboy listening to world championship boxing matches outside the *Tribune* building. "When the fight was over and the paper was easy, Mr. Rippetoe and I would get our quota, dash to Greenwood, and sell them to scores of anxious readers."

He left Tulsa as the valedictorian of the 1931 Booker T. Washington High School class. "I cannot remember the valedictory speech I gave at my high school graduation," he wrote in his autobiography. "The day's program is long lost and my memory of the event [is] clouded for having given so many commencement addresses in the last sixty years." What a flex. One year after John Hope graduated from Fisk, Buck Franklin lost their family home to foreclosure. When John Hope returned to Tulsa in the summer of 1941, a triumphing hero partnered with wife Aurelia Whittington Franklin, a Black man with a PhD in history from the country's oldest college, Harvard, his mother had passed away and his sister Mozella had moved in with their father Buck to take care of the aging man in an apartment without air-conditioning, where John Hope reported the temperature reached 115 degrees on some days. John Hope lived in Tulsa for only six years, from ages ten to sixteen.

In 1943, he became the first Booker T. graduate to deliver the commencement address to the graduating class.

Just three years earlier, John Hope's oldest brother, Buck Jr., had been a school principal in Bixby, Oklahoma, a suburb of Tulsa. He was drafted, and from indoctrination to discharge he was belittled and ridiculed by white servicemen who took great pride in reminding this former teacher and administrator he'd never do more than peel potatoes in their army. Weeks after his discharge, Buck Jr. fell into depression as he learned how little his service in defense of America mattered to white folks and how unlikely he was to find a job like the one he had before his drafting. In 1947, he traveled to Richmond, Virginia, to try to find a job among its Black business community. He booked a room at the Slaughter Hotel. That spring, just days after checking in, John Hope wrote in his autobiography, *Mirror to America*, that Buck Jr. "had fallen or jumped" from a second-story window of the hotel. He died a few days later. His father refused to allow physicians at McGuire Veterans Hospital in Richmond to perform an autopsy. Doctors suspected Buck Jr.'s lungs were riddled with cancer. Buck Sr. blamed the army for the loss of his boy. "In one of the few bitter statements I ever heard my father make," John Hope wrote, "he said they should not touch his son. They had butchered him enough, he declared, and the only thing to do now is to send him home." In fall 1947, John Hope published his first seminal work, *From Slavery to Freedom*, an early history of Black Americans, which reached a wide audience in the late 1960s.

John Hope became the first Black historian to become a full professor at a predominantly white institution, at Brooklyn College, and the first to become a chair of a history department, at the University of Chicago, a Tier One research university. He held over one hundred and thirty honorary degrees. For his work as a historian, he was awarded the Presidential Medal of Freedom in 1995. John Hope was a formidable mind and civil rights activist, but I felt the city got it wrong naming anything after him and is an example of how confused we sometimes seem in Tulsa. John Hope was a national treasure, a walking, talking Black history fact. But his best work, the work he is remembered for, did not take place in Tulsa. But his father's best work did. It's his father who was Tulsa's superhero.

And yet, there's B. C. Franklin Park, at the intersection of Virgin Street and Wheeling Avenue, tucked into the heart of North Tulsa, backed up against a dead-end road that overlooks Highway 75. There is a playground and two basketball courts with Oklahoma City Thunder logos covering both courts. In 2016, the city passed an $805,000 sales tax revenue and received gifts of $70,000 and $40,000 from the Thunder Cares foundation and Oklahoma Surgical Foundation, respectively, to renovate the park.[32] In June 2021, empty bottles of MD 20/20 wine, Mickey's malt liquor, and other trash decorated the parking lot and playground areas while nearby trash cans overflowed. Booker T. Washington High School is across the street. If you didn't already know who Buck Franklin was, you'd never know why the city named a park for him.

*

I contemplate the juxtaposition of Buck and John Hope Franklin in view of the city as Dwight steps to the microphone. Edward Joseph Dwight Jr. was born in Kansas City, Kansas, in 1933. His father, Ed Dwight Sr., played second and center fielder for the Kansas City Monarchs. Dwight Jr. became the first Black graduate at Bishop Ward High School in Kansas City in 1951. He earned an associate degree in engineering from Kansas City Junior College (now Metropolitan Community College). He enlisted in the Air Force in 1953, where he achieved the rank of captain, and he earned an aeronautics degree at Arizona State University in 1957. He graduated from ASU cum laude. At twenty-nine, in 1963, he graced the cover of *Jet* magazine after he became the first Black astronaut trainee in NASA's history.

He went on to earn an MFA in sculpting from the University of

Denver in 1977. The first major work he created was commissioned by the first Black lieutenant governor of Colorado, George Brown, in 1974.

When Dwight takes the microphone to soft applause, I am in awe. This man is walking, talking Black history—animated, alive.

At a podium in the park he created, Dwight tells us how he did not believe he was capable of creating the project for Lieutenant Governor Brown that is called *Black Frontier in the American West*. Still a student in sculpting then, he doubted his own skill. Brown told him this had to be done, and it had to be done by Dwight. Brown told Dwight he'd been to art museums all over the country, and he had not seen an exhibit created by a Black American, commenting on Black history. Dwight says he was miffed, not by the absence of Black art, by Black folks in art museums across the country, but by the notion that Black folks have done, created, built anything worthwhile. "I said, 'George, what did Black people do?'" Right then I'm sure Brown felt the shock that we do.

Here is a Black man, nearly forty years old in 1974, who had no concept of how brilliant his people were—remain—even as he is one of them. "I did not know who Harriet Tubman was until I was forty-two years old," Dwight tells us. This man, who is a walking Black history fact, admits to not knowing Black history. He tells us he is ashamed that he didn't know anything about our history at first, but that shame gave away to anger. He was angry that he'd been deprived, left ignorant, of the many triumphs of Black folks. Since then, he says he's made commemorating Black achievement his life's work. As he describes the park, the research he's performed to understand the massacre well enough to make an artful appreciation of it, I realize how little he believes us.

He refers to the massacre as a "riot." He claims there was "fighting on both sides." He tells us how the original plan wasn't for a park at all, but a single building where the signature structure, the twenty-five-foot Tower of Reconciliation, was meant to be inside of a building and not the centerpiece of the park. He tells us the reason the building never came to fruition was because of the threat of a lawsuit on behalf of survivors, and lays the blame for that at the feet of the Black attorney who'd filed the suit. "This was kind of like Black-on-Black crime," Dwight says. I wonder if he knew anything at all about Buck Franklin, about the bravery and resilience of a Black man who could've left Tulsa, opened a law office elsewhere, and been fruitful. I wonder if the attorney he speaks of in his story was not unlike Buck in ours.

I see my answer at Dwight's Hope Plaza, a sixteen-foot granite structure with three bronze men standing on it and three words written on the bottom: HOSTILITY, HUMILIATION, HOPE. Above HOSTILITY stands a white man with a rifle in each hand, one pointed toward the ground and the other perched on his shoulder. Above HUMILIATION stands a Black man with his hands raised in surrender. Above HOPE stands a white, male Red Cross worker cradling a Black infant. Then I realize this is the story white people tell about the massacre, and this is who Dwight has become: a man who believes the just and righteous thing to do is to commemorate Black Tulsans' humiliation at the hostility of white Tulsans. Only a white person's narrative of the massacre sees hope in that. After Dwight tells his story of what he felt was "Black-on-Black crime," I stand up and leave for home.

"REMEMBER & RISE" IS THE MARQUEE EVENT FOR THE centennial commission's week of activities, and people want to attend it. The concert is scheduled for Memorial Day afternoon, the day one hundred years ago when the massacre began, with headliners Stacey Abrams, John Legend, a video presentation from Mike Bloomberg, and HBO series *Watchmen* creator Damon Lindelof. Hill Harper is tapped to emcee the event from 4:00 to 6:00 p.m. Of the 6,000 tickets to the concert at ONEOK Field that went on sale at midnight on the twentieth of May, 3,500 sold in just twenty-seven minutes. The other 2,500 have been given to descendants of victims, sponsors, commissioners, and organizations in North Tulsa. Those who do not receive tickets are told the concert is going to be nationally televised—though the commission doesn't say on what network—and that other details about the schedule will be released in the coming days on the commission's website. Just an hour after I arrive home, the commission calls off the event and gives this statement to news organizations: "Due to unexpected circumstances with entertainers and speakers, the Centennial Commission is unable to fulfill our high expectations. We have hopes to reschedule later in this 100th commemorative year. We apologize for the disappointment and any inconvenience caused to ticket holders."

At first, news reports surface that the event has been canceled due to a terrorist threat from unnamed white supremacist organizations. Later in the evening, Greenwood Rising project manager Phil Armstrong, who led efforts to hold Remember & Rise, tells KWGS that those reports are false. "We're all disappointed," he says. "No one wanted to see John Legend more than myself."[33]

*

I speak with folks close to Justice for Greenwood, leading the charge to win financial compensation for Tulsa massacre survivors and victim descendants, and folks close to the centennial commission.

Damario Solomon-Simmons is executive director and founder for Justice for Greenwood, and he leads a group of attorneys who filed suit in Tulsa County court to gain reparations for survivors of the race massacre. Their lawsuit alleges that following the massacre, government officials enabled robbery, looting, and profiteering from the damage white Tulsans caused in Greenwood. The suit also alleges the local government not only did not help survivors recover the wealth they lost, but actively prevented Black Tulsans from rebuilding their businesses, rebuilding their homes. The two sides—Justice for Greenwood, and the centennial commission—cannot agree on the amount of money to be paid to survivors, who were going to act as speakers for the "Remember & Rise" event. State senator and commission chairman Kevin Matthews tells KWGS there is an agreement in place to pay the survivors $100,000 each and open an additional $2 million to establish a reparations fund. He claims that attorneys representing the three living survivors reneged and then demanded $1 million per person and an additional $50 million for the reparations fund.

"So, to be clear, I absolutely want the survivors, the descendants and others that were affected to be financially and emotionally supported," Matthews says.[34] "However, this is not the way, no matter how hard we try."

Phil Armstrong claims the same. "Those comments or whatever

your sources are for that, I would just say, hey, you're going to have to talk to them on who's directing those types of comments and ask them," Armstrong says. "I definitely wouldn't want them to speak on my behalf and I'm not going to even pretend to try to speak on their behalf. Any statements to the contrary that we have not had survivors and descendants a part of this is just false and extremely misleading. Who wouldn't want them to be there and be centered and honoring them? Again, any comment to the contrary is just false and misleading."

Armstrong is not the commission's first project manager, though. The first one was a Black man from Tulsa, a former classmate of mine at Booker T. and a former Mr. Hornet, Jamaal Nash-Dyer. When he was first hired to the project manager role in 2017, the commission was still called the 1921 Tulsa Race Riot Centennial Commission. He's the reason "Riot" was changed to "Massacre." But by 2019 he found himself forced to resign his position. He's senior pastor at North Tulsa's Friendship Church. "I'm speaking from experience," he told the *Washington Post*. "I was very vocal: 'If we are going to do this for the community, we need to allow them to be part of the decision-making body.' That was not welcomed. A year or two later, they went to them, but they had already started making decisions. They are still trying to control the narrative."

Nah, they aren't trying to control it—they do. They controlled the narrative of silence for seventy-five years. We didn't speak of it. Made each other feel crazy for saying those white folks shot us, burned us, dropped bombs from planes on us. Now, they're doing it again, making the narrative not about the Black death they wrought or the money they owe, but of an imagined Black Wall Street—a figment of their imagination birthed from the mind of a man who would rather not upset the white folks than challenge them.

The centennial commission raised $30 million and didn't put a red cent of it into the hands of the folks who need it. Instead, this is what they spent our wealth on:

- Greenwood Rising Black Wall Street History Center building and start-up operation: $20 million
- Greenwood Art Project: $1.2 million
- Pathway to Hope and Greenwood District markers: $1.75 million
- Greenwood Cultural Center Renovation: $5.3 million
- Commemoration activities—like Remember & Rise—community grants, educational programming, and economic development programming: $1.5 million

They built a Black Disney World House of Pain at the corner of Greenwood and Archer, and told us to be glad about it. But they are not the city. The centennial commission is not a city of Tulsa organization. And while the city has used this fact to try to distance itself from a discussion of financial compensation to see the lawsuit filed by the three survivors dismissed, it also highlights how little the city has been involved in performing a function that even pretends to appease Black Tulsans or care to make us whole.

*

The oldest living survivor of the Tulsa Race Massacre, 107-year-old Viola Fletcher, sits at a hearing in Washington, D.C., in May 2021, where she recalls the event and the effect it has had on her life in detailed testimony before a congressional subcommittee.

"I will never forget the violence of the white mob when we left our home," Fletcher says. "I still see Black men being shot, Black bodies lining the street. I still smell smoke and see fire. I still see Black businesses being burned. I still hear airplanes flying overhead. I hear the screams. I have lived through the massacre every day. Our country may forget this history, but I cannot. I will not, and other survivors do not. And our descendants do not."

However, the *World* publishes an account on May 29, 2021, of a video interview Fletcher sat for in 2014.[35] At 100 years old, in the interview conducted for a centenarian's project at Oklahoma State

University, she said she did not remember the massacre because she was too young. "Well, my family was, but I think they left during that time," Fletcher said. "Let's see . . . see, I was real young then, about five to six years old. I don't remember anything about that." She also said in that interview that she was not living in Tulsa when the massacre occurred. Fletcher participated in one other interview in 2014 for the Dwight Eisenhower Library, in which she said she attended school in Claremore and Nowata, moving from Claremore to Tulsa when she got married in 1932.

When the *World* reaches out to Fletcher's attorney, Solomon-Simmons, for comment, he provides this statement: "Hoping to change the subject rather than discuss a childhood trauma, Mother Fletcher simply said she was five or six years old around that time and that she didn't 'remember anything about that.' . . . It is only in more recent years that Mother Fletcher has been willing to openly discuss the massacre and her memories of that terrible night."

Two days later, folks caring for Fletcher help her into a pair of Hyper Royal Air Jordans—an expensive and difficult to procure pair of sneakers. They let an employee at Silhouette Sneakers & Art, a boutique across the street from the history center, take photos of her and post them to Instagram on the store's account.[36] "We had to gift Mother Fletcher her first pair of J's!" the caption reads.

Complex Sneakers reposts one of the pictures to its Twitter account, and the tweet receives over 5,500 retweets and 21,600 likes on the platform.[37] Silhouette Sneakers & Art turns Mother Fletcher into a mascot for its store.

It's not the gift of the shoes that angers me. It's the snapping of the photo and posting it to Instagram for the purpose of publicity. We are turning our own jewels into mascots, celebrating our destruction, and calling it commemorating. But this legacy of self-promotion, of boosterism, is one I know well. In Tulsa, if you do not

blow your own horn, there is no music. We claim John Hope Franklin, even though he lived in Tulsa for just six years. We let everyone
from our local historians to the Associated Press, *The Washington
Post*, and *The New York Times* perpetuate this myth that Booker
T. Washington called Greenwood the "Negro Wall Street of America." Even with those people so precious to us, like Mother Fletcher,
we're eager for the nation's attention and care none for each other's.
Our habit is to claim those things that are not ours and ignore those
things that can help us heal.

CBS News publishes a story on May 29, 2021, that contains part
of an email from Solomon-Simmons to the commission, accusing
Kevin Matthews of attacking "the credibility and integrity of our
survivors." The email sets terms for the survivors' participation in
"Remember & Rise." "As a result, this is where we are and/or what
we need in order to come to an agreement at this point," Solomon-
Simmons says. He writes that a $1 million fee per survivor is a "pri-
ority for us," and $50 million for a "Survivor and Descendant fund."

I reach out to a source close to the centennial commission
leadership to ask if all of this is what he's been working with over
the last two years. "If you thought Baptists could be mean to each
other," he replies, "you should see this."

"The context of the email was that a commission donor would
give $100,000 per survivor and $2 million to a reparation fund,"
a source close to the commission tells me. "Per the email, this was
supposed to remain a secret between the donor and [Solomon-
Simmons] who represents the survivors and this gift was initially
accepted by both parties."

The news about the gift is made public in a news story published on May 22, 2021, by Community Newspaper Holdings
Inc, Oklahoma: "Matthews said one of the center's donors has
independently agreed to pay the three survivors salaries and assist
with their health care costs during the remainder of their lives."[38]
When Solomon-Simmons read that the gift was made public by

the CNHI story, he countered with the $1 million per survivor and a $50 million fund. On June 3, 2021, Solomon-Simmons and Tiffany Crutcher are among those handing the three living massacre survivors—Viola Fletcher, Lessie Benningfield Randle, and Hugh Van Ellis—$100,000 gifts days after the "Remember & Rise" fallout.

In May 2021, Tulsa Metropolitan Ministries and All Souls Unitarian Church partner to facilitate raising $100,000 to be paid as reparations to survivors. On Father's Day, June 20, Tulsa's Transformation Church announces $200,000 gifts for each of the three survivors as a part of a $1 million day of giving. "Reparations start in the church," Transformation Church senior pastor Mike Todd tells his congregation while holding service in Greenwood. Todd's mentor is Gary L. McIntosh, who founded Transformation Church in 2015 before retiring. He named Todd his successor. McIntosh, a white man, is an original founding pastor at Carlton Pearson's Higher Dimensions Family Church. Pearson and McIntosh were roommates at Oral Roberts University. "We kept the leadership integrated, looking and feeling integrated, which made non-[B]lacks less intimidated to come," Pearson told the *Tulsa World* in 1996. In 2019, Todd and Transformation Church bought Spirit Bank event center for $10 million, and he told KOTV his church paid back the loan it received for the purchase in six months.[39] In December 2020, Todd and the church bought property just south of Tulsa for $20.5 million. The property, called Post Rock Plaza, is a retail shopping center that counts thirty-four businesses as tenants.

Transformation has leveraged social media to disseminate its content with more than 42,000 followers on Twitter, 481,000 on Instagram, 239,000 on Facebook, and a YouTube subscriber base of over 1.4 million as of June 1, 2021. Todd's four-part series called "Relationship Goals" generated more than 20 million total views on YouTube, and 8.4 million from the first video in the series alone by June 1, 2021. A channel the size of Tulsa's Transformation Church's

228 R J YOUNG

can generate $500,000 to $1 million from ad revenue from video-on-demand alone.

Money is made during this short period in Tulsa—millions around the centennial of a Black massacre. I see little evidence that this money benefits Black Tulsans directly, save those survivors who are gifted hundreds of thousands in what Justice for Greenwood and Transformation Church call donations. What's clear, though, is that the city of Tulsa is not tasked with this responsibility, and neither are its citizens.

"Paying reparations to the survivors, descendants and Greenwood community is a civic responsibility," TMM Executive Director Aliye Shimi tells *Tulsa World*. "Tulsa Metropolitan Ministries and Tulsa's faith communities are calling on the city to move forward with repaying the debt made by the strategic destruction that was led by the city leaders." If TMM and All Souls reach their goal, that's $400,000 raised and given to each of the survivors. When I tell one of my white friends and a lifelong Tulsan this, he is ecstatic.

"Why haven't I heard more about that?" he says.

"I don't think it's something to crow about," I say.

"Why not? Isn't it great that they got something?"

I pause, thinking through my answer, trying to unearth a part of me that I don't like displaying before white folks. "I don't think it's anything to crow about because that money was raised, donated. I'm glad people want to try to make this right for them. But you and I are not named in the lawsuit. The city of Tulsa, the sheriff department, the park authority, the chamber of commerce, the military, those are the entities, the people, responsible for making them and North Tulsa financially whole again."

"But has that happened before?"

I sigh. "When the city of Minneapolis agreed to a $27 million settlement in a federal lawsuit for the murder of George Floyd, it happened. When the city of Cleveland agreed to pay a $6 million settlement to Tamir Rice's mama, it happened. The city of Evanston, Illinois, agreed to enact a 3 percent tax on weed to raise $10 million in reparations to its Black citizens over ten years. It's happened and happening."[40]

"I didn't know that."

"Because you didn't have to."

*

By Friday, a day after I heard Dwight speak, the shape of the centennial has begun to feel surreal to me, with people slowly dividing themselves into four groups: people who do not want to reckon with the massacre, people who believe there is little to reckon with, people who believe this massacre is an event to celebrate, and finally a few Black folks who see that only a small amount of work has been done, and how much will probably never get done.

People from out of town, showing up to Tulsa on a weekend to gawk at this macabre circus, feel both obtuse and impolite when I meet them. The more people not from Tulsa I meet, the angrier I become.

As more folks from out of town descend on the district, on my city, I feel like I must defend, explain, or interrogate all of them, and my city too. We, Tulsans, are still on our bullshit. We are not reckoning, not repairing, just lapping up this attention like *Isn't this grand?* instead of *Fuck you, pay me.* I'm telling this to a tourist, a Black man wearing a BLACK WALL STREET T-shirt over his hoodie. He's a reminder of just how unseasonably cool the weather is, no higher than sixty-seven degrees with a light cool breeze.

"How does it feel to have the nation show Tulsa this kind of love?" he asks.

"Is this love?" I say.

"Yeah! People care!"

"People care, huh?" I say. "You care, huh?"

"That's what I'm saying!" he says.

"So you're saying you're down with reparations?"

He studies me like he wants to ask me something harsh and mean but can't bring himself to say it with his whole chest. It's the first time I've seen someone look at me like they don't know if I'm the wrong nigga to fuck with in more than a year. And I'm struck by how much I miss seeing that look on someone's face. Yes, fear me. I have seen and felt pain, and I'm still standing right here. "Is it just about the money to you?" he asks.

I point to his shirt. "You're the person with the Black Wall Street shirt on."

*

On the Saturday before Memorial Day, the air is crisp, the breeze cool, and the sky looks the way a child would color it. A storm has come and gone since Thursday evening, a storm so powerful that the whole of northeastern Oklahoma is under a tornado watch for most of the afternoon and through sunset in the evening. A storm so powerful it knocks the electricity out in my house for three hours with a gust that feels blown from the cheeks of an angry god. Even a day on, the temperature dares not to rise above seventy degrees in my neighborhood for the next two days.

Perhaps this angry god is washing away the refuse from a centennial commission's doings it knows are wrong. Perhaps this is one of the last beautiful days as we head toward scorched-earth temperatures. I am grateful either way when I step into my truck and drive across town to the gym. I listen to NPR's Scott Simon tell me about political gridlock in D.C., the Senate's deft use of the filibuster to crush an attempt to investigate the capitol riot, thwarted coup d'état, and successful insurrection, before turning off my radio completely.

There is still a part of me that does not want to believe this is my country, that this nation could hate us this much, when I turn off Memorial Drive and into the gym parking lot where American flags are already beginning to sprout up. The parking lot is full. The last day for many schools in Tulsa was only yesterday, and it looks as if we all had the same idea anyway: Go work out.

A year ago we were locked in our homes, or supposed to be, and just weeks after some of us have begun to get our first doses of a vaccine, everyone has begun claiming they've taken it. I believe people crowing about having received both doses of either vaccine are lying about it. In a state where many challenge science and refuse to believe in the value of vaccination, we live with more liars than not. As I put the truck into park, I lean my head back against the headrest and think about my own vaccination experience. At CVS after getting stuck for the first time, I was told to sit in a waiting area for fifteen minutes. The vaccine might give me superpowers. A Black man with a Vietnam veteran hat on his head, a Pittsburgh Steelers mask covering his face, and a toddler in his lap asked me which one I got.

"Pfizer."

"I got Moderna." He looked down at his grandson. "My daughter mad at me 'cause she wanted me to get that Pfizer. I told her I don't give a fuck. They ain't gone kill me. Soon as they said I could have it? I'm having it, goddamn it. I ain't dying. Not like that. I'm gone survive."

Survival is a Black superpower. Five weeks until I survive this virus too, I thought then. I should've expected to have to survive more, so much more.

I step out of my truck at the gym and try to squeeze between a black Toyota Sequoia and a crimson Ford Edge when the sight of that sticker on the driver's side rear of the windshield smacks me between the eyes like a punch I should've seen fit to parry long before it scored a point:

KEEP AMERICA GREAT.

Just below those three words on the bumper sticker rings out these two:

TRUMP 2020.

It's nearly June, 2021. This is where I live.

THE NEW BLACK PANTHER PARTY MAKES ITS SECOND Amendment Armed Mass March through the Greenwood District on Saturday afternoon. The Party was once led by Malik Zulu Shabazz, who also acts as attorney general for the party. He studied political science and law at Howard University and Howard University School of Law, respectively.

It is the third event of their National Convention for Black Power, which began Friday afternoon with a five-hour event called "Black Holocaust Remembrance/Reparations Night" held at Vernon Chapel AME and the Pre-Second Amendment Armed March Speakout that began at roughly 9:00 a.m. on Saturday morning and lasted until 2:00 p.m. with the march beginning at 3:00 p.m. But it is Black folks walking through the streets, wearing black, waving red, black, and green flags with guns out, who receive the most attention for the group. With a black-and-white banner stretching the width of a street that reads REPARATIONS NOW, Party members and associates march through the streets with one hand on the banner and the other raised in a fist. Others, walking behind, carry assault rifles. They follow a call-and-response chant from one man with a megaphone alternating between chants of "Black power!" and "Freedom or death!" The Party's motto for the national convention in Tulsa is "Never Again: Repair, Rebuild, Defend."

The Tulsa Police Department feels compelled to publish a release on its Facebook page after the march deviates "from its scheduled path and is now grouping outside of the entrance of the Legacy Fest. Officials with the Legacy Fest do not want visitors carrying weapons in the Greenwood area and the marchers are demanding entrance into the area." Some construe this as TPD, and perhaps the Legacy Fest officials, trying to stop the Panthers from exercising their rights as citizens. TPD updates its post shortly after publishing the first: "To be clear, this is not an issue with people marching and exercising their 2nd Amendment rights. This is a traffic issue with a group that received a permit to march during a predetermined time (6:00 p.m.) and predetermined path. At this time the group is marching through the streets of downtown Tulsa creating traffic issues for motorists. We are attempting to get in compliance with the permit and traffic regulations."

The comments below TPD's post do not agree: "'Attempting to work with the group' to get 'in compliance' should have quickly transitioned to arresting the criminals! Do your job Tulsa PD or we're going to wind up with another Portland or Seattle on our hands. We get the lawlessness that we allow." Another comment: "Why are y'all so hateful the white nationalist party can March downtown people whip Air at Trump Rally's with actual whips two comps can be gunned down by a convicted felon in which they gave multiple opportunities to step out the car kindly Mass grave sites can be found from bombings 100 years ago and people protesting about how their lives matter is what gets your blood flowing[.]"

I sometimes wonder if white Tulsans have any idea why Black folks march in Tulsa.

*

At the cultural center, at 3:00 p.m. Saturday, there is a summit featuring attorney Ben Crump, attorney Lee Merritt, Allisa Charles-Findley (sister of Botham Jean), Nyesha Barre-Hall (sister of Joshua Barre), Tulsa activist Chief Egunwale Amusan, and actor Kendrick Sampson. They sit down in a semicircle on stage at the auditorium to discuss "How to Imagine a World Where Black Lives Matter." The auditorium is full of us—Black folks. Nearly every seat has a butt in it. We wear the red, black, and green of the United Negro Improvement Association, pan-African in the house, across our chests. I take a seat in the middle section, near the back, at the end of the row. Almost as soon as I sit, a Black woman with a Kobe Bryant mural across her chest politely asks me if she could get by. I stand, give her room, and watch her embrace a friend.

A mixed family—him Black, her white, their baby caramel—sit just behind me.

"Do I look red?" she asks.

"Not *that* red," he says.

I notice a woman in a bright orange Florida A&M T-shirt and dark green mask with FAMU written on one side. Perhaps a third of the room is masked up, not unlike the population outside. I've grown so accustomed to seeing some people wear masks and some people not that I no longer feel the need to investigate this phenomenon. We're in locs and naturals and braids and perms and wave caps. We're in red house shoes and green, black and red Jordans, and highlighter-yellow Air Maxes. On stage, I notice a member of the Panthers standing nearby, providing security for the speakers.

Of the few white people I see, one, a white man, wears a Colin Kaepernick jersey. Another, a white woman, wears a T-shirt that reads USE YOUR PRIVILEGE. She scurries up to the stage to make sure each speaker has their own cordless microphone. I've been to birthday parties in this room, seen my friend Bruce fight in a boxing match for a belt no one had ever heard of in this room, and gone to a white sorority's winter formal in this room. I catch myself smiling about that when Crump stands. His black suit and white shirt make it difficult not to focus on his solid gold tie.

Crump introduces each of the panelists and then asks the crowd to give Dr. Tiffany Crutcher a round of applause. He points toward the back, and there she is in a purple suit over a black sequined blouse and black Converse. Her cheeks rise above the mask, the only indication that she is smiling.

Crutcher and her family hired Crump to represent them in seeking justice for her brother, Terrence, who was fatally shot in North Tulsa by a Tulsa Police officer with his hands still in the air. Within three days of his hiring, Crump was walking next to Crutcher, leading a protest march for justice for Terrence. Crutcher's killer was acquitted of criminal charges and hired in neighboring Rogers County. The state supreme court later dismissed a wrongful death suit against the city of Tulsa. Crump has won settlements for the families of Botham Jean, George Floyd, Breonna Taylor, and Michael Brown—all unarmed Black folks killed by police.

Crump spent his childhood in North Carolina. His mother sent him to Fort Lauderdale, Florida, as a teenager to stay with her second husband, the man he calls his father. He attended high school in Fort Lauderdale and graduated from Florida State University and its College of Law.[41] He had to write a personal statement to get into law school, in which he cited Thurgood Marshall as his hero. In 2006, he won a civil suit against Bay County, Florida, for the parents of fourteen-year-old Martin Lee Anderson, a boy beaten to death by guards at Bay County Boot Camp in Panama City, Florida. In 2012, his name became nationally known for representing the family of Trayvon Martin.[42] After the applause died down, Crump reminds the crowd why he thinks we are here.

"I will say this," he says, "just to put it in proper context before we hear from these acclaimed individuals, it is so important that we're here today to be part of this commemoration of the one-hundred-year remembrance of the Black Wall Street massacre. Because we have to understand that this injustice was probably the greatest injustice of our people other than slavery, when you put it in context. I mean, when you think about Terrence Crutcher or George

Floyd or Botham Jean, or Breonna Taylor, Ronald Greene, any of the individuals that have been killed by police violence? Multiply that by one hundred times. And that's what you will get when you think about the Black Wall Street massacre."

After he finishes explaining why he believes our participation in commemorating the massacre is important, he asks each of the speakers to answer the topic question. For Lee Merritt, the answer is accountability. Merritt, like Crump, is a civil rights attorney. He grew up in South Central Los Angeles. His father, Gregory, was a member of the Rollin 60s Crips, and Merritt learned the value of community from him. His most visceral memory of Black injustice is the infamous video of LAPD officers beating Rodney King, and he became enthralled with the idea of becoming a defender of Black folks when he watched Johnnie Cochran do the same.

Merritt attended Morehouse College and then taught for Teach for America in Camden, New Jersey, before attending and graduating from Temple University Beasley School of Law. He rose to national prominence representing victims of R. Kelly; Mark Hughes after being wrongly identified as the man who gunned down five Dallas police officers in 2016; victims of the carnage wrought by Charlottesville white supremacists; and victims of police brutality, the latter particularly in Texas.[43] Through his friendship with Shaun King, which began when they were in college together at Morehouse, he's been extremely effective in leveraging social media to gain traction for his legal cases. At the summit, Merritt stresses reverence for slain Black folks. That those deaths need to be treated with utmost respect, and the best way to do that is to seek justice under the law. Merritt represents the family of Ronald Greene, a forty-nine-year-old unarmed Black man who was stunned, choked, and punched by six Louisiana State Policemen in May 2019 after they caught up to him at the conclusion of a high-speed chase. Greene died after suffering such physical abuse. Those officers took him to a hospital, where they claimed he'd run into a tree. Doctors found two stun-gun probes in Green's body. Two years later, in May 2021, video obtained by the Associated Press showed how the officers battered Greene. The Greene family filed a federal suit against the state for wrongful death.

"In the state of Louisiana," Merritt says, "the people of Louisiana have not come to a standstill to say 'No, Ronald Greene's life mattered.' It's the same lessons that I got as a young kid in South Central every once in a while on the block at Hyde Park where I'm from when someone would die. It could be a drive-by, it could be little Latasha Harlins, when I was a kid. It could be Rodney King who wasn't killed, but he was beaten brutally. And then every once in a while, a person of Anglo-Saxon descent, someone with white skin will come to my community and die. And then we knew as kids somebody died on our block and the block is hot. You can't go outside. You're not allowed to walk to 42nd Street Elementary anymore. The block is hot because somebody died. And there must be what? Accountability. That's the reason for the existence, the purpose of, the Black Lives Matter movement. It's that our community will stop the same way the white community does and say, 'No, someone died, there must be accountability, because our lives matter.' To me, that's what Black Lives Matter means."

Kendrick Sampson, an actor, takes a more specific line, receiving applause and amens as he speaks. "We're giving representation and expected to be appeased by hyper-visibility instead," he says. "So when you look at this new administration, the Biden administration, and it's more diverse? 'Diverse' has almost become a curse word. But, you know, it's more diverse than any other administration? Of course it is. It's a white supremacist institution."

When the crowd does not immediately clap, he asked, "Oh, y'all not gone clap for that?" A few more people clap and laugh nervously. But Sampson, wearing a black track suit, looks pleased to dispel the image the audience might have had of him from his performances in *Insecure, CSI, How to Get Away with Murder,* and *The Vampire Diaries.*

"America is a white supremacist institution. We're occupying Indigenous land right now," Sampson says. "They stole resources from our community—from *Black* folks, right—and our labor, and they're living and profiting off of it still today. It's not a mistake that there was a massacre in Tulsa. After we got our shit together, right? Despite them extracting all of our resources, torturing and murdering us and enslaving us."

Crump asks Nyesha Barre-Hall to tell us what she'd tell her brother Joshua if she could see him one more time. He tried to walk into a convenience store carrying two knives and was fatally shot by two sheriff's deputies and a TPD officer for it, just a few miles north of the cultural center at Forty-Sixth Street North and Martin Luther King Boulevard, on June 9, 2017. "I would say that I love you," she says, "and mental illness matters. And even if it's one person that we can help, change, or make a difference? The Don't Hurt Them Help Them Joshua Barre Foundation will be their change. I would tell him that he didn't do anything wrong. In fact, it was your purpose to go the way that you did in order to save other lives and other souls." Barre-Hall and her family began a foundation to help Black folks find help with mental illness following his death. Her brother was diagnosed as bipolar and had stopped taking his medication days before being killed. Joshua's brother, Anthony Barre, later told KJRH that Joshua likely walked into the convenience store because it was one place where he felt safe. "He visited the convenience store almost every day," Anthony said. "He was scared. So, he was just trying to go where he felt safe."

Crump gives a similar question to Allisa Charles-Finley: if she knew she'd have one last time to talk to her brother, what would she say? "I think there's so much that I would have liked to say to him," she says. "I know one thing is that [I would say] I love you. It's something we did after every conversation." Charles-Finley is the president of the Botham Jean Foundation. Her work at the foundation focuses on building community in Saint Lucia, where Jean is from.

"Our last conversation on September 6 [2018]. We spoke about everything until he entered his apartment. And when we hung up the phone, I thought, damn, we didn't say I love you, and I was going to call back and I said, Well, I'll speak to him tomorrow. And tomorrow never came. So I would just, I would tell him, I loved him." An off-duty and five-year veteran of the Dallas Police Department, Amber Guyger, mistakenly entered Charles-Finley's brother's apartment. She thought Jean was a burglar in *her* apartment and fatally shot him in the chest.

When the speakers finish their hour of conversation, it is standing room only in the auditorium. As the speakers stand to make way for the next summit, I overhear conversation from the mixed couple behind me.

"That was so good," he says.

"It really was," she says. "It—"

She is about to say something more when a Black woman, perhaps in her late twenties, appears in front of me, bends down, and starts cooing at the baby girl in the couple's stroller. "Is this your baby?" she asks of the white woman.

The white woman looks a bit startled. "Yes, yes she's ours."

"Ooo wee, she's gorgeous." The Black woman looks up. She wears red glasses, has her hair up in a tight bun. Her gold shirt reads BLACK LIVES MATTER across the chest in black font. She takes in the white woman's face. "Now, you teach her. You teach her what went on here today, what's going on here right now. You got one of ours, and you say something if you need us." She bends over, coos at the baby girl one more time, and raises up once more. "Y'all have a good afternoon."

I stand to walk after this Gen Z Black woman. I want to know her name. I want to ask her about the conversation she had with the couple. She stops just in front of a couple of other Black women. I pull up, not wanting to intrude on her conversation.

"Who was that?" one of her friends asks.

"Another Dick and Sarah," she says.

The trio laughs.

"He'll learn," one says.

"Or he won't, but whatever," the other says.

As they laugh, continuing their conversation, my cheeks burn. I turn back to look at the family—this Black man, white woman, and their mixed baby girl—and they are gone. I scan the auditorium and don't see them. I peer around the corner toward the exit. They are leaving as the next summit begins to get underway.

Just before taking my seat again in preparation for what I suspect will be the best of the symposiums throughout the festivities, a white friend texts me.

"Are you downtown?" he asks.

"I'm at the cultural center."

"I've some friends in town. I was thinking of taking them to Reconciliation Park and a few other landmarks. What do you suggest?"

"Bring them here. Bring them to us."

When he doesn't reply immediately, I look to find my seat.

If Merritt and Crump fancy themselves following a path first cut by Thurgood Marshall, Damario Solomon-Simmons litigates in the tradition of Buck Franklin. Franklin successfully used his admission to the bar to advocate and use rule of law to get back the right of Black Tulsans to rebuild following the massacre. With his case on behalf of survivors still working through the court system, Solomon-Simmons hopes to achieve even more. Like Franklin, he is descended from Creek Freedmen who were in Oklahoma prior to statehood. In addition to graduating college and law school at the University of Oklahoma, he is a Booker T. alumnus and legacy.

His grandmother graduated from high school in 1950. Two of his uncles graduated in 1956 and 1957. He graduated in 1994 with the goal of playing professional football. "My goal in life was to play at Carver [Middle School], Booker T, OU, and the Dallas Cowboys. And I made three of those." Later, he represented fellow Booker T. alumnus and Cowboys running back Felix Jones. "So I feel like I got there too."

He attended OU's law school on a full scholarship and earned his juris doctorate in 2004, moved back to Tulsa, and opened his own practice soon after, expecting to live the life of a sports agent. But the more he looked around Tulsa, the less he saw being done for Black folks, his folks. He sought to change that first by cofounding the MVP Foundation, an organization focused on creating enrichment programs for middle-school-aged Black kids in the courts as a civil rights litigator. For the last half decade, along with a team of lawyers, he's made this case for reparations his focus.

As Solomon-Simmons takes a seat in the semicircle to begin a conversation about Tulsa's case for reparations, Texas Congresswoman Sheila Jackson Lee, Missouri Congresswoman Cori Bush, Human Rights Watch reporter Dreisen Heath, and Color of Change president Rashad Robinson take their seats while moderator and MSNBC host Tiffany Cross begins to introduce each of them. She returns to Solomon-Simmons and asks what the crux is of the suit he filed.

"The crux of it is that harm was done, and damage was done to a people one hundred years ago," he says. "We know who was harmed. We know what was stolen. It's very well documented. And we know who did it. We know the city of Tulsa authorized it, they armed them, and they gave them instruction to invade Greenwood. We know the county participated. We know the county sheriff participated. We know the Chamber of Commerce not only participated in the massacre, but after the massacre, when they put us in internment camps and forced us to work as enslaved people cleaning up our own communities. So, when they say they're not responsible, is the chamber still around? Is the city of Tulsa still around? Is the county, Tulsa County, still around? Is the state of Oklahoma? OK, so if the same entities who perpetrated the massacre, and it's one hundred years of continuing harm through policy violence are still around, they're still responsible. And we can, with the help of everyone here and everyone listening, hold them accountable."

Cross turns her focus toward Congresswoman Jackson Lee, who has succeeded in getting H.R. 40, named for the "forty acres and mule" the government claimed it would issue formerly enslaved Black folks post–Civil War, out of the House Judiciary Committee after more than three decades of effort from her peers. Lee, in her eleventh term as the representative for Texas's Eighteenth Congressional District, which counts Houston as its largest city, earned her undergraduate degree at Yale University in 1972 and her law degree at the University of Virginia in 1975. In 1987, she earned a municipal judgeship. In 1994, she ran for and won her seat and went unchallenged in the Democratic Primary for the office for twelve years. Now in her seventies, she has begun to make government-paid reparations her central fight. Cross asks her what the role of the federal government is and should be in the fight for reparations for Tulsans, and how H.R. 40 can help shape and contextualize that fight.

"It is important to take note of the fact that the H.R. 40 was written one year after a Republican president issued reparations for our brothers and sisters who are Japanese Americans," Lee says, "who, in fact, were interned in the 1940s. And we people of color, those of us who are descendants of enslaved Africans, rallied around our friends, the Japanese Americans for Ronald Reagan, to sign the Civil Liberties Act of 1988. I'm boasting about that, because I am not a fearful person, that means I do not fear you, if you're in trouble, I'm in a ditch, I'm gonna get you out of the ditch, I'm not gonna be afraid of you. And so as African Americans, my own un-angry approach is don't be afraid of us. We, too, are America. And we, too, must not be disenfranchised, and our pain must not be ignored. And our story to be told and adopted. It's ours, says the law."

As Congresswoman Lee speaks for nearly ten minutes without a break, I listen intently as heads nod. She advocates including as many people in the fight for reparations for Black folks as possible. While most in the auditorium look like agreeing, I hear nuances that irritate me. "As I close on this question, I, too, am American," Lee said. "I wear the uniform of a police officer, hear me out. When I say that, you know, your brothers, your sisters, your friends, your neighbors, etc. The one that, you know, I wear the uniform of the United States military. Uncle 'Red' [Hughes Van Ellis], one hundred and one years old, a Tulsan, went to World War II, they wanted him to be nothing. He should have been so angry that he did nothing. But he fought in World War Two. With that in mind, I too am America."

Cross then pulls Congresswoman Bush into conversation, and shares an anecdote about the freshman congresswoman from Missouri. "Every time I say her name I want to say Congresswoman Ain't Never Scared. Another member of Congress told me Marjorie Taylor Greene might be crazy, but she ain't stupid. She knows who not to run up on. She found out when she had a little encounter with Congresswoman Cori Bush."

As a registered nurse and church pastor, Bush began her career in activism and politics after former Ferguson police officer Darren Wilson fatally shot unarmed Michael Brown in 2014. As thousands took to the streets and many drove across the country to Ferguson to join the growing protests, Bush and others set up a tent feet from where Brown's body had lain and created a crisis response pop-up center for those experiencing trauma and grief. By 2020, she'd become the first Black woman elected to Congress from the state of Missouri, representing a district that includes not just Ferguson, but the St. Louis Cardinals, Anheuser-Busch's base operations, and the wealthy Central West End neighborhood in St.

Louis. She presented herself not as a congresswoman from Missouri but as a Black woman doing what she could to survive in America, like Black Tulsans, without knowing that many of the challenges she faced daily were not of her own making.

Cross asks Bush to tell her what reparations might do for Tulsans and descendants of the massacre. "Just coming from a place where I didn't understand or know that the things that I was going through was not my fault, just living the way that I was living," she says. "Just always feeling like I couldn't get anywhere. Am I a bad person? Did I do this to myself? What is wrong with me that I can't get out of debt? What is wrong with me? That I work a low wage job, even though I'm taking care of somebody else's kids all day long? And I'm teaching them how to read and teaching them Spanish, and I'm doing all of this, and I don't even have healthcare. And it's messing up my credit. And I'm in a payday loan cycle, and I just couldn't understand. Am I not worth more? How do people get them where they have a life where they don't have to worry every single day that something is going to be shut off? Like what does that look like?"

Until recently, that was her life. Two Black women sitting immediately in front me lean in, clasp their hands, and then hold each other's. Veins around their thumb knuckles pulse as their grips grow tighter as Bush describes watching not just her patients but her neighbors die because they could not afford health insurance; because they did not have access to clean water; because they had to ration insulin; because they could not afford to put food on the table. Reparations is only a start for her, because that is what is owed to victims. "I went to Congress to save lives," Bush says. "I can't even help you until I save your life first. So I went to Congress to save your life first, and then later I can help you."

Bush receives the most raucous applause of any panelist so far. Rashad Robinson follows her, feeling honored to be in Tulsa on this occasion, pitching his organization and then telling crowd members to take out their phones and send a text to a number. I watch, a bit awed, as so many follow his instructions and are willing to give their personal contact information to his organization without a second thought. He claims that by texting "Tulsa" to the designated number, his organization, Color of Change, "will sign you up to the work. It's going to ask you for your zip code and ask you to engage the people in your networks, because what we're going to be doing over the next year is working to support H.R. 40, working to fight for infrastructure, working to fight at the local level, to force prosecutors to be accountable to our communities, and working right here with you on supporting Damario and the survivors on the road ahead."

"Then what?" I say underneath my breath. I'm cynical about anyone who gets on a stage and asks a room full of strangers to give up their personal information or their money, even though Robinson and Color of Change successfully led a lobbying effort to force Facebook to independently audit its platform for hate groups, and his tactics for direct-asks work. Since becoming president of Color of Change in 2011, its membership has grown from 650,000 to 7.2 million, and the organization has made *Fast Company*'s Most Innovative Companies List in 2015, 2018, and 2020. His resume and success on a national level is substantial, but there is nothing about what he says that leads me to believe he understands the place Greenwood is, the place it could've been, or the place it still could be.

In Dreisen Heath, though, we hear from another person on the panel who has taken time to investigate and understand not only the aftermath of the massacre but its people. Indeed, by the time Cross comes to Heath, I've sat up. She is the person I want to hear from most on the panel because she quite literally wrote the case for reparations for Tulsa. It is exhaustive, damning, and underscores why she is the expert on reparations and reparatory justice at Human Rights Watch. She brings that voice to the summit. "In international human rights law, kind of wonky, but there are many forms that are reparative, and there are many forms that are necessary, specifically in the case of Tulsa," she says. "You can't just have the government throw a history center up and say, 'Here's your reparations.' Reparations is a victim-centered process. You can't handpick Black people out in the community also that you want to represent you to say 'this is our reparations.' You must have an extensive consultation process that centers the people that have been harmed from start to finish. There is no in-between. They should be a part of the decision-making, not 'we make the decisions behind closed doors, and then we're going to consult with you later.' Only communities who have been harmed can determine their recipe for repair, and we should empower each other to keep that fire up and to develop multiple remedies in Tulsa. Yes, there needs to be financial compensation. It means there's hundreds of millions of dollars that need to be paid back, not just for loss of property and economic assessment damage, but also for moral losses, loss of opportunity."

Heath cites examples where countries have quantified the damage done to communities within their borders. In 2016, Aboriginal Australians won a multi-million-dollar judgment in high court for the cultural and spiritual connection lost to their native land in New South Wales, Victoria, and South Australia due to colonization. Two months after Heath's example, on August 5, 2021, the Australian federal government agreed to pay $280 million in reparations to survivors who were severed from their families in the Northern Territory and Australian Capital Territory.[44] "But, in addition to that, trauma informed care," Heath says. "You're hearing Mother Fletcher, Mother Randle, Mr. Ellis talk, live through their trauma as they testify. How is that impacting them right now? How is that impacting the descendants who must sit in these rooms and live with whether or not their family members' bodies are in those mass graves? They must live with the loss of intergenerational wealth. They must live with the fact that they may reside in North Tulsa and then be beaten by police at three times the rate that other white people in other neighborhoods in South Tulsa are. So it's a compound issue that needs multiple solutions. And public policy is not going to do it alone, especially policies that have historically disinvested in communities like Tulsa. It emphasizes why reparations must be comprehensive and addresses the full scope of harm that has happened here in this community."

As the panel winds down and Cross asks for applause for each of the panelists, I check my phone. My white friend texts back.

"Are there any white people there? LOL."

*

The drive from my house to Silhouette Sneakers & Art is about ten minutes, and I take I-244 most of the way. When I exit onto East First Street, I cannot turn onto South Greenwood Avenue and park across the street from the boutique.

A large orange DETOUR sign directs me farther west to Elgin Street, where I need to make a loop around the block, past another large building across the street from ONEOK that will feature luxury apartments above street-level retailers. Construction fencing and signage tracks through the area, called Historic Greenwood District, that is mostly white-owned property.

I walk across the street, past street vendors selling anything they can slap "Black Wall Street" on—T-shirts, posters, koozies. There's a Black Wall Street Tees and Souvenirs on North Greenwood, inside one of the brick buildings rebuilt following the massacre. I cross the street as white folks and some Black folks take pictures and stare at the plaques of businesses destroyed in the massacre beneath their feet. Some gawk at the unfinished history center, and the parking complex being built beside it. I stare down South Greenwood Avenue with a measure of disgust, knowing why the street was closed.

A poster outside Silhouette reads BLACK LIVES MATTER above another on the shop glass that reads SAY THEIR NAMES: TERRENCE CRUTCHER, JOSHUA BARRE, JOSHUA HARVEY, all names of Black men slain by Tulsa law enforcement, all killed in the last five years. A few racks of tees, hoodies, and a jacket stand in the middle of the shop floor. I'm flanked by a curator suite of high-end sneakers. One pair has black tops with a red bottom and the iconic No. 23 on the heel. I bend over to see if those are what I think they are, and then I shoot a look at the clerk.

"Hey yo, are those the Retro 11 Breds?"

"Yup."

"Can I take a picture?"

"Do you."

I take a picture of the shoe, and the price tag on the sole. I could've walked out with those shoes for $350. The Low Spades, with the gold lining, gold swoosh, black paisley pattern on the toe, and red accents are just $190. Further down the line into the shop, the black Yeezy Boost 350s are $600. A lavender shirt that says GREENWOOD TULSA, BLACK WALL ST, FREEDOM FROM 1906 UNTIL, alongside a FIRE IN LITTLE AFRICA tee, and an olive-colored jacket with GWD AVE block-lettered in gold across a black patch against that olive catch my eye at once. The only clerk in the store pops out from behind the counter.

"That's the last one of our jackets," he says. "In case you were wondering."

"People buying these in the summer?"

"Yeah, people from out of town, coming through? With the last two festivals? They kept coming back getting stuff for their friends. We sold out of those jackets quickly."

This is the sneaker boutique that posted a photo of the oldest living survivor of the Tulsa Race Massacre, Viola Fletcher, sitting next to store owner Venita Cooper, wearing Carolina blue Hyper Royals. Since opening in 2019, Silhouette has become the kind of boutique many want to point to when asking what Greenwood could become. Mike Todd latched on to that feeling. In December 2020, Todd and Transformation Church bought out Silhouette's entire $65,000 inventory—a total of 186 pairs of shoes. The church donated the shoes to a Tulsa boys' home. The Philbrook Museum of Art created a shoe exhibit in collaboration with Cooper.[45]

The Silhouette storefront has become a hub for artists and celebrities during the centennial, with actress Alfre Woodard, the Oklahoma State men's basketball team, and Wayne Coyne visiting it or donning gear sold from it at the GreenArch building, described by the city's Tulsa Development Authority as a "[m]ixed use project with 70 apartments—studio, one-bedroom and two-bedroom; 9,000 square feet of ground floor retail; and a dedicated parking lot across Greenwood Avenue." The boutique is one of a handful of businesses that have moved into the Greenwood District just in time to be included in the centennial. Cooper operates the shop out of Suite C at 10 North Greenwood Avenue with its storefront facing Archer Street.

TDA and the Oklahoma State University system own the majority of the thirty-five blocks destroyed during the massacre. The Greenwood Chamber of Commerce owns the block-length stretch of ten brick buildings that were rebuilt after the massacre. To date, it is the only Black-owned real estate in Greenwood. The GreenArch building was completed in 2013 at a cost of $9 million. It costs $1,500 a month for a retail outlet to occupy a space at GreenArch before the centennial. A two-thousand-square-foot street-level retail space costs $24 per square foot, per year, over a five-year lease, or $4,000 a month for a term beginning in October 2021.[46]

That's not abhorrent or strange when compared to monthly rent in one of the brick buildings run by the Greenwood Chamber of Commerce. A retail space in the Bryant Building on the first floor costs $27 per square foot for 1,838 square feet over a five-year lease, or $4,135.50 per month. Renting a one-bedroom, one-bath apartment at GreenArch starts at $875 a month. The building is one of several parcels the TDA has sold to private investors in recent years. GreenArch is owned by 21 North Greenwood, LLC. The company, incorporated March 6, 2020, lists Kajeer Yar as its registered agent.

TDA general counsel Jot Hartley told the *Washington Post* that TDA sells its land to those who can afford to buy it, and that doesn't always include Black folks, let alone Black Tulsans. "That's what limits the participation of people of color—not any policy or bias on the part of the TDA or the city," Hartley said. "Some of these projects have been rather large and required capital that's not ordinarily available to just anybody unless they are already in the business of developing large projects." The *Post* also reported that $42 million in tax breaks and incentives have been parceled out to real estate development companies, mostly white-owned.

Kajeer Yar's wife, Maggie, is executive director and co-trustee of the Hille Family Charitable Foundation. She is the youngest child of Jo Bob and Mary Ann Hille, from whom the foundation gets its name. After graduating from Booker T., she attended the University of Michigan and law school at Southern Methodist. She also sat on the centennial commission's steering committee. According to the foundation's most recent tax filing in 2017,[47] she earned $122,548 in compensation as executive director. The foundation is a private firm, though it is a 501(c)(3) nonprofit. On its website, it describes its mission: "Our focus is serving the underserved." The foundation focuses its efforts on funding capital campaigns and operating expenses within its areas of interest, which range from Type 1 diabetes research to combating Alzheimer's disease.

When the foundation decided to donate the land the history center was built on, many rejoiced. The history center is expected to grow foot traffic and tourism. Directly across the street, though, is Yar's GreenArch building with a restaurant he co-owns, Lefty's On Greenwood, occupying the corner. "While we are the landowners, we have always taken great pains toward including a balanced and diverse mix of tenants," Yar told the *Post*. "We said, 'Look, let's have a tenant base that's not only reflective of Greenwood's past but also provides amenities for its future.'"[48]

Along with the Hille Foundation's donations came $500,000

from the AEP (American Electric Power) Foundation and Public Service Company of Oklahoma, $250,000 from the Oklahoma City Thunder, and $1 million from the QuikTrip Corporation. All of these companies have white CEOs or chairpersons; no Black-owned company in Tulsa was in a position to gift what Hille, the Thunder, AEP and PSO, or QuikTrip did. As we continue to talk about Greenwood's future and claim to be building it back to the Black-owned district it once was, I'm skeptical of the level of economic control asserted over it by predominantly white-run companies and a predominantly white-run city hall, who do not believe reparations to victims and their descendants is foundational to reconciling generational trauma, wealth inequality, and unequal representation in Tulsa.

T ODAY IS SUNDAY. I CHECK THE BLACK WALL STREET Legacy Festival agenda for speakers and musical acts, beginning around 2:00 p.m. The speakers, once again, look to be a brilliant mix of celebrities including actor Alfre Woodard, Wes Lowery, Jay Ellis, Brittany Packnett, Congresswoman Jackson Lee, Damon Lindelof, and Cord Jefferson. But when I check the musical acts, I stop cold when I see Taylor Hanson's name. You know—one of the Hanson brothers? I imagine a deejay ending a set with the GAP Band's "You Dropped a Bomb on Me" and Hanson walking up there on stage to do a live performance of "Mmmbop." That might be the most Tulsa thing ever, or maybe Hanson has a cover of "Lift Every Voice and Sing" in him that I'm not giving him credit for. But I never see him, which also is the most Tulsa thing ever. As I climb into my truck, taking Eleventh Street as far west as I can, past used car lots and alternative schools and dilapidated housing slowly gentrifying into a white person's version of respectable near TU before turning north toward the festival, I roll my eyes at the thought of a white man promising to show up at a Black function only to ghost us once again. That thought leads me to Lindelof and his *Watchmen*. I know I'm going to check that out, but the event doesn't start until the evening. In the meantime, Woodard and Ellis get my attention. Throughout the afternoon, they emcee the day's events. They try to lean on their Tulsa connection more than once. I park in the north parking lot at OSU and saunter toward the open grassy lot where Woodard and Ellis have begun introducing speakers.

Woodard asks the crowd if there were any Bishop Kelley Comets among us, and she is met with something worse than silence— boos. "Well, make me feel good and act like it then." I laugh. Kelley is a private Catholic school near midtown. Not too many folks in the crowd went there, or at least are smart enough not to crow about it. Ellis, though, enjoyed a short stint at Booker T. When he calls out, "Where my Hornets at?" he receives a raucous response. Even those who didn't go to Booker T. know this is the time to claim it. Such is the vibe on Sunday afternoon, and I choose to explore it. There are booths for shirts in support of United States vice president Kamala Harris, and shirts with Martin Luther King Jr. juxtaposed with Harriet Tubman. Black Lives Matter paraphernalia is outnumbered only by Black Wall Street paraphernalia, and this is what most people want. And most people are Black. This much is clear: white folks are hard to find during Legacy Fest events, easier to find at centennial commission events.

I find Roland Martin's canopy set up on Greenwood Avenue, just in front of the cultural center and across the street from Vernon AME Church. He'd begun his career as a newspaper journalist at the *Austin American-Statesman* after graduating from Texas A&M. He rose to national prominence first with his coverage of the Branch Davidian standoff for the *Fort Worth Star Telegram* in 1993 and then of the Oklahoma City bombing in 1995. In 2004, he was named executive editor of *The Chicago Defender*. Over the last decade, he has remained a fixture in Black journalism, with a daily digital show he streams across social media platforms. In some respects, I am following a path he forged. I've talked myself into walking over to him and asking to shake his hand. As I inch closer, I overhear a couple of Black men, perhaps in their forties, talking like they're from here. One of them wears an enormous black straw hat and the other a beard that looked like an homage to Dick Gregory.

"The culture of the Black man here," the bearded one says, "is to build and then rebuild."

"Mmhmm, that's right!" the hatted one says.

"They act like this is the first time we've had to build this place *Black*—you heard what I said?"

"He said 'Build it *Black*!' Yes he did!"

"I said build it *Black*, Roland!" The bearded one points at Martin then, and Martin gives him the raised fist of approval. "Tell your audience this ain't the first time we've had to build it *Black*. We built Black in 1921." He starts counting off fingers. "We built it Black when the Klan came to town in 1922. We built it Black when they denied our $2 million insurance claims in 1923—"

"Man knows his history," the hatted one says.

"We built it Black when they blamed us for the massacre of our own people. We built Black after the Depression. We built it Black after World War II, and it would've stayed that way if they didn't put that goddamn highway right—"

"Ain't no need to take the Lord's name in vain," an older Black woman breaks in. "Ain't no need."

"You right," the bearded one says. "I'm sorry. I know it's a church right there. But you hear me. They crippled Greenwood when they cut out its heart and put I-244 right through it. Tell 'em to tear out that highway, Roland. Tell 'em to give us back our community."

Two days before the bearded one's speech, the Congress for the New Urbanism included I-244's stretch through Greenwood in its "Freeways Without Futures" report. "Of course, the removal of I-244 alone won't restore Black Wall Street," the report stated. "But coordinated reparative programs, coupled with the highway's removal, can support community efforts to build a new Black Wall Street. This includes programs to help develop new Black-owned businesses and boost existing ones, leveraging the City's Affordable

Housing Trust Fund to create affordable homes within walking distance, and establishing a community land trust to rehabilitate vacant lots and abandoned houses in line with residents' interests. It will take focused investments and intentional policies like these to rebuild an expanded Greenwood district that does justice to historic Black Wall Street, while also addressing displacement concerns. This year marks the centennial of the Tulsa Race Massacre, when Black Wall Street was first destroyed. Now would be a fitting time to carry forward a conversation about I-244's removal. Preliminary investigation suggests it is more than feasible. This one-mile segment of I-244 is hardly essential for regional travel and Tulsa has a second loop highway, the Gilcrease Expressway, only a few miles to the north. The outstanding question is how to best ensure the highway's removal and a subsequent restoration of Greenwood helps Black Tulsans heal and thrive."

The bearded one goes on for a few minutes longer before he ascertains Martin is no longer interested in feeding him attention. He and the hatted one walk south, and I see my chance to introduce myself to Martin. But as I reach out my hand, another person wraps his arm around me—a stranger. I am disoriented until he shouts at Martin.

"This is our RJ Young, Roland!" he said.

I am embarrassed and don't know what to do.

"This man knows more about college football than any other person on earth, and he's from right here! Hey, Baby!" He steps between Martin and me then. "Take the picture with me and Frat." He shakes Martin's hand and then raises it into a stronger grip for the picture. As he tells Martin thank you, he turns to me. "You all right, RJ! Can I get a picture with you too?"

I take a picture with him as his Baby smiles sheepishly behind the phone. When I turn to try to shake Mr. Martin's hand, he is encumbered again by another fan. I smile. We are fanboying and fangirling so hard over this man. We are so grateful for him to think we are worthwhile. When I eventually shake his hand, I make sure not to dawdle. I want to show my appreciation with a firm grip and a kind word. Martin is kind enough to give me the same when I tell him I enjoy him and then I carry on down Greenwood Avenue to take in the rest of this Black bazaar.

By evening, people have trickled out of Greenwood. Vendors begin taking down their canopy tents, and the night air begins to still.

Matt Ruff's novel *Lovecraft Country* was published in 2016. The novel was adapted for television into something abject, elementary, obscene, and obtuse—but oh, is it *pretty*—by Misha Green, Jordan Peele, and HBO. Tulsa's history fortified the narrative that begins with Atticus Freeman—Atticus Turner in the novel—as our entry point, but he is not our most able narrator. That would be his father, Montrose. Early in the novel, we learn one of the supporting characters, George Berry, was born in Tulsa. He, too, fled Tulsa as the city burned with white flames in 1921. "In Oklahoma," Ruff writes, "a great white dragon coiled around Tulsa, breathing fire onto the neighborhood where Atticus's father and Uncle George had been born." The Klan was welcome here. The Tulsa chapter held a parade here on Earth, Wind & Fire Day—the twenty-first of September—in 1923. Just two years after burning out, killing, and ruining Black lives just miles from my house near Eleventh and Garnett, the marauders and the monsters celebrated their evil. And later we found the novel's protagonist's father, Montrose, owned a "Frankenstein Victrola" that he "had built himself, installing a modern turntable, radio receiver, and speakers into an antique phonograph cabinet salvaged from the flames of Tulsa." Near the end of the story Montrose is made to relive that experience, in detail, by the ghostly white son of a racist sorcerer, to save his child's life. Telling white folks our most traumatic stories to educate them and save their souls is an American tradition. Only a white person might think of this as a kindness. The novel's chief thesis, though, is inarguable: Black history reads like speculative fiction. The trials, the horrors, the shame of how America has brutalized Black folks is the marrow of what makes the fantasy world go. We were invaded. We were enslaved. We created our own magic and still became white folks' Magical Negroes. That Tulsa's race massacre runs adjacent to the plot is not coincidence. That Tulsa's story becomes the backbone of hate, anger, and an intense mistrust of white folks for Montrose demonstrates just how vile the massacre remains in the twenty-first century.

Atticus's clan of Berrys, Turners, Baptistes, and Lewises is remarkable. They feature an amateur astronomer, a small business owner, a medium, a comic book writer and publisher, a shapeshifter, and a man, Atticus, endowed with a talent for the occult. A group of rich white sorcerers believe the blood running through Atticus's heart makes him the strongest and most worthy of all sorcerers in their nefarious club called the Order of the Ancient Dawn. And they hate him for this. Not because he could be stronger than them, and not because he means them harm. They hate him because he is Black. Even in a world where other worlds, planets, are discovered; where beasts and beings without equal reside; and where man possesses the same ability to create as Adam in the Book of Genesis, they cannot abide Black folks.

Complicating the story further is the knowledge that Atticus is a direct descendant of the most powerful sorcerer in Ancient Dawn history—what the order calls "natural philosophers"—and so they choose not to kill him but to treat him like a trophy. They tolerate him and his family until they can tolerate them no more. And then they must kill them. 'Course there comes a white savior for Atticus and his family, or so the white savior sees himself. Like all white saviors, he manipulates and cajoles the folks he claims to rescue. He fancies himself cleverest and all the rest as simple. When the novel reaches its climax and resolution is at hand, the clan of Black folks outsmart their villain. They strip the white savior of his power and his immunity to the world's hurts; to the pains of consequences they must meet each day. The villain, named Caleb Braithwaite, realizes that he has only his truth to use to try to dissuade them. He hopes they allow him to keep his immunity by reminding the clan what the racist sorcerers will do if he is not there to stop them. In Ruff's novel, Braithwaite discusses Atticus and his family like he'd be doing him a favor: "They won't think of you as family, or even as a person, and they won't leave you alone until they get what they want from you. No matter where you go, you'll never be safe. You—" At this, the Black folks break into roaring laughter.

"What?" Braithwaite shouts, looking at them as if they are crazy. "What's so funny?" but for a long while they are laughing too hard to answer.

"Oh, Mr. Braithwaite," Atticus says finally, wiping tears from his eyes. "What is it you're trying to scare me with? You think I don't know what country I live in? I know. We all do. We always have. *You're* the one who doesn't understand." Here I'll remind you that Atticus is one half of a man, flesh of a man, born and raised in Tulsa, Oklahoma. Montrose fled this place after white Tulsans killed *his* father in the massacre. To be of this place, from Tulsa, some one hundred years after the massacre is to know that in your bones. That is the Tulsa I know as well as I know that my Black skin made me other before my Black skin made me proud.

*

The grassy lot is nowhere near full when Lindelof, Jefferson, Jeff Martin, and Nehemiah Frank step on to the Legacy Fest stage to talk about a TV show Lindelof created with Tulsa at its center. It is called *Watchmen*.

When *Watchmen* debuted in 2019, critics adored it. The show was nominated for twenty-six Emmy awards and won eleven—the most of any television show in 2020. Its Emmy victories included Outstanding Limited Series, Outstanding Lead Actress in a Limited Series, and Outstanding Supporting Actor in a Limited Series. It won awards from more than two dozen entertainment organizations and more than three times that number in trophies. But as much as critics loved it, nearly every person who watched it did too. The series was so effective that it became the point of reference for the massacre. Since the show first aired on October 20, 2019, people can be divided into two categories: those who knew about the massacre before *Watchmen*, and those who learned by watching *Watchmen*. Of course, during the centennial week and throughout the last two years, I'd encountered many who'd ask me where I was from, and then proceed to tell me they knew about Tulsa because they'd seen *Watchmen*. Then, usually awkwardly, the same people would follow up their revelation with one about the massacre itself.

I never know how to respond to someone telling me they found out about the worst act of domestic terrorism in U.S. history because of an HBO television series that centered its story and its setting on Black trauma in Tulsa. Still, there is no place I'd rather be than sitting in a large open patch of grass, across the street from the cultural center, just behind Vernon AME Church, readying myself to hear what *Watchmen*'s creator and head writer, Damon Lindelof and Cord Jefferson, have to say about their show.

They walk on stage with Jeff Martin, president at Magic City Books, and Nehemiah Frank, cofounder of the *Black Wall Street Times*. After a brief hello, Martin directs us to the movie theater–sized projector screens on either side of the stage. The screens show the cast and crew of *Watchmen* describing their experiences while making the show. One cast member describes making the show as a "harrowing, but really profound experience." Another describes the responsibility he felt in being sensitive to the subject matter.

After the short video ends, Martin introduces the other three. They each sit on a stool, four across, in the center of the stage as we, the crowd, look up at them. As Lindelof sits to Martin's right, I realize this is the first time I've seen a white guy on that stage, let alone two at the same time, all day. All four men wear jeans, though Lindelof keeps his jacket on and Jefferson drapes his khaki coat across his lap. Perhaps it was chilly in whatever room they were in as the festival went on, as the Black folks who live here enjoyed each other's fellowship and the sense of community that overtook the place. Only Frank wears a hat—and a T-shirt with the logo of his news publication on the left side of his chest.

Looking around the crowd I count perhaps two hundred people sitting across the grassy field. The field has been beaten down from three days of events. Some sit in lawn chairs, some on towels and makeshift benches they brought with them. The group is perhaps 50 percent Black and 50 percent white. The sky above has turned from its bright blue earlier this afternoon to darkening purple above the sign on top of the stage that reads LEGACY FEST in yellow letters across a black banner. The event, scheduled to begin at 7:00 p.m., is perhaps too late for folks who need to work the next morning.

In his introduction for Lindelof, Martin makes note of this being Lindelof's first-ever trip to Tulsa. That fact strikes me. The man made a television show set in Tulsa, yet had never visited the city before he was asked to as a part of the commemoration of the massacre that acts as the foundation for it. On stage, Martin acts as moderator. His first question to Lindelof is about how it felt to walk from Martin's bookstore, perhaps a mile east of where we sat, to and through what's left of Greenwood. Lindelof says he'd never heard about the massacre until he read Ta-Nehisi Coates's piece for *The Atlantic*, "The Case for Reparations."

"We always understood that what happened here was a real thing," Lindelof says, "even though we were making a piece of fiction. And when you come to a real place, you feel what happened there. So still processing it was emotionally overwhelming and intense. And we're just really grateful that we get to be here."

Martin picks up the conversation and turns to Jefferson, who he notes is credited with writing the sixth episode of the series, titled "This Extraordinary Being." The episode acts as the origin story for a prominent character in the TV show, Will Reeves, who creates the superhero identity of Hooded Justice for himself. "I personally think it's the best episode of the series," Martin tells the crowd. "And I think it's one of the great episodes of TV that we've had, in the last decade, really an amazing piece, kind of a film within the series."

Jefferson says he didn't know about the massacre until he read Tim Madigan's book *The Burning: Massacre, Destruction, and the Tulsa Race Riot of 1921*. He says he is grateful to have read the book when he did, and grateful to be in Tulsa for the commemoration. This is also his first trip to the place he was charged to write a fictional story about. He is grateful, oh so grateful, to have read enough work on this place without having to visit.

Frank, whom Martin calls Neo, is descended from victims of the massacre. His second-great-grandparents William and Virginia Clark owned a tailor shop in Greenwood in 1921. The tailor shop never reopened. He credits the show with helping launch his publication into the mainstream, as he was one of the local journalists and activists writing and talking about the massacre before *Watchmen* premiered. "Watching the first episode for the first time," Frank says, "I remember, I was sitting with my mom. And we didn't even talk. Because we were just silent, just watching the whole thing." Frank applauds Lindelof and Jefferson for their accuracy in depicting the destruction of Greenwood. "I remember after watching it, and I just kind of collapsed into myself, and just sat with that. And I actually cried. My mother cried. I was traumatized. I was traumatized thinking 'Wow, my people went through that.'"

Martin directs the conversation back to Lindelof. He wants to know what HBO first thought when he told the network executives he wanted to seat his story in the massacre. "I think HBO had the same reaction that most white people do when we hear about what happened here for the first time," Lindelof says, "which is incredulity followed by embarrassment and shame. And then, on the heels of that, hopefully, incredible curiosity."

He later tapped Regina King to play the lead character, and she told him how grateful she was. Everyone is so grateful that my teeth hurt. King knew about the massacre, and she'd tried to get a couple of projects off the ground about it in Hollywood. In the end, though, a white man needed to say he wanted to make the story for HBO to greenlight it. King was on board, though HBO did have doubts. Lindelof says the network was skeptical about a fictional limited series. They asked him to think about turning the project into a documentary or a docu-drama. Their chief concern was whether a fictional TV show could hold the Tulsa Race Massacre.

"And you know what I tried to explain to them was that for a century this story has been trying to get told, and it keeps getting erased," Lindelof says. "There's a collective historical gaslighting, and reframing of this as a riot, as opposed to a massacre. We felt like we could basically dramatize it exactly as it happened to [Frank's] point with no dramatic license whatsoever. We're just going to show you what happened."

Even that didn't satisfy executives at the network as they grew incredulous about specific details, like the planes flying overhead and dropping bombs onto Greenwood. "HBO just kept saying, 'But the planes? The planes, that didn't happen?' Yeah, that happened. And so they embraced it. Once we pitched it to them, I think that the concern from everybody's standpoint was just to try to present it in a way that never felt exploitative, or at any point unnecessarily traumatizing. Just show how it was, as it was."

After a brief back-and-forth about how their writers' room worked for the show, Martin turns the conversation back to the character of Will Reeves. "Obviously, there are tones of a Superman story here," Martin says. He asks Jefferson to explain how Reeves's superhero origin story became a central part of the show.

"I've told this to Damon before, but my secret shame is that I'm not a huge comic book fan. I didn't really read comic books until I read *Watchmen*. And so I didn't even really put together the Superman connection." He looks at Lindelof. "I don't know, did you put that together immediately? Because I know that we decided to include *Action Comics* #1 in the episode, but I didn't realize it was a Superman homage until later."

Lindelof's decision to use Superman's origin story to tell the story about *Watchmen*, a story about masked vigilantes, on top of the massacre, "was fairly immediate" once they knew they wanted to create a story about superheroes. To Lindelof, one of the most important parts of the superhero origin story is trauma, specifically emotional trauma. Superman's birth parents are killed in the destruction of Krypton when Superman is an infant. Batman's parents are murdered by a thief in an alleyway in front of him when he is a boy. Reeves (Hooded Justice) sees his parents killed during the massacre when he is little more than a toddler.

When framing their superhero origin story in their larger one about white supremacy in the early twentieth century, Lindelof says Jefferson made the point that *Watchmen* is about vigilantes—people who dress up and wear masks to fight crime in their respective communities. In a system created to sustain white supremacy, no white person needs to become a vigilante, because the law supports their way of life. The only justification for becoming a vigilante in Tulsa—then or now—is for a Black person to do it.

"And so that started to kind of click," Lindelof says. "But the idea of Tulsa always felt like Krypton to me. The beginning of the Superman story is the destruction of this planet, but also this planet of brilliant scientists." He's also clear about what the show did not do. "We did not dramatize what *was* massacred. And I think that this idea of reframing and celebrating Black Wall Street, the decade-plus that Black Wall Street was prospering, we don't need to say that that was excellence. We just need to say that that was prosperity, and that prosperity is what got it destroyed." That's also why Lindelof thought it crucial that Reeves felt "the forces of white supremacy are going to be pushing down on this character for his entire life. And that sort of really dominated a lot of our thinking."

Lindelof's answer is illuminating, but I don't agree that Greenwood needed to prosper for it to merit destruction. Greenwood merited destruction from white Tulsans simply for existing. Evidence of this is found in the hundreds of race riots throughout the country, especially during the era of Red Summer following the end of World War II. White folks killed Black folks not just for being prosperous, but for simply daring to be.

In the episode Martin likes so much, "This Extraordinary Being," Reeves moves to New York City as an adult and becomes a cop in the NYPD, where some of the first words he hears from a fellow Black police officer are "Beware the Cyclops," the Klan-like organization in the United States. Martin tells the audience that he wanted to share a scene from the episode to highlight Reeves's superhero origin story. He acknowledges that Jefferson wrote the script for the episode. "I do want to say this is a short scene," Martin says, "but it does contain an attempted lynching. So, if you are not prepared to see that, take a break. It's okay to kind of turn away from that. But we do think it's important in this context of what we're talking about."

I look around. Walk where? We're in the middle of a big-ass grassy field. You're going to show an attempted lynching on two big-ass projector screens over a bunch of big-ass loudspeakers. Where is anyone expected to go to get away from this? Stillwater? I have no sooner finished having an imaginary argument with Martin when the clip begins.

From the fifty-one minutes and thirty-three seconds that make up "This Extraordinary Being," Martin chooses to pick out three minutes and seventeen seconds, beginning with Reeves, off duty, in street clothes and walking home from work. His fellow white police officers pull up beside him in a police car as he walks along the sidewalk.

The white cop in the passenger seat rolls down his window. "Hey there, Reeves," he says. "Need a ride home?"

"No, thanks," Reeves says. "I enjoy walking."

"You sure?" the cop says. "You just got off duty. How about you come join us for a beer?"

"I appreciate it," Reeves says, "but I've got an early shift tomorrow."

"Ah, come on. We're buying."

"Maybe another time."

"OK, then," the cop says. "Another time." The police car's driver picks up speed then. As the car passes Reeves by, he and the audience see two dead Black men chained to the back of the car. Their bloodied bodies are being dragged through the street.

Reeves doesn't flinch like I did when I first saw the scene. I look at the crowd. A white man stands up, turns around, and begins walking away from the screen. A Black girl nearby scoots closer to her mama, who instinctively begins rubbing her child's head. I notice a group of four Black women sitting together who all shake their heads with disgust. I hear a Black man nearby mutter "mother*fucker*."

On the projector screen, Reeves hasn't broken stride, though he does turn right into an alleyway and off the street. He does not finish walking past the first building he encountered when the same policemen cut him off with their car. Three cops step out of the car and walk toward him.

The one who has tried to convince Reeves to let them drive him home has taken the lead. He stops just in front of Reeves and shakes his head.

"You know what?" he says. "Another time ain't gone work for us."

When Reeves tries to run, the cops beat him with their night-sticks and kick him in the face. The screen turns black. The audience understands Reeves has been beaten until he is unconscious. When the picture returns to the screen, the audience is placed in Reeves's point of view, so that we might experience, as he did, two cops dragging him by his legs through the woods. Between the two cops dragging him, another cop tosses a noose over a tree limb. While his hands are bound, one of the cops punches Reeves in his jaw. Another places the noose around Reeves's neck. Another places a hood over his head. Two others pull the rope until Reeves is dangling from the noose, his feet no longer touching the ground.

He is being lynched.

He is losing consciousness.

He is dying.

They are killing him.

We watch lights fade beneath our hood.

We are being lynched.

We are dying.

We are losing consciousness when we're cut down, fall down on our back. The white cop in charge, the instigator, is standing over us. He squats, takes the bag off of our head, and cuts the ropes off.

"You keep your Black nose out of white folks' business, nigger," he says, "or, next time, we won't cut you down."

When the clip ends, Martin picks up the conversation. "So, a very tough scene to watch," he says, "but I think it's important in that kind of origin story of this character."

He turns to Lindelof, who looks uneasy. "Damon, talk about that just for a moment, and how you worked with Cord on that?"

Lindelof hesitates, perhaps still collecting himself and his thoughts, having just looked at us, out here, in the crowd. I look for the Black girl whose mother was rubbing her head moments ago. She is firmly planted between her mother's legs, and she's thrown the blanket she was sitting on over her head. Her mother continues to rub her head anyway. The white man who got up and left has not returned.

Lindelof speaks about Hooded Justice being the first-ever vigilante in the *Watchmen* universe and his desire to create a story using that character. He discusses the choice of completely covering Hooded Justice's face and ornamenting him with a noose, as he was in Alan Moore's original comic.

However, it was Jefferson who created this origin story, this scene. "In my mind," Jefferson says, "if we're thinking about this character as being Black or thinking about this character being a Black man who wears a noose around his neck all the time, to me, there is no way to come to that conclusion, to reach that point, without thinking of some sort of racial violence. This is a person who survived a lynching of some kind. And, in order to sort of re-mind himself of the strength of not dying in that moment, he walks around with a noose around his neck all the time. So, it sort of largely came from this idea that Hooded Justice had to be Black, and I worked backward from that premise."

Martin shows one more clip at the park. This scene takes place later in the episode, after Reeves has effectively created his alter ego, Hooded Justice, and after saving a white woman and her feckless white male companion in an alleyway. As Hooded Justice, Reeves walks into a known Cyclops den. He breaks in through the back door, finds the three white men who lynched him dressed in the bed sheets and white hoods of the Cyclops, and commences whooping their asses. He throws them against garage doors, into shelves and filing cabinets—dressed in all black, black boots, black gloves, with a rope tied around his neck and waist and very little depth percep-tion. He fights one in the front of the store he'd broken into and throws him into a table of produce, startling the white customers and store owner.

A white man standing behind the counter at the store, wearing an apron, asks, "What the fuck are you supposed to be?" Before

Reeves can answer, that same white man pulls out a double-barreled shotgun and starts shooting at him. Reeves jumps through the storefront window to get away.

When the forty-five-minute conversation finishes with some congratulations for the work and its reception, I begin walking toward my truck. I stop by a Black woman wearing a Black Panther T-shirt—the comic book, not the party for self-defense. She is petting her German shepherd.

"Did it feel like they just lynched somebody at the park?" I ask her.

She looks back at me with a look of complete assurance. "Uh, yeah."

"So I'm not crazy?"

"No, my brother. *That* was crazy."

When I climb into my blue Ram and get back on I-244, heading home, I realize I am starving, and I haven't made grocery. Grandmomme warned me against making groceries on an empty stomach. "You are liable to buy the whole store," she said. But I don't want to eat fast food. I feel content, happy, and fruit and nuts and skim milk are liable to help me keep that feeling longer.

I park at the grocery store just down the block from me and begin walking toward the sliding doors. I stop abruptly when I see the bumper sticker on the back windshield of another blue Ram in a handicap space, proudly proclaiming, TRUMP/PENCE 2020. I see three other stickers on the back fender: LIB-ER-AL: 'LI-B(&-)R&, NOUN: A PERSON SO OPEN-MINDED THEIR BRAINS HAVE FALLEN OUT. Another one: POLITICALLY INCORRECT AND PROUD OF IT. A last one: A CITIZEN'S GUIDE TO REVOLUTION OF A CORRUPT GOVERNMENT: 1. STARVE THE BEAST, KEEP YOUR MONEY. 2. VOTE OUT INCUMBENTS. 3. IF STEPS 1 & 2 FAIL, PREPARE FOR WAR—LIVE FREE OR DIE.

When I finish picking up my grapes and skim milk, I watch the cashier ring up the grapes for $10.34 a pound. He is as shocked as I am. Those grapes are usually less than $3 per pound. He rings them up again, and the price is the same. "You could get, like, ten things off the dollar menu at McDonald's for this," he says. "Almost makes it feel like eating healthy ain't worth the money." I buy my grapes and eat them angrily. This is where I live.

The next day, Monday, the only event worth keeping from the centennial commission events is held. At 10:30 p.m., hundreds gather downtown inside the Greenwood District. The intersection at Greenwood Avenue and Archer is filled with people in hoodies and ponchos. The rain has come, a steady sound splashing against the pavement. The water sparks against the candlelight. Someone prays. Some of us lower our heads. Some of us grab each other's hands, even strangers. With these gestures, these genuine acts of remembrance, I am hopeful in this moment. I want this moment to be who we are: pensive, polite. One hundred years ago right now, white folks opened fire on Black Tulsans. Black Tulsans defended themselves, defended their property, and many failed to save themselves, their families, or their homes. I think about what it must've cost them, what I might have done, what I think an act of defense or stubbornness it must have been not to leave Tulsa after my friends were massacred. During this moment of silent reflection, some of us can't hold it. Some of us must sing our sorrow, sing our pain among each other, as we might have not just a century ago but two centuries ago. I want this to be where I live.

On Tuesday, Joe Biden, the president of the United States, visits the building just across the street from where the lynching happened. When news began to percolate, first on Twitter and then on local news, that Biden was headed to Tulsa on June 1, 2021, at the cultural center, I thought that made sense. President Barack Obama had made several trips to the state, and to see Obama's former vice president pick up his policy and continue a dialogue with Black Americans was meaningful to some. One of my friends, a local journalist, told me Biden was expected to arrive Tuesday afternoon, but folks who might want to catch a glimpse of him should arrive around noon.

Biden is expected to meet with the three survivors, a few local and state politicians, and then announce some form of legislation or cause to celebrate. I park in a familiar parking lot just north of the cultural center a little after noon, and I am shocked to see the lot is not even approaching full. As I walk past the park where we listened to so many speak, heard music, and fellowshipped with each other, I walk over several plaques in the sidewalk, including one for Eldridge Restaurant, which was destroyed in the massacre and never reopened.

The plaque lies directly across the street from a Secret Service agent who has set up a checkpoint about one hundred yards from the cultural center. He has on nice dress shoes, and I think that is odd as I join the growing crowd of people who have already begun congregating in front of Vernon AME, across the street from the cultural center. CBS News has taken up half the parking lot with a canopy tent, and local news stations jockey for places along the sidewalk. Among the crowd, people are guessing which direction Biden would enter from and less about what he will say.

"Gotta be coming from the south," one Black man tells another. "White folks always come from the south."

"Nah," another says. "There's buried to the south, and that overpass. You know they gotta shut down the highways for the president. They'd have stopped traffic on 244 cause, you know, snipers and shit."

"What?!" another says.

"I'm *saying*. Could be a sniper up there. You got to clear the area."

"'Clear the area'? This ain't *Call of Duty*, mu'fucka."

I move down the line and hear the newsfolks talking to one another. The local news people regard the national newsfolk with a level of reverence that is almost endearing.

"I guess this is becoming old hat for you all?" one of the national newsfolk, a white CBS cameraman, says.

"How do you mean?" a white woman wearing a local news affiliate jacket asks.

"You know?" he says. "Trump was here last year. Two presidents in two years."

I meet one more person, a marijuana dispensary owner, who is handing out flyers and wants to know if I have a medical card. When I say I don't, he looks at me like I am useless to him. I respect the hustle. But I don't respect the wait—not for Biden. Someone says they've seen his plane landing nearby. I check my watch. I have a haircut appointment in a half hour, and the barbershop is a twenty-minute drive from Greenwood. I wonder what else I might do here. What else is there for me to see? He isn't going to speak outside, and the cops are not going to let us inside. He is not likely to announce financial reparations for survivors and their descendants, either. Reporters in D.C. said he was even telling congresspeople not to expect him to publicly support H.R. 40. And that bill doesn't even call for reparations. It simply calls for the creation of a commission to study reparations.

Nah, I can't see a reason to hang. I need to see about my line-up. I've heard rich old white men talk before, and I can stand to miss a few.

Later, I learn Biden used his moment in Tulsa to call out white supremacy. "My fellow Americans: This was not a riot. This was a massacre." Thank you for calling out the obvious, Mr. President. In the same speech, he let us know *he* wasn't going to oversee restoring voting rights for Black folks across the country, *but* the Black vice president was.

Neat.

*

At the dedication for the history center on Wednesday, June 2, 2021, a day after Biden's appearance down the block, I see the full might of Tulsa rich folks on display. But it is we who have kept the streets clean. I park at the north lot of OSU-Tulsa once again and begin my walk down Greenwood Avenue. The signage on the fence in front of Vernon AME and at the corner of Cameron and Greenwood is still there, asking to DISMANTLE WHITE SUPREMACY and WHAT IS THE VALUE OF BLACK LIFE IN AMERICA?

Further down the fence line, a sampling:

WHITE GUILT IS YOUR CONSCIENCE SPEAKING. PLEASE LISTEN.

LET AMY RULE HER OWN VAGINA. NOT MINE.

BLACK LIBERATION + INDIGENOUS SOVEREIGNTY CAN HEAL THIS LAND OF COLONISTS.

LISTEN TO BLACK WOMEN.

IF THEY DON'T GIVE YOU A SEAT AT THE TABLE, BRING A FOLDING CHAIR.

PEOPLE OF QUALITY DO NOT FEAR EQUALITY.

RESPECT OUR EXISTENCE, OR EXPECT RESISTANCE.

Along with these posters and flyers and declarations, the fence line, the sidewalk, and the underpass are planted with Black Lives Matter signage and raised Black fists like weeds in a garden. The signage is in black, white, and rainbow colors. A flag advocating LGBTQ rights waves alongside a BLM one. A pink cardboard sign emblazoned with RESIST hangs next to another that says, THE POLICE WON'T PROTECT YOUR VOICE.

I take a detour after going beneath the underpass to walk the Pathway to Hope. I want to see what the $1.75 million sidewalk looks like. But it's just painted, manicured. On the plaque announcing its dedication, May 28, 2021, it notes the funding for the project. None is from the city of Tulsa. On the east side of the sidewalk, a map is mounted to show what Greenwood looked like before the massacre in 1921 and denotes where I am standing on that map. The overpass, I-244, has been refinished to look not made of concrete but of a soothing gray wood. Along with various life-size photos mounted against the overpass, which include John Hope Franklin standing in the middle of Greenwood Avenue with I-244 in the background, are quotes no could be offended by.

One from Toni Morrison, who has no ties to Tulsa: "If there's a book that you want to read, but it hasn't been written yet, you must write it."

One from Maya Angelou, who has no ties to Tulsa: "There is no greater agony than bearing an untold story inside you."

There are two from John Hope Franklin, but neither refers to Tulsa—only America. "There's no reason in the world why [B]lack [people] should not be regarded as an attribute that is not degrading but is positive. There's no reason in the world why any person should think that white is degrading." Looking at that quote from Franklin, with "[people]" in brackets inside of the poster on the wall, I know who this walkway is for, and it isn't Black folks.

The other quote: "One of the problems in the United States is the refusal on the part of our young people to remember or to want to remember, or to recognize the experiences of the past as being relevant, germane, important to the present or the future. They simply don't want anything that's painful. They want to live in a painless society where everything is pleasant and everything is joyful."

My face screws up after reading that.

First, I, a young person, am standing right fucking here. Second, who wouldn't want to live in a painless society where everything is pleasant and everything is joyful? No, this quote isn't for me either. That quote is for white folks and old folks, too.

There are blown-up photos of a Booker T. yearbook, gorgeous shrubs. The walkway itself made of brick, with modern street lightning and art deco benches. I walk the length of the Pathway, which leads to Reconciliation Park, and walk back, sound in the knowledge that this is yet another memorial to white folks' view of the massacre in the name of a Black man. I can think of several quotes, also attributable to Franklin, that they could've put on the wall of this highway that would better speak to Black folks and Black Tulsans.

In *Death in a Promised Land*, John Hope told Scott Ellsworth: "There are two ways [in] which whites destroy a [B]lack community. One is building a freeway through it, the other is by changing the zoning laws." In his autobiography, John Hope wrote: "I hardly needed to seek a way to confront American racial injustice. My ambition was sufficient to guarantee that confrontation." At a spring convocation for the University of Chicago, he said: "When one nation enslaves another people for the ostensible purpose of civilizing them, that nation merely reveals its own barbarity and invites the eternal wrath of the enslaved."

As I walk the 100 block of Greenwood to join the crowd, I pass a woman wearing a mask and a T-shirt with Terrence Crutcher's face on it and the words WILL VOTE FOR above his head. She wears a blue baseball cap and camouflage mask while holding a sign above her head: THE WHITE MAN WILL TRY TO SATISFY US WITH SYMBOLIC VICTORIES RATHER THAN ECONOMIC EQUITY, EQUALITY AND REAL JUSTICE. A quote she has repurposed from Malcolm X and cited on her sign.

The intersection at Greenwood and Archer is shut down for a fifth consecutive day, and the stage that faces north over the weekend is turned to face east as the sun travels overhead and speakers can look directly at the history center itself. Projector screens on either side give a view of every person who steps onto that stage. With perhaps five hundred people in attendance, including 160 descendants of victims of the massacre, the dedication of the history center feels like the grand opening of a car dealership, with a who's who of dignitaries on hand, from a British ambassador to city council persons, county commissioners, and state senators. Some in attendance wear suits. Some wear Black Lives Matter and Black Wall Street T-shirts. I wear black sweats, Space Jam Jordan 11s, and a white T-shirt.

There is some open seating, but all seats are full when I arrive ten minutes before the schedule starts that morning. I sit down on the freshly poured concrete underneath the awning of the history center. The speakers take the opportunity to congratulate themselves and congratulate the people of Tulsa for this building. I find myself laughing, awkwardly as the only one sometimes, when I hear one of them say something that hits my ears funny. Phil Armstrong, the project manager for the centennial commission and Greenwood Rising, gives me the heartiest chuckle when he talks about how this building is an example of "communal reparations."

"There are many forms of rock of reparations," Armstrong says, "and we believe in the most monetary and communal. This . . . portion that I'm about to share with you is what's defined as communal reparations." The project was not going to be finished in time for the centennial. Estimates from contractors are that the center might not be done until October 2021—four months past the centennial. Armstrong says that "a private community donor"—he goes out of his way to tell the crowd it is not Kaiser—called Armstrong and told him how important it was for them to see the project finished by the centennial. He asked Armstrong, as a project manager, to go to each of the contractors and ask them to resubmit a bid accounting for an accelerated construction schedule to finish by June 1, 2021. Armstrong says he gave that invoice to that private donor, who wrote the commission a check for just short of $1 million to cover the added cost.

"I also want to take time to say because this was a private development," Armstrong says, "we can decide who gets to work on this project. And I was very emphatic that I wanted African American, not minority, but specifically and with intentionality Black subcontractors and contractors on this project all throughout the process. So I'm proud to say that we've had over thirty-plus Black subcontractors to help work on Greenwood Rising in the Pathway to Hope." He receives a raucous ovation for this from the crowd. As he does, I spot my friend Kevin standing next to the stage.

I walk around one of the seated sections, slowly clearing out as Armstrong delightfully tells the crowd he's going off-script to air grievances, give verbal flowers, and soak in what he's convinced is one of the seminal achievements of life: getting to this day. I dap Kevin. We were in school together at Booker T. He went to Hampton University and earned a finance degree, became a financial advisor, and moved back to Tulsa.

"What do you think of all this?" I ask.

He hesitates, and I find myself appreciating that. People haven't made a habit of considering that question enough for my liking, especially those of us who live here, who call this place home, who have no plans to pack up with the circus.

"I think," he sighs, hesitating once more, "we'll see. There's a lot to be proud of if you want to be proud. The president speaking on it"—he casually points to the history center as Hannibal Johnson makes his way to the stage—"the center, the number of people who turned out over the last week. Even with the concert called off, there's a lot to be proud of."

I nod. I know his family has been directly involved in many of the commemoration activities, and I know he wants this to be the event that creates the kind of district so many have mythologized, one where Black enterprise funds itself and wealth is passed down not just from parent to child, but from us to our great-great-grandchildren.

"But," I say, "how is any of this going to help *us*?"

He shrugs. "We'll see." Saying it with a kind of hopeful skepticism that feels as confused as many of the commemoration events that were warped into something like celebrations. Just yesterday the centennial commission helped sponsor what it called Economic Empowerment Day with Hill Harper as its featured speaker, along with other Black and not-Black business professionals. The event went on simultaneously with the president's arrival, but I caught enough of it online to hear Harper call his business partner in the launch of his cryptocurrency "a financial Harriet Tubman leading our people out of financial slavery" before closing my laptop.

"Hey," I say, "did you go to any of Hill Harper's stuff?"

"No." His face screws up a bit.

"You buying into that Black cryptocurrency?"

"I don't think so. Feels sketchy. The million-dollar thing rubbed me the wrong way."

Harper has pledged $1 million of cryptocurrency to massacre survivors and descendants of victims. He has named the platform "The Black Wall Street," calling it a digital wallet for Black people.

"Reminds me of those Tulsa Real Estate Fund brothers."

"The what?"

Kevin looks at me like he thought I knew. "The Tulsa Real Estate Fund." He explains after Johnson receives a round of applause from the crowd. He waits for it to die down, inches closer, and then whispers to me as the Booker T. choir is invited onto the stage.

"A couple brothers came through here about three years ago talking about"—he makes air quotes with his fingers—"'buying the block back.' Called themselves the Tulsa Real Estate Fund. Saying they were forming an entity to buy property around here and invest in Black businesses. Raised about $10 million last I heard. Ain't seen those dudes since."

In June 2018, Jay Morrison announced what he called an initial public offering for the Tulsa Real Estate Fund. It was billed as "the first African American–owned Regulation A+ Tier II crowdfund designed to revitalize urban communities across the U.S." They raised $9.6 million in seven days with a goal of $50 million.

"Tulsa Real Estate Fund was created for the sole purpose of the revitalization of urban communities across America, as well as a means for working class people to own shares and equity in a portfolio of real estate assets that will combat gentrification." Morrison claimed to get inspiration for the fund name from Greenwood and the history of Black Wall Street, and he believed his fund was the best way for Black folks to pool their collective $1.3 trillion in spending power. But when attorneys and financial experts looked closer at the company, they found reason to doubt the viability of the fund and its founders.

Just two months after Morrison announced the fund, the NFL Players Association sent an alert memo to its members about the fund after an agent asked for a limited investigation into it.[49] The NFLPA found Jay Morrison listed as the fund's CEO and Tosin Oduwole as its vice president of business development. The NFLPA listed four items in its memo. The first item listed Morrison's criminal history.

"Mr. Morrison has acknowledged he was a drug dealer for several years in his youth and was incarcerated on multiple occasions as a result. Mr. Morrison contends he has not sold drugs since late 2004." Item No. 2 made members of the players association aware that Morrison filed for Chapter 7 bankruptcy in December 2016. Item No. 3 was Oduwole's criminal history: "In 2007, Mr. Oduwole was arrested in Illinois on several counts, including attempted terroristic threat, illegal possession of a firearm, theft, and computer fraud. Mr. Oduwole was either convicted or pleaded guilty to each of the above-referenced counts." Item No. 4 listed what the fund claimed were risk factors investors should be aware of before investing in the fund: the fund didn't own any assets, it had not generated any revenue or begun revenue-generating activities, and investors would have limited voting rights.

In March 2019, the Tulsa Real Estate Fund received a grand jury subpoena from the U.S. District Attorney's Office for the Northern

District of Georgia, where the fund performs its day-to-day operations, and a civil subpoena from the Securities and Exchange Commission.[50] In July 2019, the district attorney's office concluded its criminal investigation without levying charges. In May 2020, the SEC told the fund, "we do not intend to recommend an enforcement action by the Commission against Tulsa Real Estate Fund, LLC."

"While we realize that we must in no way construe the conclusions as indicating that we have been 'exonerated,' we are very pleased with the documented investigative conclusions by the Department of Justice and the SEC into the Tulsa Real Estate Fund," Morrison said.[51] "We cooperated fully with both the DOJ and the SEC investigations that led to no findings and no enforcement action, respectively; and we consider this justice for us and our more than 15,000 pledged investment partners worldwide."

The fund was created to take advantage of President Obama's 2012 JOBS Act. The act's purpose was to create an easier path for businesses with under $1 billion to obtain funding, increasing the amount of money that a small business, like the Tulsa Real Estate Fund, could raise from $5 million to $50 million.

"It also provided provisions for non-accredited investors, who are normally excluded from this process, to get involved through crowdfunding," attorney Courtney Richardson wrote at the Ivy Investor in 2018. "The act's rule, Regulation A+, essentially created a 'mini IPO' process for small businesses. Many investors are familiar with JOBS Act–facilitated IPOs such as Snapchat, Dropbox, and Blue Apron. However, potential Tulsa investors need to understand they may not be able to sell their units because 'no public market exists' and that their ability to transfer the units are limited. To withdraw, a member who has been in the investment for at least 12 months, must contact Tulsa directly."

Tulsa.

Just seeing the city's name cast like that makes my skin crawl. I think about the number of people who have or will get rich using this massacre for financial advantage. While I detest it, I can't say this is out of character for Tulsa. The city, the state, did not look at its people as human beings but as assets with a valuation. In Tulsa, you're only as good as the amount of money that can be made from you. Black folks, Black Tulsans, are familiar with white folks treating us this way. We are descended from slaves. We don't, however, expect our own people to take advantage of us, of our pain, of our stories. We expect more. Yet the Black capitalists continue to feast on their own. I dap up Kevin and tell him I'll see him later on. I take one last look at this spectacle.

When the centennial events are over, there is a slight lull between their end and the Juneteenth events that take place in just over two weeks' time. The Greenwood District still has the sheen of a jewel recently polished for display as archaeologists go back to work at Oaklawn. Before the month is over, they'll discovered those twenty-seven people buried, but locally the story will not resonate, and I will not see much about it in national news coverage. A few days later, Mama calls me. We haven't spoken much since her birthday in May.

"Hey, Mama."

"Hey, Bud!"

"What's up?"

"I need your help."

"What do you need?"

"It's about your Grandmomme. You know she's been gone awhile, and, well, a man at Forrest Lawn called."

"The cemetery?"

"Yeah, where she's buried."

"Is something wrong?"

"No, nothing's wrong. Not really. It's just—"

"It's just what?!" Saying it like I want her to get on with it. Saying it like I'm ready to be angry.

"Please don't yell at me, honey."

"I'm sorry, Mama. It's just, well, what is it?"

"She doesn't have a headstone." I can hear the shame in her voice. "And you know we don't have that kind of money."

I know, and I know how much it costs my mother personally to call me. "What's it cost? Do you know?"

She tells me.

"Do you think you have that kind of money?"

"Yes, ma'am, I do."

"Really?" She brightens up almost instantly. "I'm so grateful."

"Of course, Mama."

"I'll take care of everything else. You won't have to stop working or anything. I'll take care of it. I'll take care of all of it. Thank you so much, sweetheart."

"Yes, Mama."

"I don't think you know what this means to me that she's going to be marked. That we're going to be able to find her. She won't be lost."

At the dedication for the Greenwood Rising history center, Armstrong noted that the land the building was erected on was donated by the Hille Foundation, and an anonymous donor paid nearly $1 million to subcontractors in overtime so the building could be finished in time for the centennial. The city claims it did not make any money on the building of the history center, but it refuses to acknowledge it will benefit from its construction in the form of tourism and economic development ultimately controlled by white folks, if operated by Black folks.

Kristi Williams is the chairwoman for the Greater Tulsa African-American Affairs Commission and a descendant of Loula Williams, who opened the Dreamland Theatre on Greenwood in 1914—the same one depicted and destroyed in the HBO series *Watchmen* and *Lovecraft Country*. "I have really made a commitment to myself to no longer be a victim of symbolic gestures of the killing, the oppression and just the horrible treatment of my ancestors," Williams told the *Tulsa World*. She went on: "We have to follow that blueprint that those ancestors of Greenwood left us to create our own economy within this economy and to have a network (of) community between us as Black people. We cannot be complicit with white supremacy. That is what they taught us. That is what they left us with, and we have gotten away from that."

Vanessa Hall-Harper is a city councilor representing District 1, which includes Greenwood. She's also Tulsa's only Black elected official in the city. "It is all a farce to make Tulsa appear not to be the racist-ass city that it is as we approach the centennial. That is all it is," Hall-Harper told the *World* in May 2021. "You have been neglecting Greenwood and this part of the community all these years—for decades. Now we are rushing in to do all these things because the eyes of the world are going to be on Tulsa, and particularly Greenwood."[52]

State representative Regina Goodwin was originally appointed to the centennial commission. Greenwood Rising Black Wall Street History Center was not then in the commission's plan. The plan then was to put any money raised into the already existing Greenwood Cultural Center and develop its parking lot, next to the highway, into the history center. The commission couldn't wait for the cultural center board to figure out details, so it moved the project a block south to property donated to it by the Hille Foundation at the southwest corner of Greenwood and Archer, just in front of her uncle Joe Goodwin's newspaper, *The Oklahoma Eagle*. That was when Goodwin said she'd had enough.

"It is no secret that folks were saying that these monies were going to go to the Greenwood Cultural Center," Goodwin told the *World* in May 2021. "I took my name off of the Centennial Commission and was not participating because I thought there was an issue of integrity, and I think it has proven to be so."

Angela Robinson opened the Black Wall Street Corner Store and More just a week ago, a few steps from where the history center stands. She believes the center and the millions spent on it and other projects are only for the better. "Anything that is going to allow us to rebuild this area I think is going to benefit us, absolutely," she said.

Robinson opened her store after Tori Tyson had to close her salon, Blow Out Hair Studio, in the same space because she had been priced out of her lease. She owned the business, not the building. She was evicted in March 2021 after fourteen years at 109 N. Greenwood.[53] Her shop is now located fifteen minutes farther into North Tulsa, solidly outside of the district Tulsa officials claim their revival of for a second time since 1921. We are being pitted against each other, eating each other's wealth-building opportunities, turning trauma tricks for tourists, and killing what little we can call our own. The commission, Justice for Greenwood, and Black Tulsans have been at odds for years, though, and that animosity came to a head in the lead-up to the "Remember & Rise" concert—let alone the Greenwood Rising Black Wall Street History Center. Nearing the end of the commission's work, some resigned in May 2021.

State senator and centennial commissioner Monroe Nichols submitted his resignation on May 11, following Oklahoma governor and fellow commissioner Kevin Stitt's signing of H.B. 1775 into law, which outlaws teaching critical race theory and books like this one in Oklahoma schools.

"H.B. 1775 was a direct shot in the face for all of us who have been working hard on the commission, for all of us who have been working toward recognition, reconciliation," Nichols told KJRH on May 12, 2021. "I would have to say it was the most disruptive thing that a governor could have done. And Kevin Stitt did it with a smile on his face."[54]

The centennial commission also construed Stitt's signing of H.B. 1775 as an attack and sent him a letter that read, in part: "The Centennial Commission feels that your signature on the bill at this critical time when Oklahoma should embrace its history is diametrically opposite to the mission of the Centennial Commission and reflects your desire to end your affiliation."[55]

Oklahoma U.S. senator James Lankford resigned his position on the commission just before Memorial Day weekend. After Lankford challenged the 2020 presidential election results, helping inflame riots and insurrection at the U.S. Capitol, he was allowed to stay on the commission. In fact, when I visit Greenwood Rising at its public opening on August 4, 2021, Lankford's and Stitt's names are prominently placed on a plaque celebrating their appointments to the centennial commission.

To gain entry to the building, I reserve a ticket online. I arrive at the cultural center parking lot just a block northwest of Greenwood Rising before my tour is scheduled to begin at 12:30 p.m. I park in the lot, reminding myself this is where the museum was going to be built. The cultural center was supposed to be renovated, remain in the charge of Black Tulsans, and usher in a new narrative, a new era, of Black self-determination in my hometown. Walking south from the cultural center, over top of plaques nestled in the sidewalk where Black-owned businesses in 1921 once stood, prosperous and vibrant, has turned into something worse than a metaphor. It's a cliché. Like the rush to kneel following Kaepernick's act, it no longer has a depth of meaning

This thought hammers me when I come close enough to Greenwood Rising to read the quote on the north side of the building, stark naked for all to see: "Not everything that is faced can be changed, but nothing can be changed until it is faced." The quote was uttered by and is attributed on this wall to James Baldwin, a man whose legacy I adore, but who never set foot here in my city.

I grit my teeth because I know then the principals responsible for Greenwood Rising have co-opted yet another Black luminary who had little to do with Tulsa, the massacre at Greenwood, or the Black vitalization it represented. The people who raised money to build this museum tore that quote from an unfinished work of

Baldwin's called *Remember This House*. The work was made popularly known in Raoul Peck's documentary film about Baldwin called *I Am Not Your Negro*. Using that quote also points toward an attempt to co-opt Baldwin's language, poetic and clear, for a purpose it was not meant to be used for. His words were for his friends who were assassinated—Medgar Evers, Malcolm X, and Martin Luther King Jr.—not a Black community in North Tulsa burned and razed by its white neighbors who have yet to repair Black Tulsans.

The folks with a hand in building Greenwood Rising hide behind the words of a Black American visionary, showing a cowardice on a par with those who chose to use this opportunity to perform a kind of nefarious sincerity. I have no doubt that the principal players behind Greenwood Rising are sincere in their desire to be known as good. But white sincerity is a clever disguise for cruelty; a cruelty that does force an honest confrontation, condemnation, and reparation for the generations damaged, sullied, and forgotten; a cruelty that stabs Tulsa as a place where white lives matter and Black lives do not.

"Americans are always sincere," Baldwin said, "it is their most striking and appalling attribute . . . Nixon was perfectly sincere when lying about Watergate, the military was perfectly sincere when lying about Vietnam and Cambodia, Helms is perfectly sincere when he says that he is not a racist, and the late J. Edgar Hoover was sincere when he called the late Martin Luther King, Jr. the biggest liar in America." Tulsa mayor T. D. Evans was sincere when he said the massacre is the fault of the Black community; he was elected to serve immediately following the massacre in a refusal to allow Black homeowners and business owners to collect financial damages. Tulsa mayor G. T. Bynum was sincere when he said Tulsans will not pay reparations to its Black neighbors a century later. Richard Lloyd Jones was sincere when he backed the Ku Klux Klan in Tulsa and stoked the flame that has burned Tulsa ever since. Black Tulsans are sincere in wanting to live as social and economic peers to white Tulsans in a city that would rather have guns in school than Black history. "This sincerity covers, and pardons all," Baldwin said, "[and] is the very substance of American panic."

White Tulsans left us here in North Tulsa—buried in the rubble and refuse and blood and grief called North Tulsa—to go build their suburbs in Bixby, Broken Arrow, Jenks, Owasso, and Sand Springs, only to return to run a highway through our ruins to more easily get to their box store shrines, stick the Center of the Universe—a spot in Tulsa marked because of its peculiar acoustics, where a sound created is echoed back louder than when it was first made—near the center of mass unmarked graves of Black massacre victims, and then, in 2021, invite millions across the world to come have a gander, a look-see, at our desolation and treat our triumphs like a trinket for the price of a ticket.

Tulsans, the ones who allowed this James Baldwin quote to flash in white lettering against a black brick wall, neglect his social criticism following 1963; neglect the man who watched the civil rights movement rebuked with the assassination of his friends, the denunciation of the Black Power, the election of Ronald Reagan, and the proliferation of mass incarceration of Black bodies. Baldwin, who said, "What is most terrible is that American white men are not prepared to believe my version of the story, to believe that it happened. In order to avoid believing that, they have set up in themselves a fantastic system of evasions, denials, and justifications, a system that is about to destroy their grasp of reality, which is another way of saying their moral sense." Greenwood Rising is a multimillion-dollar symptom of that system at work in Tulsa. It's what we do. It's what we, Black Tulsans, allow, and it's what white Tulsans will stomach because the truth is so unflinching and grotesque that we refuse it, refuse to name it, set it aside. But it remains. History in Tulsa was and is written through the lens of what makes white folks feel good and doesn't make Black folks want to give up, though there are many who do. To live here, as a Black man, is to be reminded of how often people will change facts, omit facts, and assign lies in an effort to create a pleasant reading experience or, worse, turn this place made sacred into one fit for tourism, like a dastardly Disneyland of Black trauma, and call it a narrative museum of Black experience.

The truth remains because we've yet to build a mechanism that allows for reconciliation or truth-telling in the raw manner that allows for local, state, and federal policies that grant tools to repair structural racism spanning (at least) one hundred years in Tulsa. Legislation seeking the mere study of Tulsa's case for reparations was blocked by the Oklahoma House speaker Charles McCall when the state's Black caucus brought it before him, claiming, "[S]tate study on a matter now with the courts in active litigation is duplicative,"[56] rather than imperative. In place of paying what Black Tulsans are owed, we get nefariously sincere gestures like white folks tolerating acknowledgment of a Texas holiday called Juneteenth, building monuments to Dr. John Hope Franklin, misnaming Black Wall Street, and perpetuating the myth of Booker T. Washington calling Greenwood something it never was, never needed to be, never once knowing these gestures only lead to more Black trauma.

I am surprised to see Phil Armstrong greet my tour group, introduce himself as the center's interim director, and walk us through what he believes Greenwood Rising is meant to accomplish. He wears a gray blazer, white dress shirt punctuated with an ascot, blue jeans, and dress shoes made to resemble sneakers. He tells us this place is designed to make plain what, as he puts it, "was not taught in our history books," but is readily available to people who want to find it. In this mostly white-walled space at the entrance, with photos demonstrating what Greenwood looked like before 1921 and after, Armstrong directs us to a large video screen displaying the Black merchants with businesses in the Greenwood District in 2021 and the people who helped create and execute this vision of a center that teaches the massacre as a means of hope, of reconciliation, of Black pride.

Maya Angelou reads her most famous poem, "Still I Rise," as the faces and places of Greenwood are shown before us. "She wrote that poem in 1973, but it's as if she wrote it for this moment," Armstrong says. In 1991, Angelou visited the University of Tulsa to speak, though you'd never know it walking into Greenwood Rising. "Everyone is vulnerable, susceptible, to propaganda spread about him or her," Angelou said then.[57] "If it is spread around long enough, the person has to believe it. Young [B]lack men have been told, 'There is no romance.' That's not the way it is or has been," she said. "We would not have survived all we have been through if it had always been like that." This is a call to me, to Black Tulsans, nearly a decade before the massacre became a widely known national topic. Here she is, prescient and present, yet the principals behind Greenwood Rising prove blind to see her then.

At the video's conclusion, Armstrong points us to the entrance of the first exhibit, which features a quote from E. P. McCabe, one of the first Black nationalists in American history and the man who lobbied the United States to make Oklahoma, then Indian Territory, an all-Black state. "What will you be if you stay in the South?" McCabe said. "Slaves liable to be killed at any time, and never treated right. But if you come to Oklahoma, you have equal chance with the white man, free and independent." This was a half-truth at best, and perhaps no one knew that more than McCabe.

Edward Preston "E. P." McCabe hoped to become governor of Oklahoma Territory after becoming the first Black state auditor for neighboring Kansas. Kansans elected a Black man. McCabe was endorsed for the governorship of Oklahoma by President Benjamin Harrison after he helped get Harrison elected. But there were far too many white folks who would not stand to see a Black man elected governor, especially after he said he would govern "without fear or favor to white and [B]lack alike." To this, white men made themselves known. If McCabe won election, one white man said, "[I]t would take a larger army than that of the United States to keep a Negro alive in Oklahoma," according to Danney Goble's book *Progressive Oklahoma: The Making of a New Kind of State.* A government official who traveled to Oklahoma Territory claimed a Governor McCabe might be "assassinated within a week after he enters the Territory." And still another, a voting Republican, made his opinion known just as bluntly, if more profanely: "I am told that dead niggers make good fertilizer, and if Negroes try to Africanize Oklahoma, they will find that we will enrich our soil with them."

McCabe shortly thereafter decided not to pursue the Oklahoma governorship, but he was convinced that the territory itself should still be for Black folks across the country. McCabe found seventy lots for sale in the territory and acquired them. The land was just twelve miles northeast of Guthrie, Oklahoma. He renamed the area for a Black congressman from Virginia and the first dean of Howard University Law School, John Mercer Langston. McCabe developed the townsite of Langston into what he hoped would become a haven for Black folks within the borders of Oklahoma.

In its first year, two thousand Black folks moved to the town. Over time Black towns sprouted in Boley, Taft, and Rentiesville, but the Black state of Oklahoma was dashed almost as quickly as it peaked. Most of the first wave of Black migrants arrived when the time was too late to plant crops. Some left. Some stayed. Some starved. Others moved into larger cities with rising Black populations where work might be found, like Greenwood. In doing this, Black went to work for Black folks. They built each other's businesses and created their own facilities and services, until the social law of segregation became the actual law of segregation. Black folks patronized Black businesses out of necessity rather than choice. There was no problem with this among white folks. Segregation was preferred until Black success began to feel to white folks like competition, and their competitors—Black folks—were showing them up if not winning their own respect in dress, in homeownership, in prosperity. Black folks adopted the desires and means of their white capitalist neighbors. Rather than lift themselves by their bootstraps, as they told Black folks to do, white folks became bitter, mean, and violent. The city of Norman banished its Black citizens in 1896. Tulsa's neighbor, Sapulpa, expelled its Black citizens in 1901. Waurika, near the Texas border, turned itself into a sundown town—all-white communities that excluded Black folks using discriminatory laws or threats—overnight and gave its Black citizens just twenty-four hours to leave town in 1905. That same year another Tulsa neighbor, citizens in Claremore, physically assaulted Black inhabitants and drove them from the town.

Tulsan and Oklahoman white people changed the rules, quite literally. They rewrote laws to put Black Tulsans and Black Oklahomans under heel because Black folks had upset the social order in the fledgling state. In no place was the social order more upset than the Greenwood District in Tulsa, and this is where I'm inclined to see the positive nature of Armstrong's characterization of Greenwood as "a Black paradise." But that wasn't true either.

Black folks lived in Tulsa long before white folks decided to call the city that. Black folks lived in Tulsa before the city called itself a city. Black folks were among the first people to live in what became Tulsa as former slaves to Creeks. Upon taking their freedom, and then being granted that freedom under law, some Black folks even married Creeks when the nation still called Alabama home. In fact, so many Creeks looked Black that U.S. census takers were not always sure who to call Creek and who to call Black. This is where Tulsa's Black community began, and its enduring prosperity was chief among the reasons why folks burned it down, killed its residents, and buried Black folks in unmarked graves that were still being uncovered into the fall of 2021.

At the end of his introduction, Armstrong makes sure to point out that one of the descendants of the massacre survivors has joined the tour late. "Ladies and gentlemen, we are in the presence of royalty." A meek Black woman, wearing a mask, flits away applause as Armstrong leads us past McCabe's quote and into the first exhibit's space. He hangs back with the descendant for a bit while the rest of the tour moves forward, mostly at our own pace, through each of the five stages of the center. The first features the founding of Oklahoma through the eyes of Black folks and the eyes of white folks who scorned them. We are introduced to Dr. A. C. Jackson, J. B. Stradford, and Buck Colbert Franklin there. Next to their portraits is a map of the forty-six Black towns that once existed in Oklahoma. Only fourteen remain. As we make our way to the next, the descendant catches up to us. She sees my Moleskine notebook, in which I'm scribbling notes, and points to it.

"You writing a book?" she asks.

"Yes, ma'am," I say.

"Tell it right."

I tell the back of her head *Yes, ma'am* as she moves from one room to another. She is one of several Black men and women in my touring group who look so touched to be acknowledged by the existence of this museum. This is what Tulsa has done to us Black folk. We have been forced to say thank you for being treated as a commodity rather than as human beings. She looks like she is searching for something or someone. She takes a seat in front of one projector screen showing how her ancestors' world was burned, and how they were killed defending it. I watch her watch the world burn. Beneath her mask, I watch her cheeks rise and fall and a tear run a stream from her eye to the top of her mask. She catches me staring and wipes it away. She stands and walks past me, lightly tapping my shoulder.

I try to measure an appropriate amount of time to appreciate the interactive barbershop experience, meant for tourists to understand the politics and news of the day. I find myself asking a similar question: how much time should I stay and ponder here? After just a couple of minutes, we move into a room with theater-like overhead lighting as dramatic re-creations of the massacre itself play out on a projector screen made to look like broken brick walls, directly across the room from Ku Klux Klan robes, pendants, and proclamations. I stare, perhaps too long, at chains and whips used to beat slaves. Indeed, one of the items on display is called SLAVE WHIP, and its info card reads: "The whip is an enduring symbol of social control and American chattel slavery. Whips like these are a constant reminder of the violence used to reinforce a white supremacist social order." Nineteenth-century shackles are encased behind the same glass as the whip. "Shackles were used primarily to confine and restrain enslaved people, while balls and chains were used to prevent escape." A quote from the first Black Supreme Court justice, Thurgood Marshall, is framed near the shackles: "The Ku Klux Klan never dies. They just stop wearing sheets because the sheets cost too much." I meditate on the macabre humor of that quote prominently displayed in a center about racial strife with the governor on the commission, who outlawed teaching race in school because white children might feel bad.

On my way to the building's exit, I remember the construction going on next door. A large building is being erected right next door to Greenwood Rising. I notice a Black security guard sitting at the welcome counter. He dons a mask, reminding me that Armstrong had not.

"What's next door?" I ask the security guard.

"Some kind of apartments, I think," he says.

I tell him thank you and leave, knowing this place is not for me, not for Tulsans. This is a tourist destination, yet another presentation for people who aren't from here; the kind of people who take a special glee in telling me they've never heard of this tragedy that is written about widely, across the internet and in dozens of books; as if to make *me* feel better rather enraged. But I remember this

REQUIEM FOR THE MASSACRE   293

place, Greenwood Rising, is for the outside world. If it were for us, it would not exist, would not need to exist. Black Tulsans would be made whole.

I walk outside and look for the address of the building next door. It's four stories, and will include three stories of office space for rent. Greenwood Rising's address is 23 North Greenwood, and the land it's built on was gifted by the Hille Foundation to the commission expressly for this project. The address next door is 21 North Greenwood. "We feel like it will be a pretty cool addition to the neighborhood," Kajeer Yar, principal of the 21 North Greenwood LLC, told *Tulsa World*.[58] I walk back to my truck, shut myself in the heat, drenched in sweat, filled with anger, hurt. Finally, I let myself cry and cry and cry because I fear we will never recover what was lost, and our stories will continue to be so warped and twisted by others that we will shed tears at the merest recognition that we were once so brilliant.

But sometimes, I imagine what we could become. At the centennial, calls for reparations for massacre survivors, victims, and descendants of Greenwood are barely acknowledged, with only a feeble follow-up response that those alive are not responsible for the sins of those dead, we are no longer slaves, we are constantly asking for what someone else has earned and gaslit into believing we are somehow less than glorious, while they stop just short of mandating our outright extermination. We have yet to become one in the century since the massacre, least of all in Greenwood, at the centennial, where myth has taken the place of truth. If progress is defined by acknowledging the massacre that was once unmentionable in Tulsa, then progress has been made. But we still haven't grappled with horrible consequences of the massacre, made its victims whole, or acted on what we've learned. The centennial events succeeded in making someone money, but the centennial was no reckoning. This is what tell my goddaughters.

W E WALK THE LENGTH OF WHAT IS LEFT OF 1921'S Greenwood, which in November 2021 is not much more than memory.[59] My goddaughters, Weapon X and Brave, hold hands as we walk along Greenwood Avenue. Greenwood in 2021, right here, right now, is a block long, a block wide, I tell them. In five minutes, we walk from the intersection of Greenwood and Archer, north over plaques dedicated to businesses here before the massacre, past these brick buildings rebuilt to give this single block a semblance of what a community of Black apartment living, Black homes, and Black businesses teeming with ten thousand Black folks looks like. But where the ten thousand might have seen the beginning of what was once called Deep Greenwood, we encounter a graffitied overpass. It's decorated in "Black Lives Matter," "BLM," "Black Wall Street" and plaques beneath our feet commemorating businesses razed during the massacre and a handful with the courage and money to reopen afterward. We read the business names allowed as traffic on I-244 roars overhead.

On the southwest side of the overpass is the newly built Pathway to Hope, a map depicting what Greenwood looked like to a cartographer on May 29, 1921, and on the north side is the Greenwood Cultural Center. We walk the Pathway between a highway and a baseball field. The girls see portraits of Black men and women.

"Who's that lady?" Weapon X asks. "She's beautiful."

"That's Toni Morrison," I say. "She was a writer."

"A writer like you?" Brave asks.

"No, she was something much more."

At the end of the Pathway, we loop back toward Greenwood Avenue, beneath the overpass, and into the cultural center right next to the highway. The cultural center was dedicated in 1995, I tell them, and while it is leased to the Greenwood Cultural Center, the property is owned by the city of Tulsa. In 2019, Tulsans voted to approve $5.3 million in renovations for the cultural center, funded through a sales tax.[60]

"What's a sales tax?" Brave asks.

"A sales tax just means we'll pay a little extra for candy and drinks when we're done, so that some of our money goes toward making the cultural center look prettier."

She nods. "That's nice."

"It is," I say. "There's a lot of history here. Some of it's mine."

As we walk into the cultural center, I tell them, oh yes, the cultural center is the center of Black memory in Tulsa, housing a modest collection of Black art, a banquet room that has hosted more than just birthday parties, like the one where I watched their mama, Laurel, dance at a Scorpios birthday party. That so many people have held events here that it's more like a community center than a museum. I don't tell my goddaughters I was once a white girl's date at white girl sorority's winter formal here. My date, Amy, wandered off at this formal after getting drunk on liquor we weren't supposed to have, smuggled in by a brazen white girl. I waited twenty minutes before looking for Amy. I asked one of her sorority sisters who was coming out of the restroom if Amy was in there. She said no.

I located her around the corner. She was sobbing on the floor, a pale mushroom atop her billowing teal dress. Her head was down. Her shoulders pulsed like angry pistons.

"What's wrong?" I asked.

She was startled at first. Then Amy held me with her eyes, watery and not blinking, like I'd asked her if she was sane, like she might explode with sorrow. She pointed overhead to a poster. I didn't look up.

"Why is the formal *here*?" she asked. She pointed at the poster again. I looked that time. It wasn't a poster at all, but a photo memorializing the massacre.

"This is demented," she said.

I still don't know if she was asking why her sorority's winter formal was here or why the massacre was here or why her sorority was having a celebration at a place meant to remember that which so many want to forget. I took her back to the banquet hall. She drank. She passed out on the bus back to campus. I think she wanted to forget that night before it was over.

I tell the girls I don't want them to forget. There's much they have to know and hold on to knowing. I tell my goddaughters I watched my friend Bruce win a cruiserweight title boxing in a ring built in the space where Ben Crump talked in conversation with a civil rights attorney, activists, and an actor about the massacre, about Black life mattering in that same banquet hall. I tell them that I stood across the street from the cultural center waiting for a sitting United States president to address the nation in reflection on the massacre, on racial reckoning, while we Black Tulsans stood outside and waited for talk of reparations we still haven't seen in the months since the centennial. But they will remodel the cultural center; an incremental step used to placate Black Tulsans like me who know more is needed. I tell them more is owed as we make our way to a room full of faces, Black faces, Black Tulsans.

I tell my goddaughters that next to the cultural center stands Oklahoma State University at Tulsa, a mostly quiet and loveless conglomerate of buildings I have never seen filled with students. Across the street from OSU-Tulsa, across the grass park, there are train tracks separating the park from the USA BMX arena and an empty rusting building. The BMX arena, once just a brown field, has been touted by our mayor as an agent for increased tourism. He expects the park to bring one hundred thousand people in its first five years of operation. But to me and other Black Tulsans I've spoken with, the addition of a BMX arena next to train tracks looks and feels anachronistic, hollow. No one in North Tulsa asked for a BMX arena. We asked for reparations, a reckoning.

I tell them to sit with me on a bench in this room full of Black faces at the north end of the cultural center. I point out the window behind us. I tell my goddaughters if we keep heading northeast, taking a street named after the GAP Band, we'd run into what North Tulsa is and where decisions to invest in Black Tulsa fall short. I tell them that if we head northwest, we can traverse the entire OSU campus before coming to Standpipe Hill, where white Tulsans watched other white Tulsans destroy the city's Black enclave with hideous violence. If we traveled just past Standpipe, we'd no longer be in Greenwood. So this is it, I tell them. This is Greenwood in 2021, and I'm afraid, given time, this will be gone too. I tell them I will be gone too. Therefore, I brought them here.

I look at Brave, who nods at the question. They are eight and six years old. I sigh. I take them in, each to one side of me, the only children in the world I love as if they are my own. They look nothing like me.

They're long, slender, blonde like their mama, with eyes darting about this room pictured with Black Tulsans, children of the massacre. I have made them sit in silence as other folks move about the cultural center looking studious, pious. Brave's legs swing gently, perhaps six inches from the ground.

"Should we be here?" Weapon X asks. "We don't look like any of the people in here."

"Oh, yes," I say. "You should be here."

Weapon X doubts me. She was four years old when she first asked why her mother's skin is "clear," like theirs, while mine is "brown."

"You need to be here," I say, and grab their hands. "Because I am here."

And one day I won't be.

We leave the cultural center, and each girl takes turns reading the plaques in the sidewalk where 1921 Greenwood once stood. We stop at the Black Wall Street Corner Store, buy some candy and Gatorade. We sit three across on a park bench in front of the store and eat. I take pictures of them enjoying their candy, their drinks, and send those pictures to their mama. After we finish, I tell them it is time to go home.

I've yet to tell my goddaughters about Julius Jones. Five months after the centennial, in November 2021, the execution of Jones was an example of how Black folks were forced yet again to beg a white man to save the life of a Black man. On July 28, 1999, forty-five-year-old Edmond, Oklahoma, insurance executive Paul Scott Howell was shot and killed in front of his sister and his seven- and nine-year-old daughters. His SUV was stolen, too. Two days later, twenty-year-old Christopher Jordan was jailed after being accused of driving the gunman to the crime scene. On my twelfth birthday, July 31, 1999, I was reading the second Harry Potter book, *Chamber of Secrets*, in my bedroom, and Julius Darius Jones was being arrested at his parents' house where the murder weapon was located.

Two days later, Oklahoma County District Attorney Bob Macy said he'd seek the death penalty for Jones. In 2001, in a deal that granted him a thirty-year prison sentence if he testified against Jones, Jordan pleaded guilty to first-degree murder. At Jones's trial in 2002, Jordan was emphatic. "I didn't do anything," he said. "Julius did it." Jones was convicted of first-degree murder and sentenced to death. Jones's defense attorney, David McKenzie, called no witnesses in defense of his client. In an affidavit, McKenzie later said he had never tried a death penalty case and "was terrified by this case due to my inexperience." McKenzie also said he employed an investigator to help him gather evidence who was "completely untrained and unqualified to be interviewing witnesses or otherwise performing investigative functions."

After serving just half of his thirty-year sentence, Jordan was released from prison in 2014. In 2018, a red bandana, once worn by Howell and said to have his killer's DNA on it, was tested by a forensics lab in Virginia in the hopes of exonerating Jones. The result showed Jones's DNA on the bandana. Also in 2018, ABC devoted three episodes of its documentary series *The Last Defense* to Jones's trial, showing that it was riddled with errors by his defense and aided by racial bias. Still, we marched at the state capitol in Oklahoma City, demanding Jones be set free. I've yet to tell Brave that around her sixth birthday in September 2021, the Oklahoma Pardon and Parole Board voted 3–1 to recommend that Governor Kevin Stitt commute Jones's sentence to life in prison with the possibility of parole. The following week, the Oklahoma Court of Criminal Appeals scheduled Jones's execution. Requests to stay his execution in state and federal court were denied. Four hours before he was set to be killed, Jones was granted clemency on November 18, 2021, fewer than six months after the centennial anniversary of the massacre in Greenwood.

Stitt's name is among those commemorated inside Greenwood Rising, which opened to the public on August 4, 2021, Barack Obama's birthday, and is meant to honor victims of the violence against Black Oklahomans that Stitt refused to stop. Stitt later said he commuted Jones's sentence to life in prison without the possibility of parole "after prayerful consideration." I departed from God, from Christianity, because it would mean Stitt and I prayed to the same deity. A man who denies Jones's eligibility to appeal for parole for the remainder of his life is not a man I can share faith with. I've yet to tell my goddaughters that my parents are Stitt's constituents, believe Jones is guilty, and think that life in prison is the state showing mercy.

When my goddaughters are a little older, but not much older, I'll tell them that our calls to abolish prisons and defund police employed the theory and strategy of Black revolt outlined in Cedric J. Robinson's *Black Marxism*. I'll tell them Marxism is a big word that means placing a higher value on people rather than an individual person. I'll tell them defunding the police means using money accumulated from breaking the law for education, housing, and food so that most people are no longer forced to break the law for their own survival. So that we all live well. I tell my goddaughters we all deserve to live well.

I'll tell them about what Robinson called the "Black radical tradition," defined as "a revolutionary consciousness that proceeded from the whole historical experience of Black people." I'll tell them this means my Blackness cannot be separated from who I am and how I can live in this country.

I'll tell them that in the foreword of the latest edition of *Black Marxism*, marking nearly forty years of being in print, Robin D. G. Kelley thought the world was changing in the summer of 2020. My goddaughters will likely reference this moment in their lives by the murder of George Floyd. "We are witnessing the Black Radical Tradition in motion, driving what is arguably the most dynamic mass rebellion against state-sanctioned violence and racial capitalism we have ever seen in North America since the 1960s— maybe the 1860s." And I will tell them Kelley was wrong. I will tell them about the January 6 insurrection six months after Floyd's murder. I will tell them how much this scared me, and I will tell my goddaughters again about another group of white people who stormed the neighborhood in North Tulsa, where they attended preschool, when Black folks protested in the street. I'll tell them the story of two Black men from Tulsa. How one of them tried to assimilate into white Tulsa, and the other did not, and how both met the same end.

I'll tell my goddaughters that *Tulsa Star* publisher and editor A. J. Smitherman saw the millions O. W. Gurley reaped from his business ventures and how becoming rich had forced Gurley against the most aggressive ideals of Black progress, going so far as to call him an Uncle Tom in his newspaper, though his favored pejorative was "king" of "little Africa." But it wasn't just Smitherman. On June 6, 1912, the *Tulsa World* reported that along with having applied to be a reserve cop, Gurley had pleaded guilty to "keeping booze in a lodge room in his building in Darktown" and paid a $25 fine.[61] He wanted to be cozy with white folks, and white folks still mocked him. The lede in the news item also called Gurley "King of Little Africa." This is one more reason to discourage and outright detest those who still refer to Greenwood or the massacre as "Fire in Little Africa." It's a pejorative, like "nigger," and yet we let people refer to Greenwood using a slur, even carrying it forward ourselves because we've been taught Black history does not matter, measure up, or deserve our honesty. After becoming one of the richest Black men in Tulsa, the white Tulsans whom Gurley so wanted to respect him burned his life's work to the ground as he and his wife, Emma, fled south. He thought the white Tulsans he knew would save him during the massacre, according to *Black Fortunes*. When he arrived in South Tulsa, two white men shot at him. His wife fell at the sound of gunfire; Gurley left her without even saying goodbye. He chose to flee back to the North Tulsa but was picked up by National Guardsmen, who interned him at the fairgrounds just like every other Negro they saw. At the fairgrounds, most Black folks did not speak to him. He lost more than $250,000 ($3.8 million in 2021). After a white person vouched for him, Gurley was let go from the fairground. He found Emma, and he found his businesses in ruins. Months after the massacre, he sold his land, and he and his wife moved to South Los Angeles. He never fully regained the wealth he accumulated in Tulsa.

I'll tell my goddaughters that Smitherman thought Black folks should not just take care of each other, but that they should learn to harness what little financial and political power they held to collectively affect change, while men like Gurley believed in compromising with white Tulsans. Smitherman was more than willing to drag Gurley and the *Tulsa World* in his paper, but he did not stop there. In 1920, he challenged the *World*'s stance on separate but equal in the *Star*. "And why has the [B]lack man been singled out to bear the burden?" Smitherman wrote.[62] "Why don't the white man talk about social equality with the Indian whose racial qualities do not come under the ban of the white man's color prejudice: or, if so, it has been entirely overcome by the latter's avaricious proclivities, so that the Indian, who is also a colored man, has been received into the white man's home, into the white man's own terms of social equality. The [B]lack man has not failed to note that the laws of our country have been enacted and invoked to perpetuate a custom of unfairness that is aimed at no other race group under our flag, and certainly the notation is not full of pleasant memories. We are not demanding 'social equality'—that's something that regulates itself between individuals—but we are demanding all that any citizen of our country has a right to demand—Equality without discrimination." I'll tell my goddaughters that more than one hundred years after Smitherman wrote those words that we are still demanding the same.

I'll tell them that when the massacre was done, Smitherman's newspaper was too. He and his family were among the hundreds of Black folks who were homeless. His house was a two-story brick home where the Star Printing Co. was located and where he watched $40,000 dollars in assets—the equivalent of $440,000 in modern money—destroyed by white Tulsans. I'll tell my goddaughters that an arrest warrant was issued for Smitherman following the massacre, too, implicating him in the destruction of property like his own home. The Smithermans fled to St. Louis, then to Minneapolis, and then to Boston. In Boston, he gathered himself and told the Assistant Secretary for the NAACP what he planned to do. "I have decided to come out of hiding and do whatever I may to add to the splendid work you have already done to expose the atrocities of Tulsa and the massacre," he said.

The *Boston Herald* ran a story by Smitherman headlined "How Tulsa Has Treated the Negro Since the Riot," and he pleaded with white Americans to see the monster they had created. "In Tulsa, as many other parts of our country, the calloused spots of indulgence on the souls of [B]lack men have been rubbed off by the friction of race hatred, leaving the raw, bleeding sores of injustice and contumely of half century's accumulation, and they are now smarting under the sting of a growing national indifference to their cause. Will America wake?"

I'll tell my goddaughters about the publisher at the *Tulsa Tribune*, Richard Lloyd Jones—who also cofounded the church where their mother and father used to work and where Weapon X's fifth birthday party was held—responded to Smitherman's story with an editorial in the *Tribune*. The headline read: "SMITHERMAN FUGITIVE FROM JUSTICE EXTRADITION PAPERS GRANTED BY THREE GOVERNORS STOP BAD ACTOR STOP WRITING."

I'll tell my goddaughters that the city of Tulsa tried to have Smitherman extradited in Massachusetts. Eventually, he moved his family to Buffalo, New York. There he published the *Buffalo Star* and, later, the *Empire Star*. I'll tell them that after surviving the massacre, Smitherman died of a heart attack in 1961 writing an account of his life, a Black man Tulsa has tried hard to forget.

I'll tell my goddaughters that Tulsa and the massacre have taught me how much white folks want to dictate how my life is lived. I'll tell them about the Black and white Tulsans who glare at me when I hold their mama's hand. I'll tell my goddaughters about the Black and white Tulsans who screw up their faces, hold their breath, grit their teeth, when I speak with affection for them.

I will tell my goddaughters that people have all kinds of reasons for leaving home, but most Black folks have left Tulsa because they're simply not wanted here. I'll tell them I'm not wanted here. I will tell them that Tulsa tried to run me off, away from them, as Tulsa has done to so many of my friends, my sister, and thousands of Black folks who decided wherever is better, much better, than Tulsa. I will tell them that one of my most prominent acts of resistance and self-determination has been to buy a house here.

I'll tell my goddaughters that they will be two of those tasked with erecting my monument here in a cemetery around the corner from where they live now, as I was one of those tasked with erecting Grandmomme's. I will tell them that if the worst should happen and the house I own is burned to the ground, and if I survive this fire, I will fight to retain the land, rebuild my home. I have learned too much on this journey through the massacre to cede my space in Tulsa.

Acknowledgments

Laurel Williamson, my partner, my queen, who listened to me rouse and stir and then dared me to screw my courage to the sticking place. Thank you, my love.

Ron Taylor, my best and oldest friend. I have never met a better man, and I daresay I never will. Thank you, brother mine.

Thank you, Tyler Burroughs, for saving me, listening to me ramble late into the night about so much of this world. From the moment we first met, you believed I was worth the effort to know. Thank you, brother mine.

Kate Galatian-Burroughs, KGB, the Lasso of Truth still gets spins at my house. Thank you for being close to call, close to talk, to restore and repair and validate the artists in your life too, sister mine.

Katy Mullins, your unshakable belief in the work I produced fortified my own resolve. You have made me a better reader and you are the writer I most admire. Thank you, sister mine.

Thank you, Michelle Tessler, my literary agent and friend. You answered my query, believed in what this book could be, facilitated my dream.

Thank you, Mensah Demary, my editor on this book, who did not once flinch, who believed the truth of my story and that of this city I love is worth telling straight. Thank you for allowing me the chance to become the writer I always wanted to be, letting me talk at you about what I love and fear and then helping me say what I need to say.

Goddaughters, kiss my forehead. Let me kiss each of yours, and know no matter where you are, what you do or who you become, I will always love you.

Selected Bibliography

Abdurraqib, Hanif. *A Devil in Little America: Notes in Praise of Black Performance*. New York: Random House, 2021.

Askew, Rilla Askew. *Fire in Beulah*. New York: Penguin Books, 2001.

Baldwin, James, and Raoul Peck. *I Am Not Your Negro*. New York: Vintage, 2017.

Baldwin, James. *Nobody Knows My Name*. New York: Vintage, 1992.

Baldwin, James. *No Name in the Street*. New York: Knopf Doubleday Publishing Group, 2007.

Baradaran, Mehrsa. *The Color of Money: Black Banks and the Racial Wealth Gap*. Cambridge: Belknap Press, 2019.

Bell, Roger, and Jerry Hoffman. *Muskogee*. Charleston, NC: Arcadia Publishing, 2014.

Bennett, Brit. *The Vanishing Half: A Novel*. New York: Riverhead Books, 2020.

Bloom, Joshua, and Waldo E. Martin Jr. *Black against Empire: The History and Politics of the Black Panther Party*. Berkeley: University of California Press, 2016.

Coates, Ta-Nehisi. *The Beautiful Struggle: A Memoir*. New York: One World, 2009.

Cobb, Russell. *The Great Oklahoma Swindle: Race, Religion and Lies in America's Weirdest State*. Lincoln, NE: Bison Books, 2020.

Cooper, Brittney. *Eloquent Rage*. New York: St. Martin's Press, 2018.

Churchwell, T. D., et. al. *Tulsa Race Riot: A Report by the Oklahoma Commission to Study the Race Riot*. Oklahoma Commission to Study the Tulsa Race Riot of 1921, 2001.

Du Bois, W. E. B. *The Autobiography of W. E. B. Du Bois: A Soliloquy on Viewing My Life from the Last Decade of Its First Century*. New York City: International Publishers Co. Inc, 1968.

Du Bois, W. E. B. *Black Reconstruction in America: 1860-1880*. New York: Free Press, 1998.

Du Bois, W. E. B. *Darkwater: Voices from Within the Veil*. Mineola, NY: Dover Publications, 1999.

Du Bois, W. E. B. *Dusk of Dawn: An Essay Toward an Autobiography of a Race Concept*. Oxford: Oxford University Press, 2014.

Du Bois, W. E. B. *The Souls of Black Folks*. Mineola, NY: Dover Publications, 2016.

Edwards, Harry. *The Revolt of the Black Athlete*. Champaign: University of Illinois Press, 2017.

Ellsworth, Scott. *Death in a Promised Land: The Tulsa Race Riot of 1921*. Baton Rouge: LSU Press, 1992.

Ellsworth, Scott. *The Ground Breaking: An American City and its Search for Justice*. New York: Dutton, 2021.

Ferrell, James Adrian. "A Magnet School and Desegregation: A Case Study of Booker T. Washington High School, 1975–1980." PhD dissertation, Oklahoma State University, 2008.

Franklin, John Hope. *Mirror to America: The Autobiography of John Hope Franklin*. New York: Farrar, Straus and Giroux, 2005.

Franklin, John Hope, and John Whittington Franklin. *My Life and an Era: The Autobiography of Buck Colbert Franklin*. Baton Rouge: LSU Press, 1997.

Franks, Clyda R. *Tulsa: Where the Streets Were Paved with Gold.* Charleston, SC: Arcadia Publishing, 2000.

Gates, Eddie Faye. *They Came Searching: How Blacks Sought the Promised Land in Tulsa.* Fort Worth, TX: Eakin Press, 1997.

Gay, Roxane. *Hunger: A Memoir of (My) Body.* New York: Harper, 2017.

Gerkin, Steve. *Hidden History of Tulsa.* Charleston, SC: The History Press, 2014.

Glaude, Jr., Eddie S. *Begin Again: James Baldwin's America and Its Urgent Lessons for Our Own.* New York: Crown, 2020.

Goble, Danney. *Progressive Oklahoma: The Making of a New Kind of State.* Norman: University of Oklahoma Press, reprint edition, 2015

Goble, Danney. *Tulsa! Biography of American City.* Tulsa, OK: Council Oaks Books, 1997.

Hirsch, James S. *Riot and Remembrance: The Tulsa Race Riot and its Legacy.* Boston: Mariner Books, 2003.

Hurd, Michael. *Thursday Night Lights: The Story of Black High School Football in Texas.* Austin: University of Texas Press, 2017.

Jackson, David H., Jr. *Booker T. Washington and the Struggle Against White Supremacy: The Southern Educational Tours, 1908–1912.* New York: Palgrave MacMillan, 2008.

Johnson, Hannibal B. *Black Wall Street: From Riot to Renaissance in Tulsa's Historic Greenwood District.* Fort Worth, TX: Eakin Press, 2007.

Johnson, Hannibal B. *Tulsa's Historic Greenwood District.* Charleston: Arcadia Publishing, 2014.

Khan-Cullors, Patrisse, and Asha Bandele. *When They Call You a Terrorist: A Black Lives Matter Memoir.* New York: St. Martin's Press, 2018.

Kemm, James O. *Tulsa: Oil Capital of the World.* Charleston, SC: Arcadia Publishing, 2004.

Krehbiel, Randy. *Tulsa, 1921: Reporting a Massacre*. Norman: University of Oklahoma Press, 2021.

Laymon, Kiese: *An American Memoir*. New York: Scribner, 2018.

Lewis, David Levering. *W. E. B. Du Bois: A Biography: 1868–1963*. New York: Holt Paperbacks, 2009.

Loewen, James W. *Sundown Towns: A Hidden Dimension of American Racism*. New York: The New Press, 2018.

Madigan, Tim. *The Burning: Massacre, Destruction, and the Tulsa Race Riot of 1921*. New York: St. Martin's Griffin, 2003.

McWhirter, Cameron. *Red Summer: The Summer of 1919 and the Awakening of Black America*. New York: St. Martin's Griffin, 2012.

Michaeli, Ethan. *The Defender: How the Legendary Black Newspaper Changed America*. Boston: Houghton Mifflin Harcourt, 2020.

Moreno, Carlos. *The Victory of Greenwood*. Tulsa, OK: Jenkin Lloyd-Hones Press, 2021.

Nash, Jere, and Andy Taggart. *Mississippi Politics: The Struggle for Power, 1976–2008*. Oxford: University of Mississippi Press, 2009.

Onaci, Edward. *Free the Land: The Republic of New Afrika and the Pursuit of a Black Nation-State*. Chapel Hill, NC: University of North Carolina Press, 2020.

Oubre, Claude F. *Forty Acres and a Mule: The Freedmen's Bureau and Black Land Ownership*. Baton Rouge: LSU Press, 2012.

Parrish, Mary Elizabeth Jones. *The Nation Must Awake: My Witness to the Tulsa Race Massacre of 1921*. San Antonio, TX: Trinity University Press, 2021.

Pitner, Barrett Holmes. *The Crime Without a Name: Ethnocide and the Erasure of Culture in America*. Berkeley: Counterpoint, 2021.

Prager, Joshua. *The Family Roe: An American Story*. New York: W. W. Norton & Company, 2021.

Price, Asher. *Earl Campbell: Yards After Contact*. Austin: University of Texas Press, 2019.

Robertson, David. *Denmark Vesey: The Buried Story of America's Largest Slave Rebellion and the Man Who Led It*. New York: Vintage, 2000.

Robinson, Cedric J. *Black Marxism: The Making of the Black Radical Tradition*. Chapel Hill: University of North Carolina Press, 2000.

Ruff, Matt. *Lovecraft Country: A Novel*. New York: Harper Perennial, 2016.

Saunt, Claudio. *Unworthy Republic: The Dispossession of Native Americans and the Road to Indian Territory*. New York: W. W. Norton & Company, 2020.

Scott, Emmett J., and Lyman Beecher Stowe. *Booker T. Washington: Builder of a Civilization*. Garden City, NY: Doubleday, Page & Co.,1918.

Ward, Jesmyn. *Men We Reaped: A Memoir*. New York: Bloomsbury USA, 2014.

Washington, Booker T. *Up From Slavery*. Mineola, NY: Dover Publications, 1995.

Wills, Shamori. *Black Fortunes: The Story of Six African Americans Who Survived Slavery and Became Millionaires*. New York: Amistad, 2019.

Wilson, Charlie. *I Am Charlie Wilson*. New York: 37 Ink, 2016.

Young, RJ. *Let It Bang: A Young Black Man's Odyssey into Guns*. Boston: Houghton Mifflin Harcourt, 2018.

Notes

1. "William Redfearn Brief." The Tulsa Race Massacre, June 21, 2012. tulsaraceriot.wordpress.com/research-topics/accounts/william -redfearn-brief/.
2. "Timeline: The 1921 Tulsa Race Massacre." Tulsa World, May 29, 2021. tulsaworld.com/news/local/racemassacre/timeline-the-1921-tulsa -race-massacre/collection_1c02a7b4-86ce-11e8-b63d-c3bbb45d4a 6c.html#27.
3. "William Redfearn Brief."
4. Carlson, I. Marc. "Timeline of the Tulsa Race Riot." The Tulsa Race Massacre, June, 29, 2012. www.personal.utulsa.edu/~marc-carlson /riot/tulsatime.html.
5. "1921 Race Massacre Survivors." John Hope Franklin Center, June 1, 2021. www.jhfcenter.org/1921-race-massacre-survivors.
6. Hill, Rachael. "The 1921 Tulsa Massacre." *Ex Post Facto*: Volume XVIII, Spring 2009. sfsu.app.box.com/s/xip6shaw85h8js37ikpin0 fqflgmg076/file/915878877753.
7. Erling, John. "Nancy Feldman." Voices of Oklahoma, November 20, 2012. www.voicesofoklahoma.com/wp-content/uploads/2014/02 /Feldman_Transcript.pdf.
8. Glenza, Jessica. "Rosewood massacre a harrowing tale of racism and the road toward reparations." *The Guardian*, January 3, 2016. www.theguardian.com/us-news/2016/jan/03/rosewood-florida -massacre-racial-violence-reparations.
9. Fallstrom, Jerry. "SENATE OKS $2.1 MILLION FOR ROSEWOOD REPARATIONS." *South Florida Sun Sentinel*, April 8, 1994. www .sun-sentinel.com/news/fl-xpm-1994-04-09-9404080701-story.html.

10. Ferrell, James Adrian. "A MAGNET SCHOOL AND DESEGREGA-TION: A CASE STUDY OF BOOKER T. WASHINGTON HIGH SCHOOL, 1975–1980." Graduate College of Oklahoma State University, December 2008. core.ac.uk/download/pdf/215279113.pdf.

11. "SAT/ACT Conversion Tables." Oklahoma State Department of Education, November 1, 2019. sde.ok.gov/sites/default/files/documents/files/2019_SAT_ACT%20Standard%20Setting%20and%20Conversion%20Tablesv2.pdf.

12. "State Board of Education approves Oklahoma School Report Cards." Oklahoma State Department of Education, February 28, 2019. sde.ok.gov/newsblog/2019-02-28/state-board-education-approves-oklahoma-school-report-cards.

13. "Booker T. Washington High School Academic Achievement 2018–2019." The Oklahoma Schools Report Card, November 26, 2019. oklaschools.com/school/achievement/1757/.

14. Lassek, P. J. "Carlton Pearson to run for mayor." Tulsa World, October 13, 2001. tulsaworld.com/archive/carlton-pearson-to-run-for-mayor/article_c45f18ed-0a0e-5e79-8e2f-9a4f6dd1e1fe.html.

15. Hein, Anton. "Devil may go to heaven, says beleaguered preacher." Religion News Blog. May 13, 2003. www.religionnewsblog.com/3295.

16. Morehouse, Henry Lyman. "THE TALENTED TENTH." *The Independent, The American Missionary*, Volume 50, No. 6, June 1896. www.gutenberg.org/files/19890/19890-0.txt

17. Young, RJ. "OU football Q&A; Kenny Stills knows you're watching him." *The Oklahoman*, April 18, 2012. www.oklahoman.com/story/sports/college/sooners/2012/04/17/ou-football-qa-kenny-stills-knows-youre-watching-him/61080140007/.

18. Fenwick, Ben. "The Massacre That Destroyed Tulsa's 'Black Wall Street'." *The New York Times*. July 13, 2020.

19. Brown, DeNeen L. "The Devastation of the Tulsa Massacre." *Washington Post*. May 28, 2021. www.washingtonpost.com/history/interactive/2021/tulsa-race-massacre-centennial-greenwood/.

20. "In 1905 Booker T. Washington visited Tulsa." Tuskegee Institute, Facebook. June 1, 2020. www.facebook.com/tuskegeenps/posts/in-1905-booker-t-washington-visited-tulsa-oklahoma-and-dubbed-the-city-the-negro/3284221224921205/.

21. "Booker T. Washington Royally Received in Muskogee." *The

Muskogee Cimeter, November 23, 1905. www.newspapers.com
/image/664539451/.

22. "Booker T. Washington Royally Received in Muskogee." www
.newspapers.com/image/78621304/.

23. Larsen, Jonathan Z. "Tulsa Burning." *Civilization: The Magazine
of the Library of Congress*, 1997. Reprint North Tulsa. www.north
tulsa.org/index.php/blog/782-tulsa-burning.

24. Boley: A negro town in the American West (1908), n.d. www
.wwnorton.com/college/history/archive/reader/trial/directory/1890_
1914/04_ch19_05.htm.

25. Franklin, John Hope. "W.E.B Du Bois: A Personal Memoir." The
Massachusetts Review, Vol. 31, No. 3, Autumn, 1990, pp. 409–28.
www.jstor.org/stable/25090198

26. Aptheker, Herbert. "On Du Bois to Africa." Monthly Review, December 4, 1993. monthlyreviewarchives.org/index.php/mr/article
/view/MR-045-07-1993-11_4

27. "On Du Bois to Africa." monthlyreviewarchives.org/index.php/mr
/article/view/MR-045-07-1993-11_4.

28. Stackelbeck, Kary, and Stubblefield, Phoebe. "Tulsa Race Massacre
Investigation Oaklawn Cemetery Executive Summary of 2020 Test
Excavations." City of Tulsa, October 20, 2020. www.cityoftulsa
.org/media/15149/trmi_oaklawn_excavations_2020_summary_
final-2.pdf.

29. "Tulsa Race Massacre Investigation Oaklawn Cemetery Executive
Summary of 2020 Test Excavations." www.cityoftulsa.org/media
/15149/trmi_oaklawn_excavations_2020_summary_final-2.pdf.

30. "A Park Like None Other." Gathering Place. September 18, 2018.
www.gatheringplace.org/about.

31. Cook, Lisa D. "Violence and Economic Activity: Evidence from African American Patents, 1870 to 1940." Michigan State University,
October 2013. lisadcook.net/wp-content/uploads/2014/02/pats_
paper17_1013_final_web.pdf.

32. Dolman, Lucy. "Tulsa Transforms Blighted Recreation Centers into
Quality Parks." American Planning Association, August 22, 2016.
www.planning.org/blog/blogpost/9109063/.

33. Trotter, Matt. "Race Massacre Centennial Commission Cancels Main
Commemoration Event, 'Remember + Rise'." Public Radio Tulsa,
May 27, 2021. www.publicradiotulsa.org/local-regional/2021-05-27

/race-massacre-centennial-commission-cancels-main-commemoration
-event-remember-rise.

34. Trotter, Matt. "Centennial Commission Chair: Attorneys Demanded More for Massacre Survivors' Appearance at Event." Public Radio Tulsa, May 28, 2021. www.publicradiotulsa.org/local-regional /2021-05-28/centennial-commission-chair-attorneys-demanded -more-for-massacre-survivors-appearance-at-event.

35. Krehbiel, Randy. "Attorney says trauma impacted race massacre survivor's memory." Tulsa World, May 29, 2021. tulsaworld.com /news/local/racemassacre/attorney-says-trauma-impacted-race -massacre-survivor-s-memory/article_9a26a158-bf16-11eb-baf6 -7f012a5fb6fd.html.

36. "What an honor to meet Viola Fletcher, the 1921 Race Massacre's oldest living survivor." Silhouette Tulsa, Instagram, May 26, 2021. www.instagram.com/p/CPWq1iuDh46/.

37. "107-year old Viola Fletcher wearing her first-ever pair of Air Jordans." Complex Sneakers, Twitter, May 29, 2021. twitter.com /complexsneakers/status/1398679406298664971?s=21.

38. Stecklein, Janelle. "Last Tulsa Race Massacre survivors push for reparations." CNHI Oklahoma, May 22, 2021. www.enidnews.com /news/last-tulsa-race-massacre-survivors-push-for-reparations/article _cf550c14-ba7c-11eb-b273-872233bcb49b.html

39. Weaver, Kristen. "Transformation Church Buys $20M in Property Surrounding Building." News On 6, December 2, 2020. www .newson6.com/story/5fc85a0fa568200c1f990b61/transform ation-church-buys-20m-in-property-surrounding-building-.

40. Bookwalter, Genevieve. "Evanston approves housing grants as part of city's local reparations program, believed to be first of its kind in the nation." *Chicago Tribune*, March 22, 2021. www.chicago tribune.com/suburbs/evanston/ct-evr-evanston-reparations-passes -tl-0325-20210323-hjetmkcmr5g5hhxaxjohovcmii-story.html.

41. "Martin family lawyer known for civil rights cases." CBS 8, Associated Press, March 30, 2012. www.cbs8.com/article/news/martin -family-lawyer-known-for-civil-rights-cases/509-6a1556cc-8836 -4451-af17-9c9f8f5d4768.

42. Evans, Gareth. "How Ben Crump became America's go-to police brutality lawyer." BBC News, May 30, 2021. www.bbc.com/news /world-us-canada-57038162.

43. Martin, Naomi. "Lee Merritt, civil rights attorney on the rise, faces a moment of reckoning." *The Dallas Morning News*, June 2, 2018. www.dallasnews.com/news/2018/06/02/lee-merritt-civil-rights -attorney-on-the-rise-faces-a-moment-of-reckoning/.

44. Pannett, Rachel. "Australia to pay hundreds of millions in reparations to Indigenous 'stolen generations.'" *Washington Post*, August 5, 2021. www.washingtonpost.com/world/2021/08/05/australia-indigenous -school-reparation/

45. "We hope so." Philbrook Museum of Art, Twitter, March 17, 2020. twitter.com/Philbrook/status/1240016701095325698?s=20.

46. "21 N Greenwood Ave, Tulsa, OK 74120 - Office Property." LoopNet, June 1, 2021. www.loopnet.com/Listing/21-N-Greenwood -Ave-Tulsa-OK/4932899/.

47. "Public Disclosure Copy Form 990-PF 2017." Hille Family Charitable Foundation, November 15, 2018. www.hillefoundation.org /wp-content/uploads/2018/12/2017-hille-family-charitable-foundation -public-disclosure-copy.pdf.

48. Jan, Tracy. "The 'whitewashing' of Black Wall Street." *Washington Post*, January 17, 2021. www.washingtonpost.com/business/2021 /01/17/tulsa-massacre-greenwood-black-wall-street-gentrification/.

49. Christine, Tim. "Investment Alert: 'Tulsa Real Estate Fund, LLC'." NFL Players Association, August 6, 2018. nflpaweb.blob.core .windows.net/media/Default/PDFs/General/Alert_Tulsa_Real_ Estate_Investment_Fund_NFLPA.pdf.

50. "Form 1-U, Tulsa Real Estate Fund, LLC." U.S. Securities and Exchange Commission, March 7, 2019. www.sec.gov/Archives/edgar /data/1704303/000147793219000871/tulsa_1u.htm

51. "SEC Concludes Investigation into the Tulsa Real Estate Fund and Fund Manager Jay Morrison." Black PR Wire, June 3, 2020." www.blackprwire.com/press-releases/sec-concludes-investigation -into-the-tulsa-real-estate-fund.

52. Canfield, Kevin. "'A hot-button issue': Not all Black Tulsans are happy about Greenwood Rising." Tulsa World, May 28, 2021. tulsaworld.com/news/local/racemassacre/a-hot-button-issue-not-all -black-tulsans-are-happy-about-greenwood-rising/article_83c5f376 -bef0-11eb-901e-5b122f1dc1e8.html.

53. Lee, Trymaine. "Transcript: Tulsa's 1921 race massacre centennial highlights journey to reclaim Black wealth." MSNBC, May 28,

2021. www.msnbc.com/podcast/transcript-tulsa-s-1921-race-massacre
-centennial-highlights-journey-reclaim-n1269025.

54. Halbleib, Brady. "State Rep. Monroe Nichols resigns from
Tulsa Race Massacre Centennial Commission." KJRH 2 News
Oklahoma, May 12, 2021. www.kjrh.com/news/local-news/state
-rep-monroe-nichols-resigns-from-centennial-commission.

55. Farris, Emily. "Gov. Stitt responds to letter from Tulsa Race Massacre Commission." KJRH 2 News Oklahoma, May 11, 2021.
www.kjrh.com/news/local-news/tulsa-race-massacre-centennial
-commission-writes-letter-to-gov-stitt-after-signing-hb-1775-into-law.

56. Stecklein, Janelle. "Oklahoma House Speaker blocks discussion of reparations for Tulsa Race Massacre victims." CNHI Oklahoma, August
5, 2021. www.stwnewspress.com/news/oklahoma-house-speaker
-blocks-discussion-of-reparations-for-tulsa-race-massacre-victims
/article_a9375c9c-f642-11eb-af13-5f114985d444.html.

57. Graham, Doug. "Author, Actress Stresses Importance of Black
Literature." Tulsa World, February 28, 1991. tulsaworld.com
/archives/author-actress-stresses-importance-of-black-literature/article
_96b614d5-784c-5dea-a30d-9d9ace388e98.html.

58. Morgan, Rhett. "Mixed-used development 21 North Greenwood
closer to construction." Tulsa World, September 18, 2018. tulsa
world.com/business/mixed-used-development-21-north-greenwood
-closer-to-construction/article_fce1a8a5-e43a-5de8-b5ca-4d4f39
16cb6e.html.

59. "From a murder charge to the governor granting clemency, a
timeline of Julius Jones' case." The Oklahoman, March 8, 2021.
www.oklahoman.com/story/entertainment/2021/03/08/julius
-jones-timeline/336070007/.

60. "City Selects Award-winning Architecture Firm for Greenwood
Cultural Center Renovation." City of Tulsa, April 4, 2021. www
.cityoftulsa.org/press-room/city-selects-award-winning-architecture
-firm-for-greenwood-cultural-center-renovation/.

61. "Negro 'King' Pleaded Guilty in Police Court." The Morning Tulsa Daily World, June 6, 1912. www.newspapers.com
/image/665459448/?terms=gurley%20king%20africa&match=1.

62. Smitherman, A. J. "Our Religious Faith." Tulsa Star, November
27, 1920. gateway.okhistory.org/ark:/67531/metadc72827/m1/8/zoom
/?resolution=4&lat=3116&lon=2278.5.

RJ YOUNG is the author of *Let It Bang:
A Young Black Man's Reluctant Odyssey
into Guns* and a national college football
writer and analyst at FOX Sports. Find
out more at rjyoungwrites.com.